TEXTBOOK OF PHARMACOLOGICAL SCREENING METHODS

EXPERIMENTAL MODELS, CPCSEA & OECD GUIDELINES, AND DRUG EVALUATION METHODS IN PRECLINICAL RESEARCH

DR. D. SWATHI, DR. V. UMA RANI, DR. I. VEENA RANI

Contents

Textbook Of Pharmacological Screening Methods

AUTHORS
Dr. D. Swathi, M.Pharm., Ph.D.
Head of the Department
Department of Pharmacy Practice
Samskruti College of Pharmacy
Ghatkesar, Hyderabad, Telangana, India
Dr. Vadapalli Uma Rani, M.Pharm., Ph.D.
Head of the Department
Department of Pharmacology
Samskruti College of Pharmacy
Hyderabad, Telangana, India
Dr. Inugala Veena Rani, M.Pharm., Ph.D.
Head of the Department
Department of Pharmacology
SSJ College of Pharmacy
Hyderabad, Telangana, India

Editor
Dr. A. Muralidhar Rao, M.Pharm., Ph.D.
Principal,
St. Mary's College of Pharmacy,
Secunderabad, Telangana, India

Published by Notion Press
Notion Press, Inc.
800, West El Camino Real #180,
California, USA 94040
Notion Press Media Pvt Ltd
#7, Red Cross Road,
Egmore, Chennai, Tamil Nadu 600008
Email ID: publish@notionpress.com
Phone Number: +91 44 46315631

Preface

Textbook of Pharmacological Screening Methods: Experimental Models, CPCSEA & OECD Guidelines, and Drug Evaluation Methods in Preclinical Research has been written to provide a comprehensive academic and practical resource for students, educators, and early-career researchers in pharmacy and pharmacology. This book is carefully aligned with the syllabus of *PS608: Screening Methods in Pharmacology* (Open Elective – II) offered in the B.Pharm. III Year II Semester and is designed to serve as a complete guide for understanding the preclinical evaluation of drugs.

Preclinical research is the foundation of drug discovery. It requires not only knowledge of various experimental techniques but also a deep understanding of regulatory guidelines, ethical animal handling, and scientific integrity. This textbook brings all these aspects together by covering the core areas of laboratory animal science, pharmacological screening methods, toxicity studies, and internationally recognized standards such as CPCSEA and OECD guidelines.

Each chapter introduces students to essential topics like animal housing, breeding, and restraint methods, followed by the detailed screening techniques for CNS-active drugs, cardiovascular agents, metabolic disorder treatments, gastrointestinal agents, and anti-inflammatory, analgesic, and antipyretic compounds. The principles of ethical experimentation, 3Rs (Replacement, Reduction, Refinement), euthanasia protocols, and modern alternatives to animal use are also discussed with clarity and practical relevance.

Designed with simplicity and academic rigor, this textbook integrates current regulatory practices with hands-on experimental knowledge, making it especially valuable for practical training and exam preparation. Rich in protocol-based learning and evaluation techniques, it is not only a textbook but also a useful manual for pharmacology labs.

We hope this book inspires students to approach pharmacological research with curiosity, critical thinking, and ethical responsibility, and serves as a dependable reference throughout their academic and professional journey in drug development and biomedical research.

Authors

Dr. D. Swathi, Dr. V. Uma Rani, Dr. I. Veena Rani

CHAPTER ONE

Introduction to Laboratory Animal Science

1.1 Introduction to Experimental Animals

Experimental animals play a crucial role in the field of drug discovery and development. Before any new chemical entity is tested on humans, it must first undergo detailed pharmacological and toxicological testing in living systems to ensure its efficacy and safety. This is where animal models become essential. Animals are used to mimic human diseases or physiological responses, providing researchers with a reliable way to assess the pharmacodynamic and pharmacokinetic properties of new drugs. These studies help in identifying therapeutic potential, estimating dosage, understanding mechanisms of action, and predicting possible adverse effects. Using animals in research also ensures that only compounds with a favorable safety margin move forward into clinical trials, thereby reducing risks to human volunteers and patients.

The use of animals in experimentation has a long and significant history. Ancient Greek physicians such as Galen and Aristotle used animals to understand anatomy and physiology, laying the foundation for scientific inquiry. The modern era of animal experimentation began in the 19th century, when Claude Bernard, often considered the father of experimental medicine, emphasized the importance of animal models in medical research. Since then, numerous scientific breakthroughs, including the development of insulin, vaccines, and antibiotics, have relied on the use of animals. The development of smallpox vaccine by Edward Jenner, polio vaccine by Albert Sabin, and insulin therapy for diabetes are all landmark examples where animal models contributed directly to human health advancements.

In pharmacological screening, in vivo models are indispensable tools. These models allow researchers to study the complex interactions of a drug within the whole organism. Unlike in vitro systems, in vivo testing accounts for absorption, distribution, metabolism, and excretion, which are all critical in determining a drug's performance and safety. Animal models also help in evaluating drug behavior under physiological conditions such as blood flow, organ function, immune responses, and neural pathways. For instance, assessing cardiovascular safety of a new molecule requires intact circulatory and regulatory systems that can only be examined in a living animal. Therefore, in vivo models are considered a bridge between in vitro experiments and clinical application.

A variety of animal species are used in preclinical pharmacological testing, each selected based on the type of study and the desired physiological or pathological response. Rats and mice are the most commonly used species due to their small size, ease of breeding, genetic similarity to humans, and well-documented biology. Mice are often employed in genetic and molecular studies, especially when transgenic or knockout models are required. Rats, on the other hand, are preferred for behavioral, cardiovascular, and metabolic studies because of their larger size and well-characterized nervous and endocrine systems. Rabbits are frequently used in ocular, dermal, and immunogenic studies, especially in vaccine development. Guinea pigs are employed in models of asthma, tuberculosis, and nutritional studies, particularly due to their similarity to humans in terms of vitamin C metabolism and hypersensitivity reactions. The choice of species depends not only on biological similarity but also on availability, cost, ethical considerations, and the specific research objective.

1.2 Classification and Selection of Laboratory Animals

Laboratory animals used in biomedical research are broadly classified into two major categories: rodents and non-rodents. This classification is based on taxonomy, anatomy, physiology, and their suitability for different types of experiments. Rodents constitute the majority of animals used in pharmacological and toxicological research. They include species such as mice, rats, guinea pigs, and hamsters. These animals are small, easy to handle, inexpensive to maintain, and have a high reproductive rate, which makes them highly suitable for long-term and large-scale experiments. Mice and rats are the most commonly used rodents because their genetic structure is well understood, and a wide variety of inbred, outbred, and genetically modified strains are available for research.

Non-rodents include larger animals such as rabbits, dogs, cats, pigs, and non-human primates like monkeys. These animals are used in studies where rodent models are not sufficient to replicate human physiology or when specific organ systems are being investigated in detail. For example, dogs are traditionally used in cardiovascular research because of their similar heart structure and rhythm to humans. Monkeys are used in neuroscience and vaccine development due to their close genetic and immunological resemblance to humans. However, the use of non-rodents is tightly regulated due to higher ethical concerns, cost, handling difficulty, and space requirements.

Selecting an appropriate animal model for a pharmacological study requires careful consideration of several criteria. One of the most important factors is the biological relevance of the species to human physiology. For instance, in diabetes research, rats are often used because they develop hyperglycemia similar to humans when exposed to certain chemicals like streptozotocin. Another factor is the objective of the study—whether it involves acute pharmacological testing, chronic toxicity evaluation, behavioral analysis, or reproductive studies. The route of drug administration, metabolism of the compound, availability of suitable biomarkers, and ethical feasibility also influence the selection. In some cases, regulatory authorities may recommend specific animal species for particular drug categories, especially in safety pharmacology and toxicology testing.

Different species offer unique advantages and limitations, making the choice of model a strategic decision in experimental design. Mice, being small and genetically well-characterized, are ideal for genetic manipulation and molecular biology studies. However, their small size may limit blood sampling and surgical procedures. Rats are preferred in behavioral pharmacology and cardiovascular studies due to their larger size and well-documented behavior patterns. Rabbits are commonly used in immunogenicity and ocular toxicity studies but may show stress-related variability in responses. Dogs and monkeys, while providing closer physiological parallels to humans, require specialized housing and handling, and are subject to stringent ethical scrutiny. Therefore, while selecting animal models, researchers must balance scientific objectives with ethical, economic, and practical considerations to ensure reliable and humane research outcomes.

1.3 Regulatory Authorities and Guidelines

The use of laboratory animals in research is governed by national and international regulatory frameworks to ensure scientific integrity, ethical responsibility, and animal welfare. In India, the central authority responsible for regulating animal experimentation is the Committee for the Purpose of Control and Supervision of Experiments on Animals (CPCSEA). It functions under the Ministry of Fisheries, Animal Husbandry and Dairying, Government of India, and was established to oversee the ethical use of animals in research, education, and testing. CPCSEA ensures that the experiments are performed only when absolutely necessary and are conducted using the least number of animals possible with minimal pain and distress. It mandates registration of animal facilities, regular inspections, and submission of detailed protocols before experiments can begin.

Within academic and research institutions, the Institutional Animal Ethics Committee (IAEC) plays a key role in implementing CPCSEA regulations. The IAEC is constituted with a balanced representation of scientists, veterinarians, and an external social welfare member. Every research proposal involving the use of animals must be reviewed and approved by the IAEC before commencement. The committee ensures that the study design is justified, alternative methods have been considered, and animal numbers are statistically appropriate. It also ensures that animals will be handled, housed, anesthetized, and euthanized according to approved procedures. The IAEC is responsible for conducting periodic reviews of ongoing studies and reporting compliance or violations to CPCSEA.

The CPCSEA regulations applicable to academic institutions cover all aspects of animal care and experimentation. These include requirements for animal housing, personnel training, record maintenance, animal identification, veterinary care, and regular monitoring of environmental parameters. Institutions must maintain proper records of animal acquisition, breeding, use, and disposal. Housing facilities must meet the recommended standards for temperature, humidity, ventilation, lighting, and cleanliness. Special attention is given to the 3Rs principle—Replacement, Reduction, and Refinement—which emphasizes minimizing animal use, replacing animals with alternatives wherever possible, and refining procedures to reduce suffering. Educational institutions are required to use alternatives such as computer simulations and videos for undergraduate teaching wherever feasible.

In addition to national guidelines, several international regulatory frameworks are relevant to animal studies conducted in India, especially when the research is intended for global regulatory submissions. The Organisation for Economic Co-operation and Development (OECD) provides standardized guidelines for toxicity and safety studies, which are accepted by regulatory agencies across member countries. These guidelines define test procedures, animal models, dosage regimens, observation criteria, and data reporting formats. The United States Food and Drug Administration (FDA) requires Good Laboratory Practice (GLP)-compliant animal data for Investigational New Drug (IND) applications. The World Health Organization (WHO) offers guidance on animal testing for vaccines and biologicals, especially for global public health interventions. The International Council for Harmonisation of Technical Requirements for Pharmaceuticals for Human Use (ICH) provides harmonized guidelines (e.g., ICH M3(R2)) that integrate safety data requirements for regulatory approval. Together, these national and international frameworks ensure that animal experiments are scientifically valid, ethically conducted, and globally acceptable.

1.4 Ethical Considerations in Animal Experimentation

1.4.1 The 3Rs Principle: Replacement, Reduction, Refinement

The ethical foundation of animal experimentation in pharmacological research is governed by the principle of the **3Rs: Replacement, Reduction, and Refinement**. These principles were first proposed by Russell and Burch in 1959 and have since become a cornerstone of humane experimental design. **Replacement** involves using non-animal alternatives wherever feasible, such as in vitro methods, computer simulations, or lower organisms like zebrafish. **Reduction** focuses on minimizing the number of animals used by improving study design and statistical validity to obtain maximum information from the smallest sample size. **Refinement** aims to decrease pain, suffering, and distress by enhancing animal care practices, using proper anesthesia and analgesia, and training personnel for gentle handling techniques. Together, these strategies help maintain a balance between scientific goals and ethical responsibility.

1.4.2 Ethical Justification and Necessity for Animal Use

Before initiating any experimental study involving animals, researchers are ethically and legally required to demonstrate the **necessity** of animal use. This involves providing a clear scientific rationale showing that the objectives of the study cannot be achieved using alternative methods. The type and number of animals, the procedures involved, and the expected outcomes must be justified based on relevance to human or veterinary medicine. Ethical justification is closely linked to the principle of proportionality, which mandates that the anticipated benefits of the research must outweigh the potential harm or distress caused to the animals. Only experiments with sound scientific basis and minimal ethical risk are allowed to proceed under regulatory frameworks.

1.4.3 Informed Protocol Submission and Animal Use Protocol Approval

To ensure compliance with ethical norms, researchers must submit a **detailed experimental protocol** to the **Institutional Animal Ethics Committee (IAEC)** before starting any animal study. This protocol should include information on the study objectives, justification for animal use, number and species of animals, methods of anesthesia and euthanasia, handling procedures, and endpoints. The IAEC, functioning under the oversight of **CPCSEA**, critically evaluates these proposals for ethical soundness and adherence to national guidelines. Approval is granted only when the committee is convinced that the study respects the 3Rs, maintains animal welfare standards, and includes contingency measures to address unexpected distress or complications. Maintaining accurate records of animal usage and regularly updating the IAEC on study progress is also mandatory as part of ethical compliance.

1.5 Animal House Facilities and Environmental Requirements

An animal house is a dedicated facility where laboratory animals are housed, bred, and maintained under controlled conditions for research and educational purposes. The location and structural design of the animal house must follow specific guidelines to ensure the welfare of animals and the safety of personnel. It should be situated in a quiet, clean, and low-traffic area of the campus, away from chemical or industrial activity, to avoid environmental disturbances. The building should have a sturdy structure with well-insulated walls, moisture-resistant flooring, and smooth, washable surfaces to facilitate cleaning and disinfection. Separate rooms must be provided for different species to prevent cross-infection and aggression. There should also be dedicated areas for quarantine, washing and sterilization, storage of feed and bedding, experimental procedures, and necropsy. Drainage and waste disposal systems should be planned in such a way that there is no contamination or backflow. Entry should be restricted to trained personnel, and access should be controlled through airlocks or double-door entry systems where feasible.

Maintaining optimal environmental conditions inside the animal house is essential to ensure the physiological stability of the animals and the reliability of experimental data. Temperature is one of the most critical parameters. According to CPCSEA recommendations, the acceptable temperature range for most laboratory animals is between 20°C and 26°C. Temperatures outside this range may cause thermal stress, alter metabolic rates, and affect drug responses. Similarly, relative humidity must be maintained between 30% and 70%. Low humidity may lead to drying of the mucous membranes, while excessive humidity promotes microbial growth and respiratory distress. The light-dark cycle is another important factor that influences animal behavior, reproduction, and hormonal rhythms. A 12:12 hour light-dark cycle is standard, with lights typically on from 7 a.m. to 7 p.m. Artificial lighting should be uniform and flicker-free, with an intensity of about 325 lux at cage level.

Proper air circulation is vital to maintain oxygen levels and to remove ammonia, carbon dioxide, and airborne pathogens. At least 10 to 15 air changes per hour are recommended in conventional animal rooms. Air should be filtered and preferably passed through High Efficiency Particulate Air (HEPA) filters to minimize microbial contamination. Noise is a significant stressor for laboratory animals. Sudden or high-pitched sounds can trigger fear and physiological changes, affecting the outcome of experiments. Therefore, noise levels in the animal house should be kept below 85 decibels, and soundproofing materials should be used where required.

A quarantine area is an essential part of any well-managed animal facility. New or incoming animals must be kept in quarantine for a minimum of 7 to 14 days before being introduced into the main colony.

During this period, animals are monitored for any signs of disease or infection, and preventive health checks are performed. The quarantine area should be physically isolated with separate air handling and waste disposal systems. Record keeping is equally important. Accurate and up-to-date records must be maintained for animal receipt, breeding, experimental use, health status, feed and water intake, cleaning schedules, and environmental monitoring. These records are not only necessary for internal management but are also mandatory for inspection by CPCSEA and other regulatory authorities.

1.6 Animal Handling and Restraint Techniques

The humane handling of laboratory animals is a critical aspect of animal experimentation, not only for ethical reasons but also to ensure the reliability and reproducibility of experimental results. Animals that are handled properly are less likely to experience stress, which in turn minimizes physiological variations that can interfere with study outcomes. The core principle of humane handling is to minimize fear, pain, and distress by using gentle, species-appropriate techniques and by ensuring that handlers are well-trained in animal behavior. Repeated and rough handling can lead to anxiety, aggression, weight loss, and even death in sensitive species. Therefore, calm movements, consistent procedures, and adequate environmental familiarity are essential for successful handling.

Each laboratory animal species requires specific techniques for safe and effective handling. Mice are small, agile, and prone to quick movements. They are usually picked up by gently grasping the base of the tail and then supporting their body with the other hand, especially when prolonged handling is necessary. Scruffing behind the neck using the thumb and forefinger provides better control during procedures like oral gavage or subcutaneous injection. Rats are larger and stronger than mice and should never be lifted by the tail alone. They are best handled by gently encircling the shoulders and supporting the hindquarters with the other hand. Firm but gentle handling is important to avoid provoking defensive behavior. Guinea pigs are docile but can be easily startled. They should be picked up by placing one hand around the shoulders and the other under the hindquarters. Supporting the body evenly is crucial because guinea pigs have delicate spines and may struggle if not properly held. Rabbits require even more care due to their powerful hind limbs and fragile vertebrae. They should be approached calmly and lifted by placing one hand under the chest and the other supporting the hindquarters. Holding the rabbit close to the handler's body offers security and minimizes kicking. Sudden movements or loud noises should always be avoided.

Different types of restraint are used depending on the procedure being carried out, the species involved, and the duration of the restraint. Physical restraint involves manual holding of the animal in a specific position. It is suitable for short and non-invasive procedures such as weighing, dosing, or minor observations. Mechanical restraint involves the use of specialized devices like restrainer boxes, tubes, or slings to immobilize the animal. This is commonly used in blood collection, imaging studies, or prolonged dosing protocols. The device should be well-ventilated and appropriately sized to avoid discomfort or suffocation. Chemical restraint involves the use of sedatives or anesthetics to calm or immobilize the animal. It is required during painful, invasive, or time-consuming procedures such as surgery, radiological imaging, or necropsy. The choice of agent depends on the species, duration of procedure, and the pharmacological effects of the sedative or anesthetic. Proper monitoring during chemical restraint is essential to avoid overdose, respiratory depression, or delayed recovery.

1.7 Feeding, Watering, and Bedding Practices

Proper feeding, watering, and bedding practices are vital components of laboratory animal management. These factors directly affect animal health, behavior, growth, reproduction, and the outcome of pharmacological experiments. Nutritional requirements must be carefully met to support normal physiology and avoid confounding experimental results due to malnutrition or dietary imbalances. Each species has specific dietary needs based on its metabolism, body size, and physiological state. Mice and rats, for instance, require a diet rich in protein (typically 18–20%), carbohydrates, fats, fiber, and essential vitamins and minerals. Guinea pigs need a diet supplemented with vitamin C because they cannot synthesize it endogenously. Rabbits, being herbivores with a unique digestive system, require high-fiber diets (typically 15–20% crude fiber) to maintain gut motility and prevent enterotoxemia.

Feed is generally provided in one of three forms: pelleted, powdered, or liquid. Pelleted feed is the most commonly used form in animal facilities because it is uniform, easy to store, and minimizes wastage and contamination. It is formulated to meet species-specific nutritional standards and is usually heat-sterilized to reduce microbial load. Powdered diets are used less frequently but may be necessary in special experimental conditions or for animals with dental issues. Liquid diets, although rarely used in standard animal houses, are important in certain experimental models such as metabolic studies or in animals recovering from surgery when solid food is not tolerated. Feed should be stored in dry, airtight containers and used before expiry to prevent fungal growth and nutrient degradation.

Water is equally essential for maintaining hydration and metabolic functions. The water used should be clean, potable, and free from chemical contaminants like chlorine, heavy metals, or microbial pathogens. Most facilities use filtered or autoclaved water to ensure sterility. Delivery systems vary and include water bottles with sipper tubes, automatic watering lines with valves, and gravity-fed systems. Water bottles should be checked and refilled daily. In automated systems, regular flushing and microbiological testing are necessary to prevent the buildup of biofilms or blockages.

Bedding serves several purposes including absorption of urine and feces, odor control, and providing comfort and insulation. The selection of bedding material depends on the species, cost, availability, absorbency, and dust content. Commonly used bedding materials include corn cob, rice husk, wood shavings, shredded paper, and cellulose-based commercial products. Corn cob is highly absorbent and minimizes ammonia buildup but may be expensive. Rice husk is economical and widely used in Indian laboratories, although it may contain dust and sharp particles. Shredded paper is soft, clean, and biodegradable, making it ideal for animals recovering from surgery or for neonatal care. Bedding material must be non-toxic, non-allergenic, and free from pesticides or chemical residues.

The frequency of cage cleaning and bedding replacement depends on the species, number of animals, and type of experiment. Typically, cages are cleaned and bedding is changed two to three times a week for rodents. High humidity, strong ammonia odor, or visible contamination are indicators for immediate replacement. In breeding units or during experiments involving metabolic studies, daily cleaning may be necessary. During cleaning, animals must be transferred gently to clean cages with fresh bedding, and feeders and water bottles must be washed, disinfected, and refilled. All procedures should aim to minimize stress and disruption to the animals while maintaining optimal hygienic conditions.

1.8 Breeding of Laboratory Animals

The controlled breeding of laboratory animals is essential to ensure a continuous supply of healthy, genetically defined subjects for pharmacological and toxicological research. Breeding programs must be scientifically managed to maintain genetic integrity, prevent diseases, and support the specific experimental needs of the research facility. Breeding strategies vary depending on the objectives of the study—whether it requires genetically uniform animals or diverse populations. The commonly used breeding systems include inbreeding, outbreeding, crossbreeding, and hybrid breeding, each with distinct genetic outcomes and applications.

Inbreeding is the mating of closely related animals, typically siblings or parent-offspring pairs, over successive generations. This results in a genetically uniform strain with reduced variability, which is highly desirable for experiments that require consistency in response. After 20 or more generations of inbreeding, the genetic variation is reduced to less than 1%, and the animals are considered isogenic. However, inbreeding may lead to inbreeding depression, causing reduced fertility, smaller litter sizes, and increased susceptibility to disease. Outbreeding, on the other hand, involves the mating of unrelated individuals of the same stock. This maintains genetic diversity and ensures robust health and reproductive performance. It is commonly used for general-purpose experiments where genetic uniformity is not a priority.

Crossbreeding refers to the mating of animals from two different strains or stocks. The offspring may display traits from both parental lines and are useful for studying gene interactions or introducing new traits into a line. Hybrid breeding is a specialized form of crossbreeding where two inbred strains are crossed to produce the F1 generation, which is genetically uniform but heterozygous. F1 hybrids often show enhanced vigor, known as hybrid vigor or heterosis, and are widely used in immunology and vaccine research. The choice of breeding method depends on whether the experiment demands genetic stability, resistance to specific conditions, or a particular phenotype.

Understanding the estrous cycle is crucial for successful breeding. Most laboratory rodents like rats and mice have a regular estrous cycle of 4–5 days, consisting of proestrus, estrus, metestrus, and diestrus phases. The optimal time for mating is during the estrus phase, when the female is sexually receptive. Mating techniques may be natural or artificial. In natural mating, one male is housed with one or more females, either continuously (monogamous pairing) or sequentially (polygamous rotation). In timed mating, females are exposed to males during a specific estrous phase to control breeding windows. Vaginal smears are often used to identify the stage of the cycle microscopically. In some advanced facilities, artificial insemination may be employed, especially in genetically modified or high-value strains.

Pregnancy detection can be done by observing weight gain, abdominal distension, or palpation by trained personnel. In mice and rats, pregnancy lasts about 19 to 21 days. During this time, females should be provided with nesting material and kept in quiet environments to reduce stress. Parturition usually occurs during the dark phase of the light cycle and is typically uncomplicated. However, caretakers must monitor for signs of dystocia or cannibalism. After birth, pups must be left undisturbed for the first few days. Litter management includes daily observation, recording the number of pups, checking for abnormalities, and ensuring that the dam has sufficient food and water. Weaning usually takes place at around 21 days, after which pups are separated based on sex and moved to appropriate cages for further use or breeding.

1.9 Transportation and Quarantine Procedures

Transportation of laboratory animals from breeding centers to research institutions, or between laboratories, must be carried out in accordance with ethical standards and regulatory norms to ensure the welfare of animals and prevent the spread of disease. Poor transport conditions can cause immense physiological stress, lead to illness, or compromise experimental outcomes. The three main modes of transport used for laboratory animals include air transport, road transport, and institutional cage-to-cage transfer. Air transport is generally used for long-distance or international transfer and must comply with International Air Transport Association (IATA) Live Animal Regulations. Road transport is the most common and practical method for short- and medium-distance movements. In such cases, vehicles must be specially adapted for ventilation, vibration control, and thermal insulation. Cage-to-cage institutional transport is used within a facility or campus and involves direct movement of animals from one unit to another in controlled conditions, minimizing exposure to external factors.

Animals must be transported in appropriate containers that ensure safety, comfort, and containment. Containers should be species-specific and must be made of durable, non-toxic, escape-proof materials. Adequate ventilation must be provided, and the design should allow the animals to sit, stand, and lie down naturally. Absorbent bedding material must be included to manage urine and feces. Each container must be clearly labeled with details such as the species, strain, number of animals, sex, date and time of dispatch, origin, and destination. The label must also indicate special handling instructions such as "Live Animals," "Handle with Care," or "This Side Up." During transit, the containers should be secured to prevent tipping, and personnel must check environmental conditions like temperature and humidity to avoid animal distress.

Minimizing stress during transportation is a critical objective, as stress can lead to physiological changes such as elevated cortisol levels, immune suppression, dehydration, and behavioral abnormalities. To reduce these effects, animals must be acclimatized to handling before transport, and noise or light exposure should be kept to a minimum. Feeding should generally be avoided immediately before transport to reduce nausea or motion sickness, although hydration must be maintained. Transport vehicles must have shock absorbers to reduce vibration, and driving should be smooth and at moderate speed. Transportation should be scheduled during cooler parts of the day, especially in tropical climates, and the journey should be as short as possible to minimize disruption.

Upon arrival at the facility, animals must undergo a mandatory quarantine period before being introduced into the main colony. This period typically ranges from 7 to 14 days, depending on institutional policies and the source of animals. The purpose of quarantine is to monitor for clinical signs of infection or stress-related illness, prevent cross-contamination, and allow the animals to recover from transport-induced stress. During this time, animals are housed separately in a dedicated quarantine area with independent air handling and sanitation systems. Trained personnel observe the animals daily for signs such as reduced food intake, diarrhea, lethargy, nasal discharge, skin lesions, or unusual behavior. Health records must be meticulously maintained, and veterinary attention should be provided if any abnormalities are detected. Only after completing the quarantine with satisfactory health status are the animals transferred to experimental or breeding units.

1.10 Common Diseases and Health Monitoring

Maintaining the health of laboratory animals is essential for the accuracy, reproducibility, and ethical validity of experimental studies. Animals suffering from undetected infections or subclinical illnesses may exhibit altered physiological responses that can compromise experimental results. Therefore, a structured health monitoring program is required to identify, prevent, and manage diseases commonly found in laboratory animal colonies. Rodents and rabbits, being the most frequently used laboratory animals, are susceptible to a range of infectious diseases caused by bacteria, viruses, fungi, and parasites.

In rodents, some of the most common infectious diseases include respiratory infections caused by *Mycoplasma pulmonis*, murine hepatitis virus (MHV), Sendai virus, and parvovirus. These infections can lead to symptoms such as labored breathing, weight loss, rough fur, and reduced fertility. Bacterial diseases such as Tyzzer's disease, caused by *Clostridium piliforme*, and pasteurellosis may also occur in poorly managed colonies. In rabbits, pasteurellosis is a common respiratory infection caused by *Pasteurella multocida*, often presenting as nasal discharge, head tilt, and abscess formation. Other rabbit-specific infections include coccidiosis, enterotoxemia, and snuffles. Skin conditions like ringworm (dermatophytosis) and mite infestations can affect both rodents and rabbits, especially in overcrowded or poorly ventilated environments.

To detect these diseases early, many animal facilities employ sentinel animals and structured disease surveillance programs. Sentinel animals are healthy animals intentionally exposed to soiled bedding or direct contact with colony animals to detect the presence of infectious agents. These sentinels are housed under controlled conditions and are periodically tested through serological assays, culture, and histopathological examination. A sentinel program typically involves placing one or two sentinel animals per rack or room and evaluating them every three to six months. This system acts as an early warning mechanism, allowing for prompt containment measures in case of infection detection. Regular microbial screening and environmental monitoring of air, water, and surfaces further enhance surveillance.

Preventive veterinary care is a cornerstone of colony health management. Although vaccination is rarely practiced in standard laboratory rodent colonies, it may be used in specific breeding colonies or in rabbit husbandry for diseases such as myxomatosis or rabbit hemorrhagic disease in endemic areas. Deworming is necessary in colonies where gastrointestinal parasites like pinworms are a concern. Deworming agents such as piperazine or ivermectin may be administered orally or via medicated feed. Routine veterinary check-ups help detect subtle signs of illness, and procedures such as ear tagging, microchipping, or coat color marking help identify animals requiring special attention. Animals showing signs of disease must be isolated immediately, treated as per veterinary guidance, or humanely euthanized if recovery is unlikely.

The importance of maintaining detailed and accurate health records cannot be overstated. These records document each animal's health status, vaccination history, treatment, and any experimental procedures it has undergone. Records should include dates of illness onset, clinical signs observed, diagnostic test results, medications administered, and outcomes. Proper documentation supports scientific accountability, regulatory compliance, and helps in tracing the origin of outbreaks. During audits or inspections by authorities such as CPCSEA, these records serve as proof of compliance with animal welfare standards. Moreover, in long-term studies or breeding programs, health records are vital for evaluating reproductive performance, disease trends, and longevity.

Review Questions and Answers

1. **What is the primary role of laboratory animals in drug discovery?**
   Laboratory animals are used to evaluate the safety, efficacy, and pharmacological effects of new drugs before human trials.

2. **Name four commonly used laboratory animals in pharmacological screening.**
   Rat, mouse, rabbit, and guinea pig.

3. **What is in vivo testing?**
   It refers to experiments conducted in living organisms to observe physiological or pharmacological effects.

4. **Differentiate between rodents and non-rodents.**
   Rodents include rats and mice, whereas non-rodents include rabbits, dogs, and monkeys.

5. **What are the 3Rs in animal research?**
   Replacement, Reduction, and Refinement.

6. **Which committee oversees animal experimentation in India?**
   CPCSEA – Committee for the Purpose of Control and Supervision of Experiments on Animals.

7. **What is the function of the Institutional Animal Ethics Committee (IAEC)?**
   To review and approve protocols involving animal use and ensure ethical compliance.

8. **Mention two international guidelines related to animal studies.**
   OECD and ICH guidelines.

9. **What is the ideal temperature range in an animal house for rodents?**
   20–26°C.

10. **Define quarantine in animal facilities.**
    Quarantine is the isolation of newly arrived animals for observation before introduction into the main animal colony.

11. **What is the significance of light-dark cycles in animal housing?**
    They regulate circadian rhythms, which affect hormonal and behavioral responses.

12. **How are mice generally handled in laboratories?**
    By holding them at the base of the tail or scruff of the neck.

13. **Name one physical and one chemical method of animal restraint.**
    Physical: hand restraint; Chemical: anesthesia.

14. **Give two examples of bedding material used in animal cages.**
Corn cob and shredded paper.

15. **What is the weaning age for mice and rats?**
21–28 days.

16. **What is inbreeding in laboratory animal breeding?**
Mating between closely related animals to produce genetically identical strains.

17. **Name one commonly used inbred strain.**
BALB/c mouse.

18. **Why is outbreeding preferred in general toxicity studies?**
It provides genetic variability and mimics human populations better.

19. **Mention a mode of animal transport within institutions.**
Cage-to-cage transfer.

20. **What is the importance of labeling during animal transport?**
To provide information on species, number, sender, receiver, and handling instructions.

21. **Define sentinel animals.**
Animals kept in the same environment to monitor for infections or pathogens.

22. **Which tests are done during health monitoring?**
Serology, parasitology, and microbiology tests.

23. **Why is record-keeping essential in animal facilities?**
To track animal health, breeding, environmental parameters, and experimental history.

24. **What is the gestation period of a rat?**
21–23 days.

25. **What is the purpose of maintaining environmental logs in an animal facility?**
To ensure controlled conditions for animal welfare and experimental reproducibility.

MCQs

1. **Which of the following is a rodent species commonly used in pharmacological research?**
   A) Dog
   B) Monkey
   C) Mouse
   D) Cat
   Answer: C) Mouse

2. **The principle of Replacement in animal research refers to:**
   A) Using a higher number of animals
   B) Using human subjects instead
   C) Using alternatives to animals
   D) Replacing cages regularly
   Answer: C) Using alternatives to animals

3. **Which regulatory body in India governs animal experimentation?**
   A) FDA
   B) WHO
   C) CPCSEA
   D) USDA
   Answer: C) CPCSEA

4. **Outbreeding leads to:**
   A) Genetically identical animals
   B) Genetic variability
   C) Weaker offspring
   D) Unethical breeding
   Answer: B) Genetic variability

5. **What is the ideal temperature range for rodent housing?**
   A) 10–15°C
   B) 20–26°C
   C) 30–40°C
   D) 5–10°C
   Answer: B) 20–26°C

6. **Which of the following is not a component of the 3Rs?**
   A) Replacement
   B) Refinement
   C) Reduction
   D) Regulation
   Answer: D) Regulation

7. **Which type of bedding is commonly used in lab animal cages?**
   A) Sand
   B) Gravel
   C) Corn cob
   D) Cement
   Answer: C) Corn cob

8. **Who approves animal use protocols in academic institutions?**
   A) UGC
   B) AICTE
   C) IAEC
   D) DCGI
   Answer: C) IAEC

9. **Quarantine is required to:**
   A) Increase breeding
   B) Prevent escape
   C) Observe animals for infections
   D) Train new staff
   Answer: C) Observe animals for infections

10. **Which is a non-rodent animal model?**
    A) Guinea pig
    B) Rabbit
    C) Rat
    D) Mouse
    Answer: B) Rabbit

11. **The gestation period of a rat is approximately:**
    A) 10–12 days
    B) 21–23 days
    C) 30–32 days
    D) 40–45 days
    Answer: B) 21–23 days

12. **Which guideline is internationally used for animal toxicology studies?**
    A) GCP

B) ICH E6

C) OECD

D) GLP

Answer: C) OECD

13. **Which light-dark cycle is maintained in animal facilities?**

    A) 10:14

    B) 14:10

    C) 12:12

    D) 24:0

    Answer: C) 12:12

14. **In handling mice, one should preferably hold them by:**

    A) Hind legs

    B) Neck scruff or base of tail

    C) Ears

    D) Back

    Answer: B) Neck scruff or base of tail

15. **Which is a method of physical restraint in lab animals?**

    A) Tranquilizer

    B) Anesthesia

    C) Restraining box

    D) Cage washing

    Answer: C) Restraining box

16. **Animal health records include all except:**

    A) Disease surveillance

    B) Environmental parameters

    C) Financial logs

    D) Vaccination history

    Answer: C) Financial logs

17. **Inbreeding results in:**

    A) Genetically diverse offspring

    B) Genetically identical strains

    C) Random traits

    D) Sterility

    Answer: B) Genetically identical strains

18. **Which organization oversees animal experiments globally?**

    A) CPCSEA

    B) ICH

    C) OECD

D) FDA

Answer: C) OECD

19. **Water supply in animal facilities should be:**

    A) Chlorinated

    B) From natural ponds

    C) Unfiltered

    D) From drain water

    Answer: A) Chlorinated

20. **What is the preferred feed form in laboratory animals?**

    A) Raw food

    B) Canned food

    C) Pelleted diet

    D) Gravy food

    Answer: C) Pelleted diet

21. **Which method is used for euthanasia in small rodents?**

    A) Hanging

    B) Starvation

    C) Cervical dislocation

    D) Drowning

    Answer: C) Cervical dislocation

22. **Sentinel animals are used for:**

    A) Reproduction

    B) Disease monitoring

    C) Feeding trials

    D) Transportation

    Answer: B) Disease monitoring

23. **What is the purpose of animal house sanitation?**

    A) Odour control only

    B) Better feed supply

    C) Prevent disease and contamination

    D) Pest control only

    Answer: C) Prevent disease and contamination

24. **Mice are usually weaned at the age of:**

    A) 10 days

    B) 15 days

    C) 21 days

    D) 40 days

    Answer: C) 21 days

25. **Which of the following is a refinement strategy?**
    A) Avoiding anesthesia
    B) Using dirty cages
    C) Minimizing pain through analgesics
    D) Increasing animal numbers
    Answer: C) Minimizing pain through analgesics

CHAPTER TWO

Animal Handling, Housing, and Breeding

2.1 Introduction

In the field of preclinical pharmacology, the care and management of laboratory animals play a foundational role in the success and credibility of experimental research. Animals serve as in vivo models for evaluating the pharmacodynamic and toxicological profiles of investigational drugs. The quality of animal care directly influences physiological parameters such as metabolism, immune function, and stress responses, all of which are critical to experimental outcomes. Improper handling or inconsistent breeding practices may introduce variability, resulting in flawed data and misleading interpretations. Therefore, a high standard of animal welfare is not only an ethical obligation but also a scientific necessity.

Standardized handling techniques ensure that animals experience minimal distress during experimental procedures. Routine handling, if not performed properly, can alter hormonal levels and behavior, ultimately affecting drug efficacy and safety data. Trained personnel must be capable of identifying subtle signs of stress or discomfort and must follow species-specific protocols. Standard operating procedures (SOPs) must be established and strictly followed to avoid inter-experiment variability. Similarly, controlled breeding practices help maintain genetic consistency within experimental groups, especially in studies involving chronic dosing, behavioral pharmacology, or genetic models. Consistent genetic background minimizes variability in pharmacokinetics and receptor expression, enhancing reproducibility and reliability of results.

The practices of animal handling and breeding are closely governed by national regulations such as those set forth by the Committee for the Purpose of Control and Supervision of Experiments on Animals (CPCSEA). This regulatory body mandates ethical treatment, proper housing, and scientific justification for animal use in research. All animal care activities must align with CPCSEA guidelines, including the use of approved housing conditions, humane handling, veterinary oversight, and use of the minimum number of animals required to achieve statistically valid results. In addition, breeding colonies must be managed under ethical breeding plans with clearly documented lineages and health records. Failure to adhere to such standards may result not only in ethical violations but also in scientific invalidation of experimental data.

2.2 Animal Handling Techniques

Proper animal handling techniques are essential for maintaining the welfare of laboratory animals and ensuring the scientific validity of experimental results. The act of handling should always be carried out with care, calmness, and respect for the animal's behavior and biology. Humane handling minimizes physiological stress, reduces the risk of injury to both animals and handlers, and helps in achieving consistent experimental outcomes. The core principle is to cause the least amount of distress while achieving the required level of control for observation, dosing, or procedural intervention.

Each species commonly used in pharmacological research has specific anatomical and behavioral traits that determine the most appropriate handling technique. Rats are social, relatively docile animals but can become aggressive or frightened with rough handling. The most basic method for handling a rat is by grasping it gently at the base of the tail to lift it out of its cage. For transferring or restraining larger rats, additional support should be provided by placing the other hand under the chest or hindquarters to avoid unnecessary strain on the spine or limbs. Holding the rat close to the handler's body helps calm the animal during procedures such as dosing or weighing.

Mice are smaller and more agile than rats, making them more prone to escape and injury during handling. They can be picked up by gently holding the tail near its base and quickly transferring the animal onto a secure surface. For detailed procedures like injections or oral dosing, mice are often restrained by scruffing—the handler uses the thumb and forefinger to grasp the loose skin at the nape of the neck, which immobilizes the animal temporarily. This technique allows for good visibility and control while minimizing movement. Newborn mouse pups are extremely delicate and should not be handled with bare hands. Soft rubber-tipped forceps or gloves must be used to avoid skin damage or transferring scent, which can cause maternal rejection.

Rabbits are larger animals with powerful hind limbs and fragile vertebrae, making careful handling crucial. They must never be lifted by the ears or legs. The correct method involves placing one hand under the chest just behind the forelimbs and the other hand supporting the hindquarters. The rabbit should be held securely against the handler's chest or body to prevent kicking, which can lead to spinal injuries. During procedures, rabbits may be placed in restraining devices or wrapped in a towel to limit movement. Sudden noises or rough handling can easily startle rabbits, so all actions must be smooth and deliberate.

Several tools are used to facilitate safe and efficient handling of laboratory animals. These include gloves to prevent scratches or bites, restraining tubes made of plastic or acrylic for rodents, and restraining boxes for blood collection or dosing in small animals. Towels, cotton bags, or commercially available animal restrainers are often used for rabbits and guinea pigs. The choice of device depends on the species, size of the animal, and the type of procedure being performed.

Recognizing signs of distress during handling is vital for ethical and scientific reasons. Common indicators include vocalization, excessive struggling, urination or defecation, increased respiration rate, and attempts to escape. In more severe cases, animals may show signs of piloerection, hunching, aggression, or lethargy after handling. These signs suggest that the handling method is too harsh or prolonged. To minimize stress, animals should be handled regularly by the same personnel, introduced gently to new environments, and restrained only for the shortest necessary duration. Proper training of staff and a calm working environment are essential components of low-stress animal management.

2.3 Animal Housing and Environmental Requirements

Maintaining appropriate housing conditions is fundamental to the health, welfare, and performance of laboratory animals. A well-designed animal house not only meets the physical and behavioral needs of different species but also helps ensure that experimental data remains consistent and reliable. Proper housing reduces stress, prevents the spread of disease, and supports regulatory compliance, especially under frameworks such as the CPCSEA. The structural and environmental parameters of animal housing must be standardized and continuously monitored to meet both scientific and ethical obligations.

The structural design of an animal facility must provide separate rooms for different species to prevent cross-contamination and inter-species aggression. Each room should be designated for a specific purpose such as animal housing, quarantine, breeding, or experimentation. A quarantine area is essential for isolating newly received or sick animals before they are introduced into the general colony. The quarantine section should be physically separated and equipped with independent airflow and sanitation. In addition to animal rooms, the facility must have a designated wash area where cages and equipment are cleaned and disinfected. A separate record room should also be maintained for storing daily logs, breeding records, and environmental monitoring data.

CPCSEA outlines clear environmental parameters to be maintained in Indian laboratory animal facilities. The temperature for rodent housing rooms should be kept within an ideal range of 20 to 26°C. This range supports normal metabolic functions and prevents cold or heat stress. For humidity, a level between 30% and 70% is required. Too low humidity can cause dehydration and skin dryness, while excess humidity may promote fungal growth and respiratory issues. Lighting should follow a strict 12:12 hour light-dark cycle, commonly achieved through artificial fluorescent lights, ensuring consistent behavioral and hormonal rhythms. Abrupt changes in lighting can disrupt sleep patterns, affect reproduction, and induce stress.

Ventilation is critical for controlling odors, maintaining oxygen levels, and reducing the accumulation of carbon dioxide and ammonia. An air exchange rate of 10 to 15 air changes per hour is typically recommended. Facilities with high animal density or sensitive experiments may require HEPA-filtered ventilation systems to minimize microbial contamination. Noise levels should be controlled below 85 decibels to prevent auditory stress and behavioral disturbances, especially in species like rabbits and guinea pigs which are highly sensitive to sudden sounds. Use of soundproof materials and placement of animal rooms away from mechanical or human activity zones can greatly reduce noise exposure.

Regular cleaning and sanitation of animal housing equipment are essential to maintain hygiene and prevent disease transmission. Cages should be cleaned two to three times a week or more frequently based on the species and number of animals. Water bottles, feeders, and enrichment items must be cleaned and sterilized on a routine basis. Disinfectants used must be non-toxic and should not leave harmful residues. Equipment such as cage racks, trays, and bedding bins should be cleaned in designated wash areas using hot water or chemical disinfectants followed by drying. Staff must use gloves and protective gear to prevent zoonotic infections and maintain biosafety.

Accurate record maintenance is a regulatory and scientific necessity. Each animal room should maintain a logbook with entries related to the number of animals, feed and water intake, environmental conditions, cage changes, and observations of illness or mortality. Temperature and humidity should be recorded at least twice daily using calibrated instruments, and any deviations should be corrected and noted immediately. Records must be preserved for audit by regulatory authorities and for internal reviews. Proper documentation supports traceability, improves colony management, and enhances research reproducibility.

2.4 Breeding Techniques of Laboratory Animals

The systematic breeding of laboratory animals is fundamental to maintaining genetically defined colonies, ensuring a steady supply of healthy animals, and producing experimental models tailored to specific research needs. Breeding programs must be scientifically planned and ethically implemented to meet the genetic, physiological, and behavioral requirements of laboratory species. Understanding the various breeding strategies and reproductive management practices is essential for researchers and animal house personnel to maintain colony integrity and achieve consistent experimental outcomes.

Different types of breeding techniques are employed based on the desired genetic makeup and experimental utility. Inbreeding involves mating between closely related animals, such as siblings or parents with offspring, over multiple generations. This process produces genetically homogeneous populations, often referred to as inbred strains. Common examples include BALB/c and C57BL/6 mice. These strains are extensively used in immunology, oncology, and genetic studies due to their uniform responses and low inter-individual variability. However, continuous inbreeding can also lead to inbreeding depression, characterized by reduced fertility, increased disease susceptibility, and smaller litter sizes.

Outbreeding, in contrast, involves mating between unrelated individuals within the same stock. This practice maintains genetic diversity, resulting in robust health, improved reproductive performance, and resistance to disease. Outbred strains such as Wistar rats and Swiss albino mice are commonly used for general pharmacological screening, toxicology studies, and behavioral experiments where genetic variability is acceptable or desired. Crossbreeding is the mating of animals from two distinct inbred strains or stocks. It results in offspring that combine traits from both parents, which may enhance adaptability or generate specific phenotypes. This approach is used in experiments aiming to analyze genetic interactions or introduce new characteristics into a colony.

Hybridization refers to a more controlled form of crossbreeding, typically between two well-defined inbred strains, to produce F1 hybrids. These hybrids are genetically identical but heterozygous at all loci where the parents differ, exhibiting a phenomenon known as hybrid vigor or heterosis. F1 hybrids often show enhanced growth rate, reproductive performance, or immune responses, making them ideal for use in pharmacogenetics, vaccine research, and disease modeling. These hybrids are also useful in studies requiring intermediate traits not present in either parent strain alone.

Reproductive efficiency in laboratory animals depends on the proper understanding and management of the estrous cycle. Female mice and rats have a regular cycle of 4–5 days, and estrus—the period of sexual receptivity—can be identified by examining vaginal smears under a microscope. The presence of cornified epithelial cells indicates the estrus phase, which is the optimal time for mating. In typical breeding programs, one male is housed with two or three females, maintaining a male-to-female ratio of 1:2 or 1:3. Continuous or timed mating strategies can be used based on experimental design. Detection of vaginal plugs or observation of behavioral cues can confirm successful mating.

Once mating has occurred, proper care must be given during pregnancy and parturition. The gestation period is approximately 19 to 21 days in mice and 21 to 23 days in rats. Pregnant females should be separated into individual cages before parturition to prevent fighting, cannibalism, or pup injuries. Nesting material such as shredded paper or soft bedding must be provided to allow the dam to build a suitable nest. During this time, minimal handling and a quiet environment are critical to reduce stress and avoid pregnancy complications.

Litter management begins immediately after parturition. Newborn pups should be left undisturbed for the first few days to prevent maternal neglect or cannibalism. Daily observations are made to record the number of pups, detect any abnormalities, and monitor nursing behavior. Weaning generally occurs at 21 to 28 days of age, depending on the species and health status of the litter. At weaning, pups are separated from the mother and grouped by sex to prevent early or accidental mating. Sexing is done by examining the anogenital distance, which is greater in males than in females. Proper labeling, documentation, and cage assignment ensure traceability and support ethical breeding records.

2.5 Transportation and Quarantine of Laboratory Animals

The transportation and quarantine of laboratory animals are essential steps in ensuring both animal welfare and the biosecurity of animal research facilities. Movement of animals from breeding units or vendors to research institutions must be conducted in a manner that minimizes stress, prevents disease transmission, and complies with institutional and national regulatory standards. Mishandling during transport or failure to implement quarantine procedures can lead to illness, experimental errors, and loss of valuable research time.

Transportation modes commonly used for laboratory animals include road transport, air transport, and institutional cage-to-cage transfer. Road transport is the most widely practiced mode in domestic transfers and must be conducted using specially modified vehicles that provide adequate ventilation, temperature regulation, and protection from environmental stressors. Air transport is reserved for long-distance or international shipments and must comply with International Air Transport Association (IATA) Live Animal Regulations. For internal transfers within a research facility or campus, cage-to-cage institutional transfers are performed. This method offers the lowest risk of contamination and allows animals to be moved without major disruption to their routine or environment.

During transport, certain minimum requirements must be strictly followed to maintain the physiological and behavioral stability of animals.

Transport containers must be well-ventilated, secure, escape-proof, and made of durable, non-toxic materials. Each container should allow the animal to assume a natural posture without overcrowding. The internal environment of the container must be maintained within the recommended temperature and humidity range, especially for rodents where 20–26°C and 30–70% relative humidity are ideal. Containers should be fitted with absorbent bedding and should include an adequate supply of feed—preferably pelleted—and hydration in the form of gel packs or water bottles, depending on the duration of travel. Proper labeling is mandatory and should include details such as species, number of animals, sex, date of dispatch, and specific handling instructions. Transport documentation must accompany the shipment and include health certificates, source details, and any special notes regarding the animals' condition or handling needs.

Minimizing stress during transport is a critical component of animal welfare and helps preserve the animals' immune competence and behavioral stability. The duration of travel should be as short as possible and should avoid peak traffic hours or extreme weather conditions. Bedding should be placed inside the container to absorb waste and provide comfort. For longer journeys, animals should be checked periodically for signs of distress. Gentle handling, quiet surroundings, and proper ventilation significantly reduce the likelihood of transport-induced stress. Pre-conditioning the animals to handling before transport also improves their coping response.

Quarantine is a vital follow-up to transportation and serves as a protective buffer before animals are introduced into the main colony. Newly arrived animals must be kept in isolation for a period ranging from 5 to 14 days, depending on species, origin, and institutional policy. The quarantine area should be physically separated from existing colonies, with independent air handling and sanitation systems. During this period, animals are observed daily for signs of illness such as lethargy, nasal discharge, abnormal posture, or changes in feeding behavior. Baseline screening should include weight recording, fecal examinations, and serological testing if required. Veterinary staff must conduct thorough examinations, and any signs of disease must be documented and treated accordingly.

To enhance disease surveillance, sentinel animals may be used. These are healthy animals intentionally exposed to soiled bedding from the incoming or resident colony to detect subclinical infections. Sentinel animals are monitored over a defined period and then subjected to diagnostic testing, such as serology or microbiological cultures. This system provides early warnings about possible infectious agents and enables timely intervention to contain disease outbreaks. Quarantine records must be maintained meticulously, and animals should be released into the main colony only after obtaining clearance from the attending veterinarian and ethics committee.

Review Questions and Answers

1. **Why is standardized animal handling important in preclinical studies?**
   To reduce stress and variability in results, and to ensure animal welfare and data reproducibility.

2. **What is the recommended way to handle a mouse?**
   By holding it at the base of the tail or by the scruff of the neck with gentle support.

3. **How should rabbits be lifted to prevent spinal injury?**
   By supporting both forelimbs and hindquarters securely.

4. **Name one restraint device commonly used in laboratory animal handling.**
   A restraining box or cone.

5. **What signs indicate distress in laboratory animals?**
   Abnormal posture, vocalization, excessive grooming, aggression, or immobility.

6. **What is the function of a quarantine room in an animal facility?**
   To isolate newly arrived animals and monitor for diseases before introducing them to the main colony.

7. **Which animal is most commonly used in inbred strain experiments?**
   The mouse (e.g., BALB/c or C57BL/6 strains).

8. **Define inbreeding.**
   Inbreeding is the mating of closely related animals to maintain genetic consistency.

9. **What is outbreeding?**
   The mating of genetically unrelated animals to maintain genetic diversity.

10. **What is the estrous cycle duration in rats and mice?**
    Approximately 4 to 5 days.

11. **How do you detect pregnancy in rodents?**
    By observing weight gain, abdominal distension, or presence of vaginal plug post-mating.

12. **At what age are rodent pups generally weaned?**
    At 21–28 days of age.

13. **What is hybrid breeding?**
    Breeding between two different inbred strains to produce offspring with specific traits.

14. **Why is environmental control important in animal housing?**
To prevent physiological and behavioral changes due to temperature, humidity, or noise fluctuations.

15. **What is the ideal humidity range for rodents in animal houses?**
Between 30–70%.

16. **Why are HEPA filters used in ventilation systems?**
To prevent contamination from airborne pathogens and maintain sterile conditions.

17. **What is the standard light-dark cycle maintained in an animal facility?**
12:12 hours (12 hours light, 12 hours dark).

18. **What kind of containers are used for animal transport?**
Ventilated, escape-proof, and labeled containers with bedding and food provisions.

19. **Name one way to minimize stress during animal transport.**
Minimize travel duration and avoid loud noises and vibrations.

20. **How often should bedding in animal cages be replaced?**
At least twice a week or as per animal load and cleanliness.

21. **Why are guinea pigs more sensitive to environmental noise?**
They have a higher auditory range and easily experience stress-induced physiological changes.

22. **Which method is used to identify the estrous cycle stage in rodents?**
Vaginal smear cytology.

23. **What is the purpose of sexing before weaning?**
To separate male and female pups and prevent early, unplanned breeding.

24. **List any two common bedding materials used in rodent cages.**
Corn cob and shredded paper.

25. **What is the function of an animal logbook?**
To record animal-related details such as date of arrival, health status, procedures performed, and environmental records.

26. **What are the structural components of a standard animal house?**
Species-specific rooms, quarantine area, washroom, record room, and storage.

27. **How does cage cleaning contribute to animal health?**
Removes waste and reduces microbial load, preventing infections.

28. **Why is a male-to-female ratio of 1:2 or 1:3 preferred in breeding?**
To increase the chances of successful mating while preventing aggressive

behavior among males.

29. **What is crossbreeding?**
Breeding between animals of different genetic backgrounds or strains to combine beneficial traits.

30. **How long is the gestation period for mice and rats?**
Mice: around 19–21 days; Rats: around 21–23 days.

MCQs

1. **What is the correct way to hold a mouse?**
   A) By the hind legs
   B) By the ear
   C) By the tail base or neck scruff
   D) By the abdomen
   Answer: C) By the tail base or neck scruff

2. **Rabbits should be lifted by supporting:**
   A) Only the forelimbs
   B) Only the ears
   C) Only the abdomen
   D) Both hindquarters and forelimbs
   Answer: D) Both hindquarters and forelimbs

3. **Which of the following is a restraint device?**
   A) Syringe
   B) Cone
   C) Pipette
   D) Balance
   Answer: B) Cone

4. **Signs of animal distress include all EXCEPT:**
   A) Immobility
   B) Bright eyes
   C) Excessive grooming
   D) Aggression
   Answer: B) Bright eyes

5. **Ideal temperature for rodent housing is:**
   A) 10–15°C
   B) 16–19°C
   C) 20–26°C
   D) 30–35°C
   Answer: C) 20–26°C

6. **What is the function of a quarantine room?**
   A) Feed storage
   B) Disease observation
   C) Animal sacrifice
   D) Surgery

Answer: B) Disease observation

7. **Which of the following is an inbred strain?**
   A) Wistar rat
   B) Swiss albino mouse
   C) BALB/c mouse
   D) Rabbit
   Answer: C) BALB/c mouse

8. **Outbreeding results in:**
   A) Genetically identical animals
   B) Deformities
   C) Reduced variability
   D) Increased genetic variability
   Answer: D) Increased genetic variability

9. **What is the average duration of the estrous cycle in mice?**
   A) 7–10 days
   B) 4–5 days
   C) 12–14 days
   D) 20 days
   Answer: B) 4–5 days

10. **How are pregnant rodents generally identified?**
    A) Aggression
    B) Weight loss
    C) Weight gain and abdominal distension
    D) Bright fur
    Answer: C) Weight gain and abdominal distension

11. **What is hybrid breeding?**
    A) Mating animals of the same litter
    B) Mating different species
    C) Crossing different strains for desirable traits
    D) Random mating
    Answer: C) Crossing different strains for desirable traits

12. **Which is NOT a structural component of an animal house?**
    A) Record room
    B) Operating theatre
    C) Wash area
    D) Quarantine area
    Answer: B) Operating theatre

13. **Ideal humidity range in animal rooms is:**
    A) 10–20%
    B) 30–70%
    C) 80–90%
    D) 0–10%
    Answer: B) 30–70%

14. **What does HEPA stand for in ventilation systems?**
    A) High Efficiency Particulate Air
    B) High Energy Power Access
    C) Heat Exchange Pressure Air
    D) None of the above
    Answer: A) High Efficiency Particulate Air

15. **What is the standard light-dark cycle maintained?**
    A) 8:16
    B) 12:12
    C) 10:14
    D) 14:10
    Answer: B) 12:12

16. **Which container is suitable for animal transport?**
    A) Transparent glass box
    B) Ventilated and escape-proof box
    C) Plastic bag
    D) Metal bin
    Answer: B) Ventilated and escape-proof box

17. **What type of breeding is used to produce genetically identical animals?**
    A) Outbreeding
    B) Crossbreeding
    C) Inbreeding
    D) Hybridization
    Answer: C) Inbreeding

18. **Which of the following is used for sexing rodents?**
    A) Body weight
    B) Fur color
    C) Distance between anus and genital opening
    D) Cage location
    Answer: C) Distance between anus and genital opening

19. **Which bedding material is preferred for rodents?**
    A) Sand
    B) Corn cob
    C) Wood chips with oil
    D) Stone powder
    Answer: B) Corn cob

20. **Rodents are generally weaned at what age?**
    A) 5 days
    B) 10 days
    C) 21 days
    D) 40 days
    Answer: C) 21 days

21. **Purpose of animal logbooks includes all EXCEPT:**
    A) Monitoring temperature
    B) Tracking animal health
    C) Feeding records
    D) Auditing exam results
    Answer: D) Auditing exam results

22. **What is the male:female ratio for rodent breeding?**
    A) 1:1
    B) 2:2
    C) 1:2 or 1:3
    D) 3:1
    Answer: C) 1:2 or 1:3

23. **Which method is used to detect the stage of the estrous cycle?**
    A) Blood pressure
    B) Vaginal smear
    C) Fecal analysis
    D) Food intake
    Answer: B) Vaginal smear

24. **Crossbreeding is done to:**
    A) Eliminate mutations
    B) Increase muscle mass
    C) Combine beneficial traits
    D) Stop fertility
    Answer: C) Combine beneficial traits

25. **What is the function of bedding in cages?**
    A) Decoration

B) Play surface

C) Absorb moisture and waste

D) Source of food

Answer: C) Absorb moisture and waste

26. **Which species is more sensitive to noise?**

A) Rabbits

B) Guinea pigs

C) Mice

D) Frogs

Answer: B) Guinea pigs

27. **Which animals are commonly used in hybridization studies?**

A) Monkeys

B) Dogs

C) Mice

D) Pigs

Answer: C) Mice

28. **What is the most humane way to transport animals over long distances?**

A) Truck with loud music

B) Cage without ventilation

C) Air-conditioned, ventilated transport containers

D) Open baskets

Answer: C) Air-conditioned, ventilated transport containers

29. **Which parameter is monitored in breeding performance?**

A) Number of cage cleanings

B) Number of mating attempts

C) Litter size

D) Fur length

Answer: C) Litter size

30. **Pregnant rodents are usually separated to prevent:**

A) Overeating

B) Stress from crowding

C) Aggression from pups

D) Early weaning

Answer: B) Stress from crowding

CHAPTER THREE

Euthanasia and Alternatives to Animal Use

3.1 Introduction

Euthanasia, in the context of laboratory animal science, refers to the humane, painless, and rapid termination of an animal's life when its continued existence is no longer scientifically justified or ethically acceptable. It is an essential practice in biomedical research and pharmacological testing, particularly when animals experience unrelieved pain, suffering, or when they reach pre-defined humane endpoints. Euthanasia must be carried out in a manner that prioritizes the animal's welfare while fulfilling scientific or educational objectives responsibly. The decision to euthanize an animal should always be based on ethical judgment, scientific rationale, and regulatory compliance.

The practice of euthanasia is grounded in the principle of ethical necessity. Humane endpoints are clearly defined criteria used to determine when an animal should be removed from an experiment or euthanized to prevent unnecessary pain or distress. These endpoints may include significant weight loss, severe infection, immobility, loss of grooming behavior, or unresponsiveness. Recognizing these indicators early allows for timely intervention and minimizes unnecessary suffering. Humane euthanasia is not only a moral responsibility but also enhances the credibility and ethical standing of research programs. Researchers must balance the acquisition of meaningful scientific data with the duty to preserve animal welfare.

The Committee for the Purpose of Control and Supervision of Experiments on Animals (CPCSEA) strongly emphasizes that every attempt should be made to reduce pain and distress in laboratory animals. According to CPCSEA guidelines, euthanasia must be carried out only by trained personnel using approved techniques and should never be delayed once the humane endpoint is reached. The method used must be appropriate for the species, age, health status, and type of research. Facilities are required to maintain standard operating procedures (SOPs) for euthanasia and ensure the availability of necessary equipment and agents. CPCSEA also mandates that records of euthanasia events be maintained for verification and ethical review.

The Institutional Animal Ethics Committee (IAEC) plays a central role in overseeing euthanasia practices in research institutions. Before starting any experiment, the IAEC must review and approve protocols, including the defined endpoints and proposed euthanasia methods. The committee ensures that the methods are scientifically justified, ethically appropriate, and compliant with CPCSEA regulations. In cases where unexpected suffering arises during a study, IAEC members are authorized to recommend immediate euthanasia or cessation of the experiment. Their role extends to training personnel, inspecting euthanasia facilities, and monitoring adherence to approved practices. By doing so, the IAEC ensures that the dignity and welfare of laboratory animals are protected throughout the research process.

3.2 CPCSEA-Approved Euthanasia Methods

The CPCSEA provides structured and humane guidelines for the euthanasia of laboratory animals in India. These guidelines are designed to ensure that the method chosen results in a rapid loss of consciousness followed by cardiac or respiratory arrest without causing pain or distress. While scientific goals are important, ethical responsibility toward the animals remains the top priority during euthanasia. The method must be appropriate for the species and circumstance and must be applied by trained personnel in accordance with institutional protocols.

Selecting an appropriate method of euthanasia requires consideration of several key guidelines. The chosen technique must be capable of producing quick unconsciousness followed by irreversible death. It should not cause physical discomfort, anxiety, or pain. Animals should be handled gently and calmly during the procedure, and if the method requires the use of anesthetics or chemicals, these must be pharmaceutically approved and used in correct dosages. CPCSEA-approved methods are categorized broadly into physical (e.g., cervical dislocation, decapitation) and chemical (e.g., overdose of anesthetics like sodium pentobarbital or isoflurane) methods, with specific guidelines for different species. In all cases, a secondary physical method (confirmation of death) may be required to ensure that euthanasia is complete.

Several factors influence the selection of a euthanasia method. The species of animal is a primary consideration, as different animals respond differently to specific techniques. For instance, cervical dislocation is acceptable for small rodents like mice but not for larger animals like rabbits. The age of the animal also plays a role; neonatal animals may be more resistant to certain chemical agents due to immature organ systems and may require alternative methods like hypothermia or decapitation. The nature of the experimental procedure also determines the method—some studies require tissue collection free of chemical interference, which may favor physical methods. The type of endpoint, whether planned (as per protocol) or emergency (due to suffering), may also influence the choice and urgency of euthanasia. In all cases, the animal's welfare must take precedence over convenience or tradition.

CPCSEA mandates proper legal and ethical documentation of every euthanasia event. This includes the recording of the animal identification number, species, weight, reason for euthanasia, method used, name of the personnel involved, date and time, and any deviations from standard procedures. These records must be maintained in a central log and submitted to the IAEC for review. Personnel involved in euthanasia must receive adequate training in both the theoretical and practical aspects of the procedure. Training records must also be maintained as part of regulatory compliance. Before using a specific method, a justification must be included in the experimental protocol submitted to the IAEC, explaining why the chosen technique is appropriate for the given situation. The IAEC will evaluate the scientific rationale, ethical validity, and technical feasibility before approval.

3.3 Classification of Euthanasia Techniques

Euthanasia techniques are broadly classified into **physical methods** and **chemical methods**, each with specific indications based on species, age, health status, and research objectives. Physical methods cause death by mechanically disrupting brain activity or circulation and are commonly employed where chemical agents are either unsuitable or may interfere with the intended study outcome. These methods must be executed with precision by trained personnel, as improper technique can cause severe distress or incomplete death. The CPCSEA permits certain physical methods under specific circumstances, particularly in small laboratory animals.

3.3.1 Physical Methods

3.3.1.1 Cervical Dislocation

Cervical dislocation involves dislocating the cervical vertebrae from the skull to rapidly disrupt the spinal cord and brainstem. It is commonly used in mice and very small rodents, typically weighing less than 200 grams. The technique is performed by firmly holding the animal's tail or hind limbs and applying a quick, sharp traction at the neck base to separate the spinal cord from the brain. When performed correctly, it leads to immediate unconsciousness and death due to cessation of brain activity. However, it requires significant training and confidence to ensure effectiveness and prevent suffering.

3.3.1.2 Decapitation

Decapitation is another physical method, mainly used in small animals like mice and rats when tissue samples are needed without chemical interference, especially in neurochemical or endocrine studies. The animal is restrained, and the head is quickly severed using a well-maintained guillotine. Properly performed decapitation results in immediate unconsciousness. However, ethical concerns exist due to the appearance of post-decapitation movements, which are reflexive but may be distressing to observers. The guillotine must be sharp, rust-free, and regularly inspected to ensure humane application.

3.3.1.3 Stunning Followed by Exsanguination

This method is more applicable to large animals like rabbits, pigs, or goats. Stunning refers to rendering the animal unconscious using a blow to the head or captive bolt pistol, followed by rapid bleeding (exsanguination) to ensure death. It is generally used in slaughter or terminal experiments where large volumes of blood are required. While effective, this technique involves a greater risk of operator error and must only be done by highly experienced personnel under veterinary supervision.

3.3.1.4 Advantages of Physical Methods

Physical euthanasia methods are rapid, cost-effective, and require minimal chemical inputs. They eliminate the need for drugs that may contaminate tissues and are ideal in settings where chemical residue may interfere with postmortem analysis. Additionally, physical techniques are often more practical in field conditions or in facilities lacking access to anesthetic gases or injectable euthanasia agents.

3.3.1.5 Disadvantages of Physical Methods

Despite their speed, physical methods carry a high risk of causing distress or incomplete death if not performed correctly. Improper execution can lead to pain, vocalization, or prolonged suffering, making operator skill and training essential. Some physical methods, such as decapitation, can also be visually distressing to observers and may raise ethical objections even when carried out correctly. Therefore, physical euthanasia is only justified when chemical methods are contraindicated or would compromise the research outcome.

3.3.2 Chemical Methods

Chemical methods of euthanasia involve the use of pharmaceutical agents to induce unconsciousness and death in a humane and controlled manner. These methods are widely accepted and recommended for most laboratory species due to their reliability and minimal discomfort to animals when administered correctly. The choice of chemical agent depends on factors such as species, age, health status, and the need for tissue preservation. All chemical euthanasia agents must be administered by trained personnel, and the process should be carefully monitored to confirm the absence of pain and consciousness.

3.3.2.1 Inhalation Agents

Inhalational euthanasia is commonly used in small animals such as mice, rats, and guinea pigs. Agents like **isoflurane** and **carbon dioxide (CO_2)** are frequently employed. Isoflurane is a volatile anesthetic that induces rapid anesthesia followed by death when delivered in high concentrations using a vaporizer and sealed chamber. It is well-tolerated and allows for controlled loss of consciousness, making it suitable for sensitive procedures. Carbon dioxide is also widely used, especially in rodents. It is introduced into a chamber in a gradual-fill method to prevent anxiety or distress. The gas displaces oxygen, leading to hypoxia and eventual death. However, proper concentration, flow rate, and equipment design are critical to avoid distress during exposure.

3.3.2.2 Injectable Agents

Injectable chemical euthanasia involves the intravenous, intraperitoneal, or intracardiac administration of pharmacological agents. **Pentobarbitone sodium**, a barbiturate, is one of the most commonly used agents. It acts as a central nervous system depressant, causing rapid unconsciousness, respiratory depression, and cardiac arrest. The standard dose is generally 150–200 mg/kg for most rodents, administered intravenously or intraperitoneally. Another alternative is the overdose of a **ketamine-xylazine** combination, which produces deep anesthesia followed by death when used at high concentrations. Injectable agents are especially useful for individual euthanasia and situations where inhalational methods are not feasible.

3.3.2.3 Advantages

Chemical methods are widely preferred due to their **painless and less distressing** nature. When administered correctly, they lead to a smooth transition from consciousness to unconsciousness and finally death, minimizing animal suffering. They are also useful in terminal surgical procedures or in cases where accurate control over depth of anesthesia is essential. The availability of standard dosing and the ability to combine with sedatives further enhance their humane profile.

3.3.2.4 Disadvantages

Despite their advantages, chemical euthanasia methods have certain limitations. One major concern is the **cost**, especially in large-scale studies or in resource-limited institutions. The requirement for equipment like vaporizers, gas chambers, or sterile injectable setups adds to operational expenses. Another limitation is the **potential for chemical residues** in animal tissues, which can interfere with downstream biochemical or histological analysis. This is especially important in pharmacological and toxicological studies where clean tissue samples are needed. Moreover, improper dosing or route of administration can lead to prolonged or incomplete euthanasia, emphasizing the need for proper training and monitoring.

3.4 Alternatives to Animal Experiments

Modern pharmacological research increasingly emphasizes the ethical and scientific responsibility of reducing dependence on animal experimentation wherever possible. This shift is supported by the globally recognized **3Rs principle—Replacement**, **Reduction**, and **Refinement**—which serves as a foundational guideline for ethical animal use. These alternatives are not only aligned with animal welfare but also enhance scientific rigor by offering models that may better reflect human biology in certain contexts. Regulatory bodies like CPCSEA, OECD, and international research organizations now strongly encourage the integration of non-animal methods in research protocols wherever feasible.

3.4.1 Introduction to the 3Rs: Replacement, Reduction, Refinement

Replacement refers to the use of methods that avoid or replace the use of live animals in research. This includes the use of in vitro techniques, computer simulations, and human-based studies. **Reduction** focuses on strategies that minimize the number of animals used without compromising the statistical power or scientific validity of the study. Techniques such as improved experimental design, shared control groups, and advanced data analysis tools contribute to this goal. **Refinement** involves modifying experimental procedures to minimize pain, distress, or lasting harm to animals. This includes better handling techniques, improved housing, and the use of anesthetics or analgesics. Together, the 3Rs guide researchers in developing humane, efficient, and scientifically advanced approaches to pharmacological testing.

3.4.2 In Vitro Methods

One of the most practical and widely adopted replacements for animal use is the application of **in vitro methods**. These techniques involve the study of biological processes in controlled environments outside a living organism, typically in test tubes, culture dishes, or bioreactors. In vitro systems are particularly valuable for initial toxicity screening, drug metabolism studies, receptor binding assays, and cytotoxicity tests.

3.4.2.1 Use of Cell Cultures and Human Tissues

Cell culture techniques use isolated cells from human or animal tissues, which are grown under sterile conditions in artificial media. These cells can be primary cultures taken directly from tissues or immortalized cell lines that can be maintained over multiple generations. Human tissue samples, such as those obtained post-surgery or from organ donors, provide more accurate data on drug effects in human physiology, reducing species-to-species variability seen in animal models. Cell culture models also allow high-throughput screening of multiple compounds simultaneously, saving time and resources.

3.4.2.2 Example: Hepatocyte Culture for Hepatotoxicity Studies

A notable example of an in vitro model is the use of **hepatocyte culture** for studying drug-induced liver toxicity. Human or rat hepatocytes can be isolated and maintained in culture to assess the metabolism of drugs and their potential to cause hepatocellular injury. These models help in early identification of compounds with liver toxicity risks, thereby avoiding unnecessary animal use in later stages. The expression of metabolic enzymes, transporters, and cell viability markers can be monitored using colorimetric or fluorescent assays, providing rich mechanistic insights into drug safety.

3.4.3 Ex Vivo Methods

Ex vivo methods serve as an intermediate approach between in vitro and in vivo experimentation, offering a way to study intact tissues or organs outside the living body while preserving their physiological functions. These techniques retain the structural and functional integrity of biological systems better than isolated cell models and are widely used in pharmacology for studying drug effects on specific organs. Ex vivo setups are valuable alternatives that reduce the number of animals used, as multiple experiments can be conducted using tissues from a single animal.

3.4.3.1 Isolated Organ Models (e.g., Frog Heart, Guinea Pig Ileum)

Ex vivo models often involve the removal of an organ or tissue from an animal and its maintenance in a controlled experimental environment. The **isolated frog heart** is one of the oldest and most classic models used to assess cardiac pharmacology. The heart is dissected and placed in a physiological solution like Ringer's or Tyrode's, where its contractions can be observed in response to drugs. This model helps evaluate the chronotropic (heart rate) and inotropic (contractile force) effects of test compounds.

Another frequently used ex vivo model is the **guinea pig ileum**, which is a reliable preparation for studying drug actions on smooth muscle. The excised segment of ileum is mounted in an organ bath filled with aerated physiological saline and connected to a recording device like a kymograph or data acquisition system. Drugs affecting muscarinic receptors, histamine receptors, or serotonin receptors can be evaluated based on changes in ileal contractions. This model is particularly useful for screening **gastrointestinal**, **cholinergic**, and **antispasmodic** agents.

3.4.3.2 Use in Screening for Cardiac, GIT, and Smooth Muscle Effects

Ex vivo techniques allow researchers to observe direct drug responses on cardiac and smooth muscle tissues without systemic influences like metabolism or distribution. For example, **isolated atria or vas deferens** from rats or guinea pigs can be used to study adrenergic or purinergic responses. The **isolated rat uterus** is another model used in reproductive pharmacology, especially for screening uterotonic or tocolytic agents. Since these tissues maintain their receptor systems and physiological responsiveness, they serve as reliable tools to predict in vivo pharmacological actions while using fewer animals.

These models are cost-effective, provide reproducible results, and allow controlled testing of concentration-response relationships. However, they do not fully mimic the complexities of a whole living system, such as drug absorption or biotransformation. Nonetheless, in early drug discovery phases or mechanism-specific investigations, ex vivo methods represent a valuable alternative to whole-animal experimentation.

3.4.4 In Silico / Computer Simulation Models

In silico models—also known as computer-based simulation techniques—represent a cutting-edge alternative to animal use in pharmacological research. These methods utilize computational power to simulate biological processes, predict drug behavior, and analyze pharmacokinetic and pharmacodynamic properties. In silico tools significantly contribute to **Replacement** under the 3Rs principle, reducing the need for animal experiments, especially in early drug development. They are cost-effective, fast, and scalable, allowing researchers to evaluate hundreds of compounds within a short time frame.

3.4.4.1 Predictive Software and AI Models

Modern in silico techniques are powered by **predictive software platforms and artificial intelligence (AI) algorithms**. These systems simulate drug absorption, distribution, metabolism, excretion (ADME), and toxicity profiles using available experimental or molecular data. AI models can analyze complex datasets to identify patterns and predict how a compound will behave in human or animal systems. These models continuously improve as more data is added, enabling better predictions with each iteration. For example, AI-based platforms can forecast adverse drug reactions or suggest optimal dosage regimens, thereby narrowing down candidates before in vivo testing begins.

3.4.4.2 QSAR Models for Drug-Receptor Interactions

Quantitative Structure-Activity Relationship (QSAR) models are widely used in computational pharmacology. These models establish mathematical relationships between the chemical structure of a compound and its biological activity, such as receptor binding or enzyme inhibition. QSAR tools help identify potential pharmacophores, optimize lead compounds, and predict the likelihood of success in target-specific drug development. They are especially useful in receptor-ligand interaction studies, toxicity screening, and virtual compound libraries. By predicting how a drug molecule might interact with a biological target, QSAR models help eliminate ineffective or unsafe compounds early in the drug discovery process.

3.4.4.3 Examples: GastroPlus, Simcyp

Several sophisticated software platforms are commercially available for in silico pharmacology. **GastroPlus** is a physiologically-based pharmacokinetic (PBPK) modeling tool used to predict oral drug absorption, intestinal metabolism, and pharmacokinetics in humans and animals. It simulates how drugs dissolve, permeate through membranes, and reach systemic circulation, thereby assisting in dose optimization and formulation design. **Simcyp** is another powerful simulation tool that predicts drug-drug interactions, variability in populations, and virtual clinical trials using demographic and genetic data. Both platforms are extensively used by pharmaceutical companies and regulatory agencies to support non-animal-based risk assessment and decision-making.

In silico tools are transforming the landscape of pharmacological research, enabling **ethical, efficient, and highly informative alternatives** to traditional animal models. However, they are not yet complete replacements for all experimental needs and are best used in combination with other methods to support informed and humane research strategies.

3.4.5 Zebrafish Models

Zebrafish (*Danio rerio*) have emerged as one of the most promising and widely accepted alternatives to traditional mammalian models in pharmacological and toxicological research. Their unique physiological and genetic features, combined with practical advantages such as low maintenance cost and ethical acceptability, make them ideal for early-stage drug screening and mechanistic studies. As a vertebrate species, zebrafish share a high degree of genetic and organ system similarity with humans, enabling meaningful extrapolation of results, especially in areas like developmental biology, neuropharmacology, and toxicology.

3.4.5.1 Why Zebrafish Are Preferred: Transparent Body, Rapid Growth

Zebrafish embryos and larvae are naturally transparent, allowing researchers to visually observe organ development, blood flow, neuronal activity, and cellular responses in real-time without invasive procedures. This transparency enables direct visualization of drug effects on live tissues under a microscope, offering dynamic insights into pharmacological responses. Additionally, zebrafish have a rapid reproductive cycle—females can lay hundreds of eggs weekly, and embryonic development is extremely fast, with most organs formed within 48 to 72 hours post-fertilization. These features facilitate high-throughput screening of multiple compounds within short timeframes.

3.4.5.2 Use in Toxicology, Cardiology, and Neuropharmacology Screening

Zebrafish are extensively used in **toxicological studies** to assess acute, subacute, and developmental toxicity of drugs and environmental chemicals. Standardized tests such as the Fish Embryo Toxicity (FET) assay are recognized by international bodies like OECD. In **cardiology**, zebrafish heart rate, blood flow, and vascular structure can be measured in response to test compounds, making them a valuable model for screening cardiotoxicity and vasodilatory drugs. **Neuropharmacology** applications include behavioral assays for anxiety, locomotion, and seizure activity using larval and adult zebrafish. These models help in identifying CNS-active compounds, studying neurodegenerative disease pathways, and screening antiepileptic or antidepressant drugs.

3.4.5.3 Ethical and Cost Benefits Over Rodents

Zebrafish offer significant **ethical advantages** over mammalian models, particularly in early developmental stages where they are not classified under higher animal use regulations in many countries. This simplifies approval processes and allows for broader experimental flexibility. Moreover, zebrafish require **less space, water, and feed** compared to rodents, making them a **cost-effective** alternative, especially for high-volume screening. Their housing infrastructure is scalable and automated systems are available for egg sorting, imaging, and data analysis, further reducing labor and operational expenses.

Due to their unique blend of **biological relevance, experimental convenience**, and **regulatory flexibility**, zebrafish are now widely adopted in academia, pharmaceutical companies, and regulatory bodies as a powerful complement or alternative to traditional animal models.

3.5 Advantages and Limitations of Alternative Methods

The integration of alternative methods into pharmacological research reflects a significant advancement in both scientific innovation and ethical responsibility. As awareness of animal welfare increases and regulatory standards evolve, alternative techniques are gaining widespread adoption across drug discovery, toxicity testing, and mechanistic studies. These methods provide several important advantages, especially in early stages of compound evaluation, while also presenting certain limitations that must be considered before replacing in vivo models entirely.

3.5.1 Advantages

One of the most important benefits of alternative methods is the **reduction in the use of live animals**, which aligns directly with ethical principles and the 3Rs (Replacement, Reduction, Refinement). By substituting or supplementing animal use, these methods promote humane science while still enabling valuable experimental outcomes. Techniques such as in vitro assays, in silico models, and zebrafish testing allow researchers to conduct meaningful evaluations without the need for large numbers of rodents or higher mammals.

Another advantage is the **faster turnaround time** and **cost-effectiveness** of alternative systems. For instance, cell-based assays and computer models can process hundreds of compounds in days, compared to the weeks or months required for animal studies. This rapid screening accelerates drug development and helps eliminate non-viable candidates early in the process, thereby saving significant time and resources. Models like zebrafish and organ-on-chip devices also offer high-throughput compatibility, further enhancing research efficiency.

Alternative techniques are particularly **valuable in early screening and toxicity prediction**, allowing the identification of compounds with hepatotoxic, cardiotoxic, or neurotoxic potential before entering animal or clinical trials. This early detection not only protects animal welfare but also improves overall drug safety and decreases the risk of failure in later phases of development. In vitro models such as hepatocyte cultures or cardiac myocytes can yield mechanistic data on metabolism, enzyme inhibition, and receptor interactions that guide decision-making in preclinical pipelines.

Furthermore, alternative methods enjoy **better acceptance in modern regulatory environments**, especially for initial toxicity and safety evaluations. Agencies such as OECD, US FDA, and ECHA have recognized and validated several in vitro and computational assays, and international guidelines are now being updated to incorporate non-animal data in risk assessment. This regulatory shift supports global harmonization and encourages institutions to adopt validated alternatives as part of ethical compliance and scientific transparency.

3.5.2 Limitations

Despite their many benefits, alternative methods are not without limitations, particularly when it comes to replicating the complex, systemic nature of whole-animal biology. While they can complement or reduce reliance on animal experiments, in many cases they cannot completely replace them—especially in regulatory toxicology, behavioral pharmacology, and long-term safety studies. Understanding these limitations is important when designing ethically sound and scientifically reliable research protocols.

One of the key limitations is their **limited predictive value for whole-body responses**. In vitro and in silico models, though powerful, cannot replicate the complex interplay between multiple organs, hormonal systems, immune responses, and physiological feedback mechanisms. For example, a compound might appear safe in a liver cell line but may show toxicity only after being metabolized in the body or interacting with other organs. Whole-body absorption, distribution, and clearance of drugs can only be assessed through live systems, which is essential for finalizing dosage regimens and predicting adverse effects.

Alternative methods also **cannot assess behavioral, metabolic, or chronic toxicity** with the same accuracy as in vivo models. Behavioral responses such as anxiety, depression, cognition, or pain—critical endpoints in CNS drug development—can only be evaluated in conscious animals through validated behavioral assays. Similarly, chronic toxicity, carcinogenicity, or reproductive effects that develop over weeks or months cannot be captured using short-term cellular or computational models. This makes animal models indispensable for certain types of safety evaluations and pharmacodynamic profiling.

Even though regulatory frameworks are evolving, **many agencies still require animal data**, especially for late-stage toxicological assessment, investigational new drug (IND) applications, and certain pharmacokinetic parameters. While alternative methods are increasingly accepted for early-stage testing and as supporting evidence, they often must be paired with confirmatory in vivo results to meet global regulatory requirements. This reflects a cautious approach to ensure public safety, especially when data from alternatives alone is insufficient or lacks long-term validation.

Finally, these methods require **skilled personnel and specialized infrastructure**. In vitro models demand expertise in sterile techniques, cell culture, and assay validation, while in silico tools require bioinformatics knowledge and access to high-end computing systems. Establishing and maintaining zebrafish labs, microfluidic chips, or 3D culture systems involves significant setup costs, technical training, and ongoing maintenance. Institutions lacking such resources may find it challenging to implement these methods effectively without collaboration or funding support.

Hence, while alternative approaches offer remarkable potential, they must be applied with awareness of their scope and constraints. In most cases, the most effective strategy is a combined model—integrating alternatives to reduce animal use where possible, while retaining critical in vivo studies where necessary for holistic evaluation.

MCQs

1. **What does "euthanasia" mean in the context of laboratory animal science?**
   A) Sterilization of animals
   B) Humane killing to prevent pain and suffering
   C) Transfer to another lab
   D) Quarantine
   Answer: B) Humane killing to prevent pain and suffering

2. **Which Indian regulatory body approves euthanasia methods?**
   A) WHO
   B) FDA
   C) CPCSEA
   D) ICMR
   Answer: C) CPCSEA

3. **Which of the following is a physical method of euthanasia?**
   A) Isoflurane overdose
   B) Cervical dislocation
   C) Ketamine injection
   D) CO_2 inhalation
   Answer: B) Cervical dislocation

4. **Inhalation of CO_2 is classified as a:**
   A) Physical method
   B) Mechanical method
   C) Chemical method
   D) Behavioral method
   Answer: C) Chemical method

5. **Cervical dislocation is commonly used in which species?**
   A) Guinea pigs
   B) Monkeys
   C) Mice
   D) Rabbits
   Answer: C) Mice

6. **Which factor is NOT considered when selecting a euthanasia method?**
   A) Animal age
   B) Lab color
   C) Species
   D) Procedure type
   Answer: B) Lab color

7. **Which injectable drug is commonly used for euthanasia?**
   A) Glucose
   B) Saline
   C) Pentobarbitone
   D) Insulin
   Answer: C) Pentobarbitone

8. **The concept of '3Rs' stands for:**
   A) Reduce, Recycle, Reuse
   B) Replace, Reduce, Refine
   C) Recognize, Record, Report
   D) Rescue, Return, Rehouse
   Answer: B) Replace, Reduce, Refine

9. **Which of the following is NOT a goal of the 3Rs?**
   A) Use more animals
   B) Use alternatives
   C) Improve animal welfare
   D) Reduce pain
   Answer: A) Use more animals

10. **Zebrafish are considered a useful alternative model because:**
    A) They are mammals

B) They are cheap and transparent

C) They are genetically identical to humans

D) They are nocturnal

Answer: B) They are cheap and transparent

11. **What is the main disadvantage of physical euthanasia methods?**

A) High cost

B) Residue interference

C) Potential distress if done improperly

D) No equipment needed

Answer: C) Potential distress if done improperly

12. **Which CPCSEA committee approves animal experimentation protocols?**

A) IAEC

B) ICMR

C) FDA

D) GCP

Answer: A) IAEC

13. **Which of the following is an example of in vitro method?**

A) Frog heart experiment

B) Hepatocyte culture

C) Mouse climbing test

D) Tail flick test

Answer: B) Hepatocyte culture

14. **The term "refinement" in 3Rs refers to:**

A) Using more chemicals

B) Decreasing data quality

C) Improving techniques to reduce suffering

D) Repeating the experiment

Answer: C) Improving techniques to reduce suffering

15. **Which method uses organ systems removed from animals for testing?**

A) In vivo

B) Ex vivo

C) In silico

D) Placebo

Answer: B) Ex vivo

16. **What does 'in silico' refer to in research?**

A) Testing in animals

B) Testing in humans

C) Computer-based simulations

D) Testing on organs

Answer: C) Computer-based simulations

17. **Which software is used for in silico pharmacokinetic modeling?**

A) GraphPad

B) Excel

C) GastroPlus

D) Zoom

Answer: C) GastroPlus

18. **Which chemical method is preferred for small rodents?**

A) Morphine

B) CO_2 inhalation

C) Ether

D) Saline

Answer: B) CO_2 inhalation

19. **Why are zebrafish used in toxicity screening?**

A) They do not feel pain

B) They are mammals

C) They allow real-time observation of organs

D) They live in water

Answer: C) They allow real-time observation of organs

20. **What does $ED_5{}^0$ mean?**

A) Dose that kills 50% animals

B) Dose that shows 50% response

C) Expiry dose

D) Emergency dose

Answer: B) Dose that shows 50% response

21. **Which of the following is a disadvantage of alternatives to animal use?**

A) Quick results

B) Limited whole-body prediction

C) Cost-effective

D) Accepted globally

Answer: B) Limited whole-body prediction

22. **Which method uses isolated tissue but not the whole animal?**

A) In vivo

B) Ex vivo

C) In vitro

D) In silico

Answer: B) Ex vivo

23. **What is a common example of ex vivo preparation?**

    A) Frog heart

    B) Cell line

    C) Software

    D) ELISA

    Answer: A) Frog heart

24. **Who is responsible for maintaining euthanasia records?**

    A) Pharmacist

    B) IAEC

    C) Animal caretaker

    D) Trained personnel

    Answer: D) Trained personnel

25. **Why is pentobarbitone used in euthanasia?**

    A) Causes vomiting

    B) Increases BP

    C) Induces deep anesthesia and death

    D) Stimulates appetite

    Answer: C) Induces deep anesthesia and death

26. **Which of the following is a benefit of computer simulation in pharmacology?**

    A) Ethical issues

    B) Predicts organ toxicity

    C) Time-consuming

    D) Requires animal blood

    Answer: B) Predicts organ toxicity

27. **Which in vitro technique is used for liver toxicity?**

    A) Tail flick test

    B) Frog ileum

    C) Hepatocyte culture

    D) Open field test

    Answer: C) Hepatocyte culture

28. **Which ethical principle is followed before animal sacrifice?**

    A) Clinical trial report

    B) GCP

    C) Humane endpoint

    D) Quarantine report

    Answer: C) Humane endpoint

29. **Sentinel animals are used to:**
    A) Guard cages
    B) Reproduce faster
    C) Monitor disease spread
    D) Administer drugs
    Answer: C) Monitor disease spread

30. **Which of the following is required for a legal euthanasia process?**
    A) IAEC approval
    B) Fast results
    C) Old animals only
    D) Personal choice
    Answer: A) IAEC approval

Short Answer Questions

1. **What is euthanasia in laboratory animals?**
   Euthanasia is the humane, painless, and rapid killing of laboratory animals to minimize suffering, often at the end of an experiment.

2. **Why is euthanasia necessary in animal experiments?**
   It is used to prevent or end severe pain and distress in animals that cannot be rehabilitated or reused.

3. **Name the Indian authority that regulates euthanasia in research animals.**
   CPCSEA (Committee for the Purpose of Control and Supervision of Experiments on Animals).

4. **What is the humane endpoint?**
   A predefined point during an experiment at which an animal is euthanized to avoid unnecessary pain or distress.

5. **Mention two physical methods of euthanasia.**
   Cervical dislocation and decapitation.

6. **Give two chemical methods of euthanasia.**
   CO_2 inhalation and pentobarbitone sodium injection.

7. **What factors are considered before selecting a euthanasia method?**
   Species, age, type of procedure, and endpoint requirements.

8. **What does '3Rs' stand for in animal ethics?**
   Replacement, Reduction, and Refinement.

9. **What is meant by 'Replacement' in the 3Rs principle?**
   Using non-animal methods such as in vitro, in silico, or computer-based simulations instead of live animals.

10. **Define 'Reduction' in animal use.**
    Minimizing the number of animals used without compromising the quality of scientific results.

11. **What is 'Refinement' in animal research ethics?**
    Improving experimental techniques to reduce pain and enhance animal welfare.

12. **Name two in vitro alternatives to animal use.**
    Hepatocyte cultures and human skin cell cultures.

13. **What are ex vivo methods?**
    Experiments done on isolated organs or tissues taken from an animal, like frog heart or guinea pig ileum.

14. **What is meant by in silico testing?**

Use of computer-based simulations and software models to predict drug actions or toxicity.

15. **Give one example of an in silico model.**

GastroPlus or Simcyp.

16. **Why are zebrafish used in place of rodents in some experiments?**

They are transparent, cost-effective, and have rapid development, allowing real-time study of organ functions.

17. **What is the principle of CO_2 inhalation in euthanasia?**

CO_2 causes unconsciousness and death by hypoxia when inhaled in a controlled environment.

18. **What is cervical dislocation?**

A physical method where the spinal cord is dislocated from the skull, leading to rapid death, used in small rodents.

19. **Name one disadvantage of chemical euthanasia.**

It may interfere with tissue samples used for biochemical or histological analysis.

20. **What is the role of the IAEC in euthanasia approval?**

To review and approve all procedures involving euthanasia, ensuring ethical and humane practices.

21. **Which injectable drug is commonly used for euthanasia in rodents?**

Pentobarbitone sodium.

22. **What is an advantage of using alternative methods?**

They reduce the number of animals used and often provide quicker, cost-effective results.

23. **What is the limitation of in vitro models?**

They cannot replicate full-body responses such as behavior or immune function.

24. **Why is record keeping important in euthanasia procedures?**

To ensure transparency, accountability, and compliance with CPCSEA guidelines.

25. **What is a sentinel animal?**

An animal used to monitor the health status of a colony, especially for detecting infectious diseases.

26. **What is meant by justification of euthanasia method?**

Explaining why a particular method was chosen based on animal type and scientific goals.

27. **Which guidelines should be followed when using euthanasia methods in India?**
CPCSEA guidelines and IAEC-approved SOPs.
28. **Which cell line is commonly used for liver toxicity testing?**
Hepatocyte cell line.
29. **What is the difference between in vitro and ex vivo methods?**
In vitro uses isolated cells or tissues outside the organism, while ex vivo uses intact organs removed from the body.
30. **How can animal stress during euthanasia be minimized?**
By handling animals gently, using appropriate anesthesia, and choosing the least distressful method.

Fill in the Blanks

1. Euthanasia refers to the ___________, painless, and quick killing of laboratory animals.
   Answer: humane

2. The regulatory authority for animal experiments in India is ___________.
   Answer: CPCSEA

3. Cervical dislocation is a ___________ method of euthanasia.
   Answer: physical

4. Pentobarbitone sodium is an example of a ___________ agent used for euthanasia.
   Answer: chemical

5. The 3Rs in animal ethics stand for Replacement, ___________, and Refinement.
   Answer: Reduction

6. The ethical endpoint at which an animal must be euthanized to avoid pain is called the ___________ endpoint.
   Answer: humane

7. Hepatocyte cultures are used in ___________ methods of toxicity screening.
   Answer: in vitro

8. Computer-based simulations in pharmacology are called ___________ methods.
   Answer: in silico

9. The software ___________ is used to simulate drug absorption and metabolism.
   Answer: GastroPlus

10. Zebrafish are preferred as alternative models due to their ___________ body and rapid development.
    Answer: transparent

11. ___________ animals are used to monitor disease in laboratory animal colonies.
    Answer: Sentinel

12. Inhalation of ___________ gas is a commonly used chemical euthanasia method for rodents.
    Answer: carbon dioxide

13. The principle of ___________ in the 3Rs aims at minimizing the number of animals used.

    Answer: Reduction

14. Cervical dislocation is commonly performed in ___________ and other small rodents.

    Answer: mice

15. ___________ animals should always be used for training before performing euthanasia.

    Answer: Dead

16. Ethical approval for any euthanasia method must be obtained from the ___________.

    Answer: IAEC

17. The principle of Replacement encourages using ___________ instcad of live animals.

    Answer: alternatives

18. Ex vivo models involve using ___________ organs from animals for pharmacological studies.

    Answer: isolated

19. The chemical agent ___________ can be administered to cause overdose and euthanasia.

    Answer: pentobarbitone

20. Ethical and scientific justification must be included in the ___________ before conducting animal studies.

    Answer: protocol

CHAPTER FOUR

Toxicity Testing and OECD Guidelines

4.1 Introduction to Toxicity Studies

In the field of pharmacology and drug development, **toxicity** refers to the degree to which a substance can cause harm to an organism. In simple terms, it is the potential of a chemical or drug to damage biological systems. Understanding a compound's toxicity profile is essential to ensure its safe use in humans, especially before advancing to clinical trials. Toxicity studies are designed to evaluate the harmful effects of drugs on various organs and biological functions and to establish safe exposure limits.

Toxicity testing plays a **vital role in the early phases of drug development**. Before a new drug can be administered to human volunteers or patients, it must undergo rigorous safety evaluation in laboratory animals or alternative models. These studies help determine the doses at which a drug becomes harmful, the type of damage it can cause (acute or chronic), the organs it affects most, and how it behaves over time inside the body. Data from toxicity studies are used to calculate safety margins, decide dose ranges for clinical trials, and design risk mitigation strategies.

Regulatory toxicology is the discipline that ensures toxicological assessments are standardized, validated, and acceptable to authorities such as the US FDA, European Medicines Agency (EMA), and Indian regulators like CDSCO. These bodies rely on guidelines issued by the **Organisation for Economic Co-operation and Development (OECD)**, which provide internationally accepted methods for conducting various types of toxicity tests. Regulatory toxicology ensures consistency, ethical compliance, and public safety by enforcing these structured testing protocols. As a result, every new drug must pass a series of toxicity tests—including acute, sub-acute, chronic, reproductive, and genotoxicity studies—before it can reach the market.

4.1.4 Concept of NOAEL, LOAEL, and Therapeutic Index

In toxicological evaluations, three critical concepts help in determining the safety margins of drug candidates: **NOAEL (No Observed Adverse Effect Level)**, **LOAEL (Lowest Observed Adverse Effect Level)**, and the **Therapeutic Index (TI)**. These parameters are fundamental in deciding appropriate dose ranges for both animal studies and human clinical trials.

The **NOAEL** is defined as the highest dose at which there are **no statistically or biologically significant adverse effects** observed in the test subjects compared to the control group. This value is crucial because it represents a threshold below which the drug can be considered safe, at least within the tested conditions. NOAEL is typically determined through repeated dose toxicity studies (such as sub-acute or chronic toxicity tests), where animals are exposed to multiple dose levels over a specified time. NOAEL serves as a reference point to derive the **human equivalent dose (HED)** and calculate **safety factors** for first-in-human dosing.

The **LOAEL**, on the other hand, is the **lowest dose at which adverse effects begin to appear** in the test population. It marks the point where toxicity becomes detectable and provides insight into the drug's risk potential. The difference between NOAEL and LOAEL helps define the steepness of the dose-response curve and is especially important in setting regulatory exposure limits such as the **Acceptable Daily Intake (ADI)** for long-term exposure or **Reference Dose (RfD)** in environmental toxicology.

The **Therapeutic Index (TI)** is a ratio that quantifies the safety margin of a drug. It is typically calculated as:

$$TI = LD_{50} / ED_{50}$$

Where:

- **LD_{50}** is the median lethal dose—the dose at which 50% of the test population dies.
- **ED_{50}** is the median effective dose—the dose that produces the desired therapeutic effect in 50% of the population.

A **high therapeutic index** indicates a large margin between effective and toxic doses, suggesting that the drug is relatively safe. Conversely, a **narrow TI** means there is a small window between efficacy and toxicity, requiring precise dosing and careful monitoring (e.g., in drugs like digoxin or lithium). In modern pharmacology, a drug's therapeutic index is critical not only for regulatory approval but also for clinical safety and patient-specific dosing decisions.

4.2 Types of Toxicity Studies

4.2.1 Acute Toxicity

Acute toxicity studies are conducted to evaluate the toxic effects of a **single dose** of a drug or chemical substance administered by a particular route (oral, dermal, or inhalational). These studies are generally the **first step in safety evaluation** of new compounds and are used to estimate the immediate hazard of exposure. The primary aim is to identify the dose that causes observable adverse effects or death and to determine an approximate LD_5^0 **(median lethal dose)** if applicable.

4.2.1.1 Definition: Single Dose Study

An acute toxicity test typically involves the administration of a single, well-defined dose or a short-term exposure (usually less than 24 hours). The study design may include various dose levels to observe a range of responses. Based on OECD guidelines (such as Test Guideline 423 or 425), rodents like mice or rats are most commonly used, and the substance is usually given orally unless otherwise specified by the intended route of human administration.

4.2.1.2 Observation Period (14 Days)

After dosing, the animals are carefully monitored for **14 days**, which is the standard observation period in acute toxicity studies. This timeframe allows for the detection of **delayed toxic effects** and helps assess both immediate and sub-acute symptoms following the exposure. Observations are recorded at multiple time intervals—initially frequent (e.g., every 30 minutes for the first few hours) and then at least once daily until the end of the study. Any clinical symptoms or abnormal behaviors are noted in detail.

4.2.1.3 Parameters: Behavioural Signs, Mortality, Body Weight

Key parameters assessed during acute toxicity testing include:

- **Behavioural signs:** These include changes in gait, posture, grooming, locomotion, respiration, convulsions, tremors, piloerection, and reflexes. Any sign of pain, distress, or neurological alteration is recorded.

- **Mortality**: The number and timing of deaths in each dose group are carefully documented. This information is critical in estimating the lethal dose or establishing a safe upper limit for future dosing.
- **Body weight monitoring**: Animals are weighed at the start, periodically during the study, and at termination. A significant loss in body weight (more than 10%) may indicate systemic toxicity or impaired metabolic functions.

Other assessments may include food and water intake, gross necropsy at the end of the study, and histopathological analysis of key organs in some cases. Acute toxicity studies form the basis for defining dose ranges in sub-acute and chronic studies, and they are essential for risk classification and labeling of chemicals.

4.2.2 Sub-Acute Toxicity

Sub-acute toxicity studies are designed to evaluate the adverse effects of repeated dosing over a **short-term period, typically 14 to 28 days.** These studies help identify target organs, cumulative toxicity, and early biomarkers of organ damage. Sub-acute testing also helps to determine the **No Observed Adverse Effect Level (NOAEL)**, which is crucial for calculating the safe starting dose in humans and for planning long-term toxicity studies.

4.2.2.1 Exposure for 14–28 Days

In a sub-acute toxicity protocol, the test compound is administered daily to animals over a period of **14 to 28 consecutive days**, depending on the study design and regulatory requirements. The **oral route** is most commonly used, although dermal, inhalation, or parenteral routes may be applied based on the intended human exposure. Animals are observed throughout the treatment period and at the end of the study for any clinical or pathological changes.

4.2.2.2 Common Doses: Low, Medium, High

Typically, **three dose levels** are selected—**low**, **medium**, and **high**—based on the results of acute toxicity data. The **high dose** should produce signs of toxicity but not mortality, the **medium dose** may show minimal effects, and the **low dose** should ideally represent a no-effect level. A **control group** receiving only the vehicle is also included for comparison. Dose selection must be scientifically justified and supported by preliminary data.

4.2.2.3 Endpoints: Organ Weight, Histopathology, Hematology

Several **critical endpoints** are assessed during and after the dosing period:

- **Organ weight**: Major organs such as liver, kidneys, spleen, heart, brain, and testes are removed and weighed at necropsy. Changes in organ weight can be an early sign of toxicity even before microscopic alterations are visible.
- **Histopathology**: Tissue samples from target organs are fixed, sectioned, and stained for microscopic examination. Pathological changes such as inflammation, necrosis, fibrosis, or cellular degeneration are evaluated to identify the extent and nature of organ damage.
- **Hematology**: Blood samples are collected to analyze parameters like hemoglobin concentration, red and white blood cell counts, platelet count, and differential leukocyte count. These parameters indicate the compound's effect on the **hematopoietic system** and immune response.

Additional evaluations may include **biochemical assays** (e.g., liver enzymes, renal markers), **urinalysis**, and **gross pathology** to provide a comprehensive toxicological profile. Sub-acute studies are vital in screening drugs for **early organ-specific toxicities**, especially liver, kidney, and blood-related effects, and serve as a bridge to more extensive **sub-chronic or chronic toxicity studies**.

4.2.3 Sub-Chronic Toxicity

Sub-chronic toxicity studies are conducted to evaluate the adverse effects of **repeated administration** of a test substance over an **intermediate duration**, typically **90 days**. These studies provide deeper insights into the **cumulative toxic potential**, **organ-specific damage**, and **reversibility** of effects induced by repeated exposure. Sub-chronic studies are required by regulatory agencies before long-term (chronic) studies are initiated and are considered a vital step in the risk assessment process.

4.2.3.1 Duration: 90 Days Repeated Dose

In sub-chronic studies, the test compound is administered daily to laboratory animals—commonly **rats or mice**—for a period of **90 consecutive days**. Dosing may be oral, dermal, or inhalational, depending on the expected human exposure. The study design includes at least three dose levels (low, mid, high) along with a control group. Satellite groups may also be included to evaluate **recovery** after a withdrawal period, typically lasting 14–28 days post-treatment. This helps in identifying whether observed effects are reversible, persistent, or progressive.

4.2.3.2 Toxicokinetic Studies and Biomarker Evaluation

Sub-chronic studies often include **toxicokinetic analysis**, which involves measuring **plasma or tissue concentrations** of the drug or its metabolites at multiple time points. This helps correlate **systemic exposure** with observed toxicological effects and supports pharmacokinetic modeling. In addition, researchers evaluate **biomarkers**—specific biochemical or molecular indicators of organ injury or dysfunction. Examples include serum **ALT and AST** levels (for liver damage), **creatinine and BUN** (for renal toxicity), or **troponins** (for cardiac effects). The use of validated biomarkers helps in early detection of toxicity before pathological changes become apparent.

4.2.3.3 Used in Dose-Range Finding for Chronic Studies

Sub-chronic toxicity studies are critical in determining the **dose range** and **target organs** for subsequent **chronic toxicity studies**, which may last six months to two years. The **NOAEL** derived from sub-chronic studies is often used to set the highest dose in long-term studies and contributes to setting **human exposure limits** such as the **ADI (Acceptable Daily Intake)** and **TDI (Tolerable Daily Intake)**. Sub-chronic results are also used to predict **species sensitivity**, identify **cumulative effects**, and guide safety decisions in both regulatory submissions and clinical trial planning.

4.2.4 Chronic Toxicity

Chronic toxicity studies are designed to evaluate the harmful effects of a drug or chemical when administered over an extended period, typically ranging from **6 months to 2 years**. These studies simulate prolonged human exposure and are especially important for **drugs intended for long-term use**, such as those for diabetes, hypertension, asthma, or psychiatric disorders. Chronic studies help identify **cumulative toxicities**, delayed adverse effects, **organ degeneration**, and potential **carcinogenic risks**.

4.2.4.1 Long-Term Exposure: 6 Months to 2 Years

Chronic studies generally involve **daily administration** of the test substance over a long period—**at least 6 months in rodents** and **up to 2 years in non-rodents** (like dogs or primates), depending on the regulatory requirement. The choice of species, route of administration, and dose levels are determined based on data from sub-acute and sub-chronic studies. Animals are monitored for mortality, body weight, behavioral changes, food and water intake, and general health status throughout the study. Interim and terminal sacrifices are scheduled for **gross pathology and histopathological evaluation**.

4.2.4.2 Goal: Detect Cumulative Toxicity and Carcinogenicity

The main objective of chronic toxicity testing is to detect **cumulative toxicity**, which may not be visible in shorter studies. Long-term exposure may reveal **progressive organ damage**, **immune suppression**, or **neurotoxicity**. Chronic studies are also used to evaluate the **carcinogenic potential** of a compound by monitoring for **tumor formation** in organs over time. This is essential for chemicals or drugs that may interact with DNA or cause prolonged cellular stress, such as industrial chemicals, hormonal agents, or certain antibiotics.

4.2.4.3 Essential for Drugs Meant for Chronic Use

For any drug intended for **chronic human administration**, such as those used in **cardiovascular, neurological, endocrine, or autoimmune conditions**, chronic toxicity data is a mandatory requirement for regulatory submission. These studies help define **long-term safety profiles**, establish **maximum safe daily doses**, and support the design of **Phase III and post-marketing surveillance** plans. The data obtained are also critical in determining if **special monitoring** is needed in clinical use (e.g., liver function tests, blood counts, or ECGs).

Chronic toxicity studies are expensive, time-consuming, and ethically intensive, but they remain the **gold standard** for assessing the full spectrum of toxic effects that may arise from lifelong drug exposure.

4.3 $LD_5{}^0$ and $ED_5{}^0$ Determination

Understanding the relationship between a drug's dose and its biological effect is central to toxicology and pharmacology. Two commonly used quantitative indicators for this purpose are $LD_5{}^0$ **(Lethal Dose for 50% of the test population)** and $ED_5{}^0$ **(Effective Dose for 50%)**. While $LD_5{}^0$ measures toxicity, $ED_5{}^0$ evaluates pharmacological efficacy. These values help in determining the **therapeutic index** of a drug and guide its safe and effective use.

4.3.1 $LD_5{}^0$ (Lethal Dose 50%)

4.3.1.1 Definition and Significance

$LD_5{}^0$ is defined as the **single dose of a substance** that causes death in **50% of the experimental animals,** typically within a defined observation period (usually 14 days). It is expressed in terms of mg or g of substance per kg of body weight (mg/kg or g/kg). $LD_5{}^0$ serves as a benchmark for comparing the **acute toxicity** of different substances and helps in classifying chemicals into hazard categories. Although modern toxicology is shifting towards non-lethal methods, LD_{50} remains an important historical and reference measure.

4.3.1.2 Traditional Methods: Karber's, Miller and Tainter

Earlier, the determination of LD_{50} was done using **classical methods** involving multiple animal groups and observation of mortality rates:

- **Karber's Method**: This statistical approach estimates LD_{50} using the arithmetic mean of dose intervals and the corresponding mortality fractions. It is relatively simple but assumes linearity in dose-response relationships.
- **Miller and Tainter Method**: A more refined approach that uses **probit analysis**—a statistical transformation of the sigmoid dose-response curve into a straight line. It calculates the log-dose versus probit mortality to determine the LD_{50} with greater precision.

Both methods required **large numbers of animals** and often resulted in significant animal distress and death, leading to ethical concerns and a push for refinement.

4.3.1.3 OECD Alternatives to LD_{50}: Up-and-Down Method (OECD 425)

To reduce animal use and align with ethical practices, the **OECD has introduced alternative methods** for acute toxicity testing. One of the most accepted alternatives is the **Up-and-Down Procedure (UDP)** described under **OECD Test Guideline 425**. In this method:

- A single animal is dosed and observed.
- If the animal survives, the next animal receives a higher dose.
- If the animal dies, the next animal is given a lower dose.
- This continues until a statistically valid estimation of LD_{50} is obtained with **fewer animals** and **reduced mortality**.

The **UDP approach minimizes suffering**, improves data reliability, and complies with the **3Rs principle**, making it a preferred method in modern regulatory toxicology.

4.3.2 ED_{50} (Effective Dose 50%)

While LD_{50} represents a measure of toxicity, **ED_{50}** is a key indicator of **therapeutic efficacy**. It allows researchers to identify the minimum dose at which a drug produces a meaningful effect in 50% of the test population. This helps in **dose standardization, therapeutic window estimation**, and **comparison of potency** between drugs. ED_{50} is essential in both preclinical and clinical phases of drug development.

4.3.2.1 Definition and Role in Efficacy Measurement

ED_{50}, or the **Effective Dose 50%**, is the dose at which **50% of the subjects** exhibit the desired pharmacological effect. It is a **quantitative measure of a drug's potency** and is commonly expressed in mg/kg or µg/kg body weight. ED_{50} is fundamental in selecting doses for therapeutic use, determining the therapeutic index (TI), and designing further efficacy studies. In preclinical pharmacology, it provides a basis to evaluate how well a drug performs in comparison to a standard reference compound.

4.3.2.2 Graphical Method Using Dose-Response Curves

The most common way to determine ED_{50} is by constructing a **dose-response curve**, where:

- The **x-axis** represents the **logarithm of the dose.**
- The **y-axis** represents the **percentage of animals showing the desired effect.**

The resulting sigmoidal curve helps visualize the range of effective doses. The point on the curve corresponding to **50% of the maximum response** is identified as the **ED_{50}**. This graphical method allows researchers to assess the drug's **onset, peak activity**, and **saturation point**. Probit analysis or nonlinear regression models may be used for more accurate estimation.

4.3.2.3 Example: Analgesic ED_{50} Using Tail Flick Latency

A practical example of ED_{50} determination is seen in **analgesic testing** using the **tail flick test** in rats. In this method:

- Animals are exposed to a heat source at the tail, and the **reaction time (latency)** to flick the tail is recorded.
- A compound is administered at different dose levels.
- If a specific dose produces a latency above a defined threshold in **50% of the animals,** that dose is considered the **ED_{50}** for analgesic action.

This method is widely used in preclinical studies for opioids, NSAIDs, and other central analgesics, providing a reliable measure of their **pain-relieving potency.**

4.4 Overview of OECD Guidelines in Toxicology

Toxicological research and regulatory testing require internationally accepted procedures to ensure consistency, reliability, and ethical compliance. The **Organisation for Economic Co-operation and Development (OECD)** plays a central role in this domain by providing validated and globally recognized testing protocols. These **OECD Test Guidelines (TGs)** form the backbone of non-clinical safety evaluations of chemicals, pharmaceuticals, pesticides, and cosmetics across member and non-member countries.

4.4.1 Introduction to OECD and Its Importance in Global Harmonization

The **OECD** is an international organization that promotes policies to improve the economic and social well-being of people worldwide. One of its key contributions in the life sciences is the development of the **OECD Guidelines for the Testing of Chemicals,** which ensure that safety assessments of drugs and chemicals are **scientifically sound, ethically conducted, and mutually accepted** across regulatory authorities. This concept of **Mutual Acceptance of Data (MAD)** minimizes duplication of tests, reduces animal usage, and promotes faster regulatory approvals on a global scale.

4.4.2 Numbering and Naming of Test Guidelines (TGs)

Each **Test Guideline (TG)** is assigned a **unique numerical identifier,** and its title indicates the type of toxicity being evaluated (e.g., acute, chronic, reproductive). The numbering also loosely corresponds to the category of testing: for instance, guidelines in the **400 series** are mainly related to toxicology. The guidelines are updated regularly based on new scientific developments and ethical considerations. They contain detailed protocols covering test design, animal species, dose selection, observation parameters, data analysis, and reporting format.

4.4.3 Key Guidelines

4.4.3.1 OECD TG 425: Acute Oral Toxicity – Up-and-Down Procedure

This guideline outlines the **up-and-down method** for determining acute oral toxicity in rodents. Instead of using large animal groups, it sequentially doses single animals and adjusts the next dose based on the survival of the previous one. This significantly reduces animal usage and aligns with ethical testing principles. The endpoint is the **estimation of LD_{50}**, using a statistical model based on survival outcomes.

4.4.3.2 OECD TG 407: Repeated Dose 28-Day Oral Toxicity Study in Rodents

TG 407 is used for evaluating **sub-acute toxicity** by administering the test substance orally for **28 consecutive days** in rats. The study includes three dose groups and a control, with endpoints such as clinical signs, hematology, clinical biochemistry, organ weights, and histopathology. This guideline is important for identifying early organ-specific toxicities and establishing **NOAEL values**.

4.4.3.3 OECD TG 408: 90-Day (Sub-chronic) Toxicity

TG 408 provides a framework for conducting **90-day repeated dose studies** in rodents, typically rats. It helps assess **sub-chronic toxicity** and includes a detailed evaluation of systemic effects, toxicokinetics, and target organ damage. Satellite recovery groups may also be included. This study is usually required before initiating chronic toxicity or carcinogenicity tests.

4.4.3.4 OECD TG 414: Prenatal Developmental Toxicity

This guideline addresses **teratogenic and developmental toxicity** by assessing the effects of test substances on pregnant animals and their fetuses. Typically conducted in rats or rabbits, TG 414 involves daily dosing from implantation to late gestation. It evaluates parameters like **implantation loss, fetal abnormalities, maternal toxicity, and organ development**. This guideline is essential for reproductive safety assessments.

OECD guidelines form a **scientific and ethical foundation** for toxicity testing and are widely accepted by regulatory bodies worldwide. Their adoption ensures uniformity, promotes international trade, and upholds animal welfare through structured and validated approaches.

4.4.4 Parameters Monitored: Food/Water Intake, Clinical Signs, Hematology, Organ Weight

In all toxicity studies conducted under OECD guidelines, **specific parameters are mandatorily monitored** to assess the physiological and pathological impact of the test substance. These parameters help detect subtle and overt toxic effects and are essential for determining the **NOAEL, LOAEL**, and potential target organ toxicity.

- **Food and water intake** are measured periodically to detect any changes in consumption patterns, which may indicate **gastrointestinal toxicity, metabolic alterations, or general malaise.** A consistent reduction in intake may signal systemic toxicity or palatability issues with the test compound.
- **Clinical signs** are observed daily and include changes in behavior, posture, locomotion, grooming, respiration, and neurological status. Signs like tremors, convulsions, salivation, lethargy, piloerection, or skin changes can suggest **central nervous system, cardiac,** or **dermal toxicity.** The **onset, duration, and severity** of symptoms are recorded systematically.
- **Hematological parameters** are evaluated at the end of the study using blood samples. These include **hemoglobin, red blood cell (RBC) count, white blood cell (WBC) count, platelet count,** and **differential leukocyte counts.** These tests provide insight into **bone marrow function, immune status,** and **systemic inflammation or bleeding tendencies.**
- **Organ weights** are measured post-mortem, especially for **liver, kidneys, heart, lungs, spleen, brain, and reproductive organs.** Changes in organ weight—either hypertrophy or atrophy—can be early indicators of **organ-specific toxicity** even when no visible lesions are present. Absolute and relative organ weights are compared between treated and control groups.

These parameters collectively help in making a comprehensive assessment of a compound's safety profile and potential risks.

4.4.5 Reporting and Documentation as per GLP Norms

All toxicity studies under OECD guidelines must comply with **Good Laboratory Practice (GLP)** standards. GLP is a set of principles that ensure the **integrity, reliability, reproducibility, and transparency** of data submitted to regulatory agencies.

Key documentation and reporting elements include:

- **Detailed study protocol** approved by the Quality Assurance (QA) unit.
- **Raw data records,** including body weights, food intake, clinical observations, and laboratory results.
- **Analytical data** of the test and control substances (identity, purity, stability).

- **Histopathology and necropsy reports** with photographs if applicable.
- **Statistical analysis** and interpretation of findings with reference to historical control data.
- **Final study report** signed by the Study Director, including summary, methodology, results, discussion, conclusions, and compliance statements.

All documents must be stored securely and retained for regulatory audits and future reference. GLP compliance enhances **regulatory acceptability**, reduces duplication of studies, and strengthens the scientific credibility of toxicological findings.

4.5 Reproductive and Teratogenic Toxicity Testing

Testing for reproductive and teratogenic toxicity is crucial in determining the **impact of a drug or chemical on reproductive health and fetal development**. These studies are performed to ensure that exposure to a substance does not adversely affect fertility, embryo-fetal development, or postnatal outcomes. Regulatory authorities require this data before approving any drug for **chronic use, especially in pregnant women or reproductive-age populations.**

4.5.1 Reproductive Toxicity Testing

Reproductive toxicity testing investigates the ability of a compound to **interfere with sexual function, fertility, and reproductive outcomes** in both male and female animals. It includes several phases that examine different stages of reproduction, from gamete formation to neonatal growth.

4.5.1.1 Phases: Fertility Study, Pre-natal, Peri-natal, Post-natal

Reproductive toxicity testing is conducted in **four main phases**, each targeting a specific reproductive stage:

- **Fertility studies** evaluate the effects of the test compound on **spermatogenesis, ovulation, mating behavior, and conception rates.** Both male and female animals are dosed for several weeks before and during mating.
- **Pre-natal studies** involve dosing pregnant females during organogenesis (days 6–15 in rats), a critical period for structural development. The focus is on **embryonic resorption, implantation success, and gross fetal malformations.**

- **Peri-natal studies** begin in the late stages of pregnancy and continue through delivery. These assess the effects of the substance on **parturition, birth survival rates, and maternal behavior.**
- **Post-natal studies** follow the offspring until weaning and sometimes into adolescence to assess **developmental milestones**, growth patterns, and neurobehavioral effects.

Each phase can be conducted separately or as part of **Segment I, II, and III studies**, as defined by regulatory frameworks such as those of the ICH and OECD.

4.5.1.2 Common Models: Rats, Rabbits

Rats and rabbits are the most commonly used species for reproductive toxicity studies due to their **predictable reproductive cycles**, short gestation periods, and **high sensitivity to teratogenic agents**. Rats are preferred for fertility and peri-/post-natal studies, while rabbits are often used in prenatal teratogenicity testing due to their higher susceptibility to developmental defects. Both species allow for **detailed observation of mating, pregnancy, fetal development, and birth outcomes.**

4.5.1.3 Parameters: Mating Behavior, Gestation Length, Litter Size

Important parameters monitored in reproductive toxicity studies include:

- **Mating behavior**: Frequency and timing of copulation, mating index, and time to successful mating.
- **Gestation length**: Normal duration is about **21–23 days in rats** and **28–31 days in rabbits**. Any shortening or prolongation indicates potential reproductive disruption.
- **Litter size and viability**: Number of live births, stillbirths, and survival rate up to weaning are recorded. Smaller litter sizes, increased postnatal deaths, or malformations indicate **adverse effects on reproductive or fetal health.**

Other parameters may include **birth weight, sex ratio, external malformations, organ development,** and **skeletal anomalies** in fetuses. These studies are crucial for assessing the safety of drugs used by **pregnant or potentially pregnant individuals** and for identifying risks to reproductive health.

4.5.2 Teratogenicity Testing

Teratogenicity testing is a specific branch of reproductive toxicity that evaluates whether a substance can cause **structural or functional malformations in the developing fetus** when administered during pregnancy. These studies are essential for assessing the **safety of drugs, chemicals, and environmental agents** that may be used or encountered by pregnant women. Regulatory agencies require teratogenicity data to prevent fetal injury, congenital anomalies, or pregnancy-related complications caused by drug exposure.

4.5.2.1 Definition and Importance

Teratogenicity refers to the **ability of a substance to cause birth defects**, such as malformations in the limbs, heart, brain, eyes, or skeletal system. Teratogenic testing detects such effects through **prenatal studies** conducted in pregnant animals exposed to a test compound during the **most sensitive developmental window**. The data from these studies are used to determine **whether the drug is contraindicated in pregnancy** and to guide appropriate **pregnancy category labeling**.

4.5.2.2 Critical Period: Organogenesis (Day 6–15 in Rats)

The **organogenesis period**—typically **Day 6 to Day 15 in rats** and **Day 6 to Day 18 in rabbits**—is the most critical phase for teratogenic studies. This is the window when major **organ systems and anatomical structures are being formed**. Exposure to teratogens during this period can result in serious structural abnormalities, fetal death, or growth retardation. Consequently, test substances are administered daily during this window, and animals are sacrificed just before parturition to assess fetal outcomes.

4.5.2.3 Agents Tested: Thalidomide (Historical), Valproic Acid

Historical cases like **thalidomide**—a sedative once prescribed to pregnant women—demonstrated catastrophic teratogenic outcomes such as **phocomelia (limb malformations)**. This led to the development of stringent testing regulations. Another widely studied teratogen is **valproic acid**, an antiepileptic drug known to cause **neural tube defects, craniofacial anomalies, and skeletal deformities** when administered during pregnancy. These agents serve as **positive controls** and historical benchmarks in teratogenicity studies.

4.5.2.4 Gross Malformation Scoring, Fetal Resorption, Skeletal Abnormalities

Assessment in teratogenicity studies includes:

- **Gross malformation scoring**: External examination of fetuses for abnormalities in limbs, eyes, mouth, tail, or abdominal wall.
- **Fetal resorption rate**: Indicates **embryo lethality or early developmental arrest**. Increased resorptions suggest high embryotoxic potential.
- **Skeletal abnormalities**: Fetuses are stained using agents like **Alizarin Red** to visualize bones. Observations include **delayed ossification, bent ribs, vertebral deformities**, or **missing digits**.

Each fetus is examined thoroughly, and findings are quantified to compare treatment and control groups statistically.

4.5.2.5 OECD TG 414 Applicability

OECD Test Guideline 414 is the internationally accepted protocol for **prenatal developmental toxicity studies**. It recommends daily dosing of pregnant animals during organogenesis, followed by caesarean section and fetal evaluation. The guideline provides a structured framework for assessing **maternal toxicity, fetal viability, growth, and malformations**, ensuring harmonization of teratogenicity data across global regulatory submissions.

Teratogenicity testing remains an essential safety requirement for all **new chemical entities (NCEs)** intended for human use, particularly when exposure in pregnancy is possible or unavoidable.

Short Answer Questions

1. **What is toxicity in pharmacological studies?**
   Toxicity refers to the ability of a substance to cause harmful effects on living organisms.

2. **Why are toxicity studies important in drug development?**
   They help assess the safety of drugs before human use by identifying potential harmful effects.

3. **Define acute toxicity.**
   Acute toxicity refers to adverse effects from a single dose or short-term exposure, usually observed over 14 days.

4. **What is sub-acute toxicity?**
   It is the study of toxic effects following repeated dosing for 14–28 days.

5. **Define sub-chronic toxicity.**
   It involves repeated drug administration for 90 days to assess medium-term effects.

6. **What is chronic toxicity?**
   It refers to long-term exposure studies lasting 6 months to 2 years to detect cumulative toxicity.

7. **Name any two endpoints observed in acute toxicity studies.**
   Mortality and behavioral changes.

8. **What is the typical duration of sub-acute toxicity testing?**
   14 to 28 days.

9. **What parameters are monitored in sub-chronic studies?**
   Hematology, organ weight, histopathology, and body weight.

10. **Why is chronic toxicity testing required for certain drugs?**
    For drugs meant for long-term use, to evaluate carcinogenicity and cumulative toxicity.

11. **What does LD_{50} stand for?**
    Lethal Dose 50%, the dose at which 50% of the test animals die.

12. **How is LD_{50} traditionally calculated?**
    Using Karber's or Miller and Tainter methods.

13. **What is ED_{50}?**
    Effective Dose 50%, the dose at which 50% of animals show the desired therapeutic effect.

14. **Mention one method used for ED_{50} determination.**
    Graphical plotting of dose-response curves.

15. **Give an example of a test used to determine ED_{50}.**
Tail flick test for analgesic drugs.

16. **What is OECD TG 425 used for?**
Acute oral toxicity using the up-and-down procedure.

17. **What is the significance of OECD guidelines?**
They standardize toxicity testing across countries for regulatory acceptance.

18. **Name the OECD guideline for 28-day repeated dose toxicity.**
OECD TG 407.

19. **What does OECD TG 408 refer to?**
90-day sub-chronic toxicity study in rodents.

20. **Name the OECD test guideline for reproductive toxicity.**
OECD TG 414 (Prenatal Developmental Toxicity).

21. **What is NOAEL?**
No Observed Adverse Effect Level – the highest dose with no toxic effect.

22. **What is LOAEL?**
Lowest Observed Adverse Effect Level – the lowest dose showing toxicity.

23. **What is the therapeutic index?**
A ratio of LD_{50} to ED_{50}, indicating drug safety margin.

24. **Name one alternative method to traditional LD_{50}.**
Up-and-down method (OECD 425).

25. **What is a toxicokinetic study?**
It studies the absorption, distribution, metabolism, and excretion of toxic doses.

26. **Which organ systems are commonly affected in chronic toxicity?**
Liver, kidney, cardiovascular, and nervous system.

27. **What is reproductive toxicity?**
Adverse effects on sexual function, fertility, and reproductive organs.

28. **Name two phases of reproductive toxicity studies.**
Pre-natal and post-natal phases.

29. **What is teratogenicity?**
The ability of a substance to cause birth defects or fetal malformations.

30. **What is the critical period of organogenesis in rats?**
Day 6 to Day 15 of gestation.

31. **Which drug historically caused teratogenicity in humans?**
Thalidomide.

32. **What is the endpoint in teratogenic studies?**
Fetal malformations, resorption, and skeletal abnormalities.

33. **Why are rats and rabbits used in teratogenic studies?**
They are sensitive models and have known gestational timelines.

34. **What is the duration of observation in acute toxicity?**
14 days after a single dose.

35. **What is the purpose of sub-acute toxicity study?**
To identify target organ toxicity from repeated dosing.

36. **What is the advantage of OECD TG 425 over LD_{50}?**
It uses fewer animals and gives reliable results with ethical compliance.

37. **Which instrument is used to assess body temperature in toxicity studies?**
Rectal thermometer.

38. **Which parameters are included in hematological analysis?**
Hemoglobin, WBC count, RBC count, platelet count.

39. **Which liver function test is important in toxicity evaluation?**
ALT and AST levels.

40. **How is food consumption recorded in toxicity studies?**
Measured daily or weekly and compared with control.

41. **What is organ-to-body weight ratio?**
Weight of specific organs normalized to body weight, used to assess toxicity.

42. **Why is histopathology important in toxicity testing?**
To observe cellular damage and tissue architecture changes.

43. **What is GLP in toxicology?**
Good Laboratory Practice – ensures proper documentation and conduct of studies.

44. **What kind of documentation is required for OECD studies?**
Daily records, dose logs, clinical signs, necropsy findings, final report.

45. **What is used as a control in toxicity studies?**
Vehicle-treated animals.

46. **What does OECD TG 414 focus on?**
Prenatal developmental toxicity in pregnant animals.

47. **Which samples are collected at necropsy in toxicity testing?**
Blood, liver, kidney, spleen, brain, heart.

48. **What is one indicator of nephrotoxicity?**
Increased serum creatinine and urea.

49. **How is statistical analysis done in toxicity studies?**
Using t-test or ANOVA, with data expressed as Mean ± SEM.

50. **Why are toxicity studies done before clinical trials?**
To ensure drug safety in humans by predicting potential risks.

MCQs

1. **What does LD_{50} represent?**
   A) Lowest effective dose
   B) Dose causing 100% death
   C) Dose killing 50% of test animals
   D) Safe dose for humans
   Answer: C

2. **Acute toxicity is observed over a period of:**
   A) 48 hours
   B) 7 days
   C) 14 days
   D) 30 days
   Answer: C

3. **Which OECD guideline describes the 28-day oral toxicity study in rodents?**
   A) TG 425
   B) TG 408
   C) TG 407
   D) TG 420
   Answer: C

4. **NOAEL stands for:**
   A) No Observed Adverse Event Limit
   B) No Observable Adverse Effect Level
   C) No Outcome After Experimental Loss
   D) New Observation About Experimental Life
   Answer: B

5. **Which animal is commonly used for reproductive toxicity testing?**
   A) Dog
   B) Rabbit
   C) Monkey
   D) Cat
   Answer: B

6. **The therapeutic index is calculated by:**
   A) ED_{50}/LD_{50}
   B) LD_{50}/ED_{50}
   C) $ED_{50} \times LD_{50}$

D) $LD_{50} - ED_{50}$

Answer: B

7. **Karber's method is used to calculate:**

A) ED_{50}

B) LOAEL

C) LD_{50}

D) MTD

Answer: C

8. **Which of the following is a sub-chronic study?**

A) 7-day study

B) 28-day study

C) 90-day study

D) 180-day study

Answer: C

9. **OECD TG 425 describes which method?**

A) Prenatal developmental toxicity

B) Acute oral toxicity – up-and-down procedure

C) 90-day toxicity

D) Inhalation toxicity

Answer: B

10. **What is LOAEL?**

A) Lowest Observed Adverse Effect Level

B) Local Organ Affected Expression Level

C) Last Oral Absorption Efficiency Level

D) Limit of Adverse Evaluation Level

Answer: A

11. **Which is the standard drug in analgesic ED_{50} tests?**

A) Aspirin

B) Diclofenac

C) Morphine

D) Paracetamol

Answer: C

12. **Which phase is included in reproductive toxicity studies?**

A) Teratogenic phase

B) Peri-natal phase

C) Post-marketing phase

D) Acute phase

Answer: B

13. **Which of the following is used to assess teratogenicity?**
    A) Liver weight
    B) Ulcer index
    C) Fetal malformation scoring
    D) Blood pressure
    Answer: C

14. **Which test guideline focuses on prenatal developmental toxicity?**
    A) TG 410
    B) TG 414
    C) TG 416
    D) TG 420
    Answer: B

15. **The critical period of organogenesis in rats is:**
    A) Day 1–7
    B) Day 6–15
    C) Day 10–18
    D) Day 3–8
    Answer: B

16. **Which parameter is NOT usually studied in toxicity testing?**
    A) Hematology
    B) Biochemistry
    C) Weather reports
    D) Histopathology
    Answer: C

17. **Which organ is most commonly affected in chronic toxicity?**
    A) Pancreas
    B) Liver
    C) Eye
    D) Spleen
    Answer: B

18. **Which of the following is a reproductive toxin historically known for causing birth defects?**
    A) Paracetamol
    B) Thalidomide
    C) Ibuprofen
    D) Aspirin
    Answer: B

19. **Sub-acute toxicity duration is typically:**
    A) 5–10 days
    B) 30–45 days
    C) 14–28 days
    D) 60–90 days
    Answer: C

20. **OECD guidelines are followed to ensure:**
    A) Profitability
    B) Global harmonization
    C) Animal preservation only
    D) Quick drug marketing
    Answer: B

21. **Which method uses fewer animals and is OECD approved for acute toxicity?**
    A) Karber's method
    B) Miller's method
    C) Up-and-down method
    D) Reversal method
    Answer: C

22. **The primary endpoint in reproductive toxicity studies includes:**
    A) Ulcer count
    B) ECG change
    C) Litter size and gestation length
    D) Reflex activity
    Answer: C

23. **A substance is teratogenic if it causes:**
    A) Hair loss
    B) Fetal malformation
    C) Weight gain
    D) Joint inflammation
    Answer: B

24. **Which test is NOT a part of toxicity testing?**
    A) Tail-flick test
    B) $LD_5{}^0$ estimation
    C) Hematology
    D) Organ weight
    Answer: A

25. **Which of the following statements is true?**
A) ED_{50} is the dose that kills half of the animals.
B) Chronic studies are shorter than sub-acute studies.
C) OECD TG 407 relates to 28-day repeated dose toxicity.
D) Teratogenicity studies are done in adult male rats only.
Answer: C

Fill in the Blanks

1. The term **LD_{50}** refers to the dose that causes death in ___% of the test animals.
   Answer: 50

2. The **ED_{50}** value represents the dose at which ___% of the population shows the desired therapeutic effect.
   Answer: 50

3. **NOAEL** stands for **No Observed __________ Effect Level.**
   Answer: Adverse

4. Acute toxicity studies are typically observed for a period of ___ days.
   Answer: 14

5. **OECD Guideline 407** is used for ___-day repeated dose oral toxicity studies.
   Answer: 28

6. **Sub-chronic** toxicity studies are generally conducted for ___ days.
   Answer: 90

7. The **therapeutic index** is calculated using the formula ___ $\div ED_{50}$.
   Answer: LD_{50}

8. **Chronic** toxicity studies may extend up to ___ years in duration.
   Answer: 2

9. **Karber's method** is a classical technique used to determine ___.
   Answer: LD_{50}

10. The principle of **teratogenicity testing** is to identify substances that cause ___ defects.
    Answer: congenital

11. **OECD Guideline 425** describes the ___-and-down method for acute toxicity.
    Answer: up

12. **LOAEL** is the abbreviation for **Lowest Observed __________ Effect Level.**
    Answer: Adverse

13. In **reproductive toxicity**, common models used include rats and ___.
    Answer: rabbits

14. The **critical window of organogenesis** in rats occurs between days ___ and 15 of gestation.
    Answer: 6

15. **OECD TG 414** deals with ___ developmental toxicity studies.
   Answer: prenatal

16. **Histopathology** is the microscopic examination of ___ tissues for signs of toxicity.
   Answer: organ

17. One of the most famous teratogenic drugs historically is ___.
   Answer: thalidomide

18. **Up-and-down** method helps reduce the number of ___ used in acute toxicity testing.
   Answer: animals

19. In toxicity testing, parameters like hematology and ___ chemistry are commonly studied.
   Answer: clinical

20. **Repeated dose toxicity** is studied to determine the effect of drug administered over a ___ period.
   Answer: prolonged

21. In **OECD 407**, at least ___ dose levels are tested along with a control group.
   Answer: three

22. In **chronic studies**, animals are observed for signs of ___ toxicity or carcinogenicity.
   Answer: cumulative

23. A high **therapeutic index** indicates a ___ drug.
   Answer: safer

24. **Teratogenicity testing** includes evaluation of fetal resorption and ___ malformations.
   Answer: skeletal

25. **Toxicokinetics** deals with the absorption, distribution, metabolism, and ___ of toxic substances.
   Answer: excretion

True or False

1. LD_{50} represents the dose that produces a therapeutic effect in 50% of animals.
   False (It refers to lethal dose causing death in 50%)
2. Acute toxicity testing is conducted over a period of 14 days.
   True
3. OECD TG 407 is used for chronic toxicity testing.
   False (It is for 28-day repeated dose testing)
4. The therapeutic index is calculated as LD_{50} divided by ED_{50}.
   True
5. Sub-chronic toxicity studies usually last for 90 days.
   True
6. Chronic toxicity studies are shorter than sub-acute studies.
   False (Chronic studies are longer)
7. NOAEL is the highest dose that causes a significant toxic effect.
   False (It is the dose at which no adverse effect is observed)
8. Teratogenicity testing is only conducted in adult male rats.
   False (It involves pregnant females, usually rats or rabbits)
9. The up-and-down procedure uses fewer animals than traditional LD_{50} tests.
   True
10. LOAEL stands for Lowest Observed Adverse Effect Level.
    True
11. ED_{50} indicates the dose at which 50% of animals die.
    False (It indicates the dose at which 50% show therapeutic effect)
12. OECD TG 414 refers to prenatal developmental toxicity testing.
    True
13. Histopathology involves examining organs under the microscope.
    True
14. All toxicity studies must include teratogenicity assessment.
    False (It depends on the type of study)
15. Sub-acute toxicity studies last between 14–28 days.
    True
16. Karber's method is used to calculate ED_{50}.
    False (It is used to calculate LD_{50})

17. Chronic toxicity studies help in evaluating cumulative and long-term effects.
    True

18. Reproductive toxicity tests include pre-natal and post-natal evaluations.
    True

19. The critical period of organ development in rats is between Day 6 and 15 of gestation.
    True

20. Blood glucose is the only parameter checked during toxicity testing.
    False (Other parameters like hematology, organ weight, histology are also checked)

21. Thalidomide is a well-known example of a teratogen.
    True

22. OECD guidelines ensure global harmonization in drug testing.
    True

23. All OECD toxicity guidelines are numbered above 500.
    False (Many are in the 400 range)

24. Clinical signs such as salivation and convulsions are observed in toxicity tests.
    True

25. Up-and-down method is recommended under OECD TG 425 for acute oral toxicity.
    True

DR. D. SWATHI, DR. V. UMA RANI, DR. I. VEENA RANI

CHAPTER FIVE

Screening for CNS Activity – I (Antipsychotic and Antidepressant Drugs)

5.1 Introduction to CNS Screening

The central nervous system (CNS) is a critical target for pharmacological intervention, as **neurological and psychiatric disorders** affect millions of people globally and often lead to long-term disability. CNS disorders such as **schizophrenia, depression, bipolar disorder, and anxiety** require long-term treatment and significantly influence patient quality of life. As a result, discovering and evaluating **neuroactive agents** remains a central focus in drug development.

5.1.1 Importance of CNS Disorders in Drug Discovery

CNS-related illnesses account for a significant proportion of the **global disease burden**, and their management is often complex due to **heterogeneous symptoms, treatment resistance,** and **delayed onset of therapeutic effects.** Because of this, there is an urgent need for **novel therapeutic agents** that are more effective, safer, and faster-acting. Screening studies play a vital role in **identifying lead compounds** with potential CNS activity during the preclinical phase, using reproducible and validated animal models.

5.1.2 Common Categories of CNS Drugs: Antipsychotics, Antidepressants, Anxiolytics

CNS drugs can be broadly classified into several categories depending on the nature of the condition:

- **Antipsychotics**: Used to manage symptoms of psychosis, particularly in conditions like schizophrenia and bipolar disorder. These drugs act primarily on **dopaminergic (D_2) and serotonergic (5-HT$_2$A) receptors**.
- **Antidepressants**: Indicated for **major depressive disorder (MDD)**, **anxiety disorders**, and some chronic pain conditions. They often work through **modulation of monoamines** such as serotonin, norepinephrine, and dopamine.
- **Anxiolytics**: Target **anxiety and panic disorders**, typically by enhancing **GABAergic transmission**, as seen with benzodiazepines.

The classification is not always rigid, as some agents exhibit overlapping activities (e.g., atypical antipsychotics with antidepressant effects).

5.1.3 Role of Animal Models in Screening Neuroactive Agents

Preclinical screening of CNS drugs relies heavily on **animal models** that replicate the behavioral and physiological characteristics of human psychiatric conditions. These models are essential for:

- Assessing **mechanism of action** through receptor or neurotransmitter interactions.
- Evaluating **dose-dependent behavioral effects**, such as sedation, locomotion, or agitation.
- Identifying **side effect profiles**, including extrapyramidal symptoms, cognitive impairment, or dependency risks.

Rodents, particularly **rats and mice**, are widely used because of their **predictable behavioral responses**, ease of genetic manipulation, and compatibility with validated behavioral paradigms. These animal models help in shortlisting compounds that can proceed to further pharmacological and toxicological evaluations.

5.2 Screening Methods for Antipsychotic Drugs

Antipsychotic drugs primarily act by **modulating dopamine and serotonin receptors**, and their efficacy can be assessed using **behavioral models** that simulate psychotic-like symptoms in animals. Among these models, **amphetamine-induced hyperactivity** is one of the most widely accepted for screening drugs targeting the **positive symptoms of schizophrenia**, such as hallucinations and delusions.

5.2.1 Amphetamine-Induced Hyperactivity Test

5.2.1.1 Principle: Antipsychotics Reduce Dopamine-Mediated Hyperactivity

Amphetamines stimulate the central nervous system by **increasing synaptic dopamine levels**, particularly in the **mesolimbic pathway**, which is associated with **psychotic behaviors**. This leads to **increased locomotor activity** in animals. Antipsychotic drugs, particularly **dopamine D₂ receptor antagonists, reduce this hyperactivity** by inhibiting dopamine signaling. Therefore, a significant decrease in motor activity following drug administration indicates **potential antipsychotic efficacy.**

5.2.1.2 Animal Model: Rats or Mice

Male Swiss albino mice or **Wistar rats** are typically used for this test due to their well-characterized behavioral responses and compatibility with locomotor tracking systems. Animals are usually **acclimatized** for several days before the test and fasted for 12–16 hours to improve drug absorption consistency.

5.2.1.3 Procedure

- **Induction of Hyperactivity**: Animals are first administered **d-amphetamine**, usually at a dose of **2–5 mg/kg intraperitoneally (i.p.),** to induce hyperlocomotion.
- **Drug Administration**: Test compound or reference antipsychotic (e.g., chlorpromazine or haloperidol) is administered **30–60 minutes before amphetamine.**
- **Observation**: Locomotor activity is recorded using **actophotometers, open-field arenas,** or **video-tracking software** for a standard observation period (usually 60 minutes).
- **Control Group**: A group receiving amphetamine alone (without any antipsychotic) is included for baseline comparison.

5.2.1.4 Interpretation: Drugs That Reduce Locomotion Suggest Dopamine Blockade

If the test compound **significantly reduces amphetamine-induced locomotion** compared to the control group, it suggests that the drug is **antagonizing dopamine-mediated pathways.** A dose-dependent inhibition supports **dopaminergic receptor blockade**, which is a hallmark mechanism of most first-generation (typical) and some second-generation (atypical) antipsychotics.

However, it is also important to differentiate between **true antipsychotic activity and non-specific CNS depression**. Therefore, additional tests (e.g., rotarod, catalepsy) are conducted in parallel to rule out **motor impairment or sedation**.

5.2.1.5 Relevance to Schizophrenia (Positive Symptoms)

This model is particularly relevant for screening agents targeting the **positive symptoms** of schizophrenia, which are largely mediated by **hyperdopaminergic activity in the mesolimbic system**. The amphetamine-induced hyperactivity paradigm closely mimics this pathophysiological mechanism, making it a **predictive model for antipsychotic efficacy**. Drugs that succeed in this model often proceed to **clinical trials targeting schizophrenia** and related psychotic disorders.

5.2.2 Conditioned Avoidance Response Test

The **Conditioned Avoidance Response (CAR) test** is a classic and highly predictive behavioral model for evaluating the **efficacy of antipsychotic agents**. It is particularly effective in distinguishing compounds that possess **dopamine antagonistic activity**, and it is sensitive enough to differentiate between **typical and atypical antipsychotics** based on their behavioral profiles.

5.2.2.1 Principle: Antipsychotics Suppress Learned Avoidance Without Affecting Escape

The principle of the CAR test is based on **Pavlovian conditioning**, where an animal learns to associate a **warning cue (like a tone or light)** with an impending **aversive stimulus (usually a mild foot shock)**. After training, the animal consistently performs an **avoidance response** (moving to the other compartment) to prevent the shock. Antipsychotics **selectively suppress the conditioned avoidance response**, while the animal retains the ability to escape if the shock is actually delivered. This **selective suppression of learned behavior** mimics their clinical effect of reducing delusional and hypervigilant behaviors in psychotic patients, without producing gross motor impairment.

5.2.2.2 Equipment: Shuttle Box

The experiment is conducted using a **shuttle box**, which consists of **two equal-sized compartments separated by a central partition**. The floor is electrically wired to deliver mild shocks, and speakers or lights provide the conditioned stimulus (CS). The animal can freely move between compartments.

5.2.2.3 Procedure

- **Training Phase**: Animals (commonly rats) undergo **conditioning sessions** over several days. A **tone or light** (CS) is given a few seconds before the floor shock. The animal learns to move to the other compartment to avoid the shock, which is termed an **avoidance response**.
- **Drug Administration**: On the test day, the **test compound or reference antipsychotic** is administered 30–60 minutes prior to the session.
- **Testing Phase**: After drug administration, the animal is exposed to the CS. Two types of behaviors are observed:

  - **Avoidance response**: Animal moves before the shock begins.
  - **Escape response**: Animal moves after the shock begins.

- **Evaluation**: A decrease in **avoidance responses with preservation of escape responses** is interpreted as **antipsychotic-like activity**.

5.2.2.4 Differentiation of Antipsychotic Classes (Typical vs Atypical)

- **Typical antipsychotics** (e.g., haloperidol) significantly suppress avoidance behavior but may also impair escape responses at higher doses, indicating **motor side effects** like catalepsy or extrapyramidal symptoms.
- **Atypical antipsychotics** (e.g., clozapine, risperidone) also reduce avoidance responses but **preserve escape behavior more effectively**, suggesting **lower liability for motor impairment**. Therefore, this test can be used to **functionally differentiate** between drug classes.

5.2.2.5 Predictive Value for Antipsychotic Efficacy

The CAR test has **high predictive validity** for **dopaminergic antagonists**, especially those targeting D_2 receptors involved in positive symptoms of schizophrenia. However, it is less sensitive to drugs acting on **glutamatergic or serotonergic targets** unless they indirectly modulate dopamine signaling. Despite its limitations, it remains a **standard tool in the screening of novel antipsychotic agents** and supports further pharmacodynamic and safety testing.

5.3 Screening Methods for Antidepressant Drugs

Antidepressant drug screening involves **behavioral models** that replicate features of **depressive disorders**, particularly behavioral despair, learned helplessness, or anhedonia. These models help identify compounds that improve mood or motivation by **modulating monoaminergic systems,** especially **serotonin, norepinephrine, and dopamine**. One of the most widely used and validated animal models for antidepressant screening is the **Forced Swim Test (FST)**.

5.3.1 Forced Swim Test (FST)

5.3.1.1 Principle: Immobility Reflects Behavioral Despair

The Forced Swim Test, also known as the **Porsolt swim test**, is based on the premise that when placed in an inescapable water-filled container, rodents initially attempt to escape. Over time, they adopt an **immobile posture**, which is interpreted as a state of **behavioral despair**, mimicking depressive-like behavior. **Antidepressant drugs reduce the duration of immobility**, suggesting a **restoration of coping behavior** or increased motivation to escape.

5.3.1.2 Model: Rat or Mouse Placed in Water Cylinder

The test is typically conducted using **albino rats or mice**. Each animal is placed individually in a **transparent glass or plexiglass cylinder** (height ~40 cm, diameter ~20 cm for rats; smaller for mice) filled to about two-thirds with water maintained at $25 \pm 1°C$. The cylinder should be deep enough to prevent the animal from touching the bottom or escaping.

5.3.1.3 Procedure

- **Pre-Test Session**: Animals are first exposed to a **15-minute swimming session** (for rats) or **2–5 minutes** (for mice) one day before the test. This allows habituation and standardization of baseline responses.
- **Test Session**: On the next day, animals are placed in the cylinder again for a **6-minute session**. The first 2 minutes are considered an acclimatization period, and data are usually collected for the last 4 minutes.
- **Observation Parameters:**

  - **Immobility Time**: The primary measure; time spent floating passively with minimal movement to keep the head above water.

- ○ **Swimming Time**: Indicates **serotonergic activity** (especially with SSRIs like fluoxetine).
- ○ **Climbing Time**: Reflects **noradrenergic activation** (increased by drugs like desipramine).

Video recordings or automated behavior analysis systems can be used to ensure accurate scoring and eliminate observer bias.

Antidepressants reduce immobility either by **increasing swimming (serotoninergic action)** or **climbing (noradrenergic action)**, depending on their pharmacological class. The test is sensitive to **acute and sub-chronic administration**, though chronic dosing more closely mirrors clinical treatment regimens.

5.3.2 Tail Suspension Test (TST)

The Tail Suspension Test (TST) is a rapid and reliable behavioral model used to assess antidepressant-like activity in mice. It is based on the concept of behavioral despair, similar to the Forced Swim Test, but does not involve water, making it easier to execute and less stressful in terms of post-test recovery. It is particularly suitable for high-throughput screening of test compounds.

5.3.2.1 Principle: Suspension Causes Behavioral Despair

When a mouse is suspended by its tail, it initially exhibits escape-oriented movements such as struggling and swinging. Over time, the mouse becomes immobile, which is interpreted as a sign of despair or helplessness. Administration of antidepressant agents reduces the duration of immobility, indicating a restoration of escape motivation and central monoaminergic stimulation.

5.3.2.2 Species: Mouse

The TST is conducted exclusively in **mice**—typically **Swiss albino** or **C57BL/6 strains**—as **rats are too large and strong** for standardized tail suspension. Mice used for the test are usually **male**, aged between **6 to 8 weeks**, and housed under standard laboratory conditions.

5.3.2.3 Setup: Mouse Suspended by Tail on Hook or Stand

- Each mouse is suspended by the **distal end of its tail (approximately 1 cm from the tip)** using **adhesive tape**.
- The tape is attached to a **horizontal bar or suspension hook** placed at a height of **50–60 cm** above a padded surface to prevent injury if the animal falls.

- The mouse should be suspended in a **vertical position**, with its body freely hanging and limbs exposed.
- The duration of the test is typically **6 minutes**, and **immobility is recorded** during the final 4 minutes after a 2-minute acclimatization period.

Immobility is defined as **absence of initiated movements**, with the mouse hanging passively and making only the minimal motions necessary to maintain balance.

Antidepressants, especially **tricyclics and SSRIs**, decrease immobility time in this model. For example:

- **Imipramine** increases active escape behaviors.
- **Fluoxetine** increases limb movements and swinging.

The TST is valued for its **simplicity, reproducibility, and sensitivity** to a wide range of antidepressant classes. However, it is **not ideal for drugs with strong sedative or anxiolytic effects**, as they may reduce movement non-specifically.

5.3.2.4 Observation: Duration of Immobility vs Active Movement

During the test, two key behaviors are closely observed:

- Immobility: Defined as a complete lack of initiated movement, where the mouse hangs passively without attempting to swing, climb, or struggle. Minor movements made only to maintain balance are not counted as active.
- Active movement: Includes vigorous struggling, twisting of the body, or attempts to climb back up the suspended surface. These behaviors are indicative of motivated effort to escape the stressful situation.

Observers typically use a stopwatch or automated video tracking system to record the duration (in seconds) of immobility and movement over a 6-minute session. The test is often conducted under silent conditions to avoid external stimuli that may alter behavior.

5.3.2.5 Reduction in Immobility = Antidepressant-Like Activity

The primary index of antidepressant activity in the TST is a statistically significant reduction in immobility time compared to vehicle-treated controls. Antidepressants, by stimulating monoaminergic neurotransmission, increase the active effort to escape, reducing passive behavior.

For instance:

- A typical control mouse may show immobility for about 180–200 seconds during the 6-minute test.
- An animal treated with an effective antidepressant (e.g., imipramine 15 mg/kg i.p.) may show immobility reduced to 80–120 seconds, with corresponding increases in struggling and swinging behavior.

Thus, the TST offers a quantitative, reproducible, and ethically less invasive model for detecting central antidepressant activity, especially in the early stages of preclinical drug screening.

5.3.3 Apomorphine-Induced Climbing Behavior

The Apomorphine-Induced Climbing Behavior test is a well-established animal model for studying the dopaminergic activity of test compounds. It is primarily used in the screening of antidepressant and antipsychotic drugs, especially those that modulate dopamine receptor-mediated effects. This model provides valuable insights into whether a compound acts as a dopamine agonist or antagonist, aiding in the classification of CNS-active drugs.

5.3.3.1 Principle: Apomorphine Stimulates Dopamine Receptors

Apomorphine is a non-selective dopamine agonist that primarily stimulates D_1 and D_2 receptors in the central nervous system. When administered to mice, it induces a stereotyped climbing behavior, especially on vertical surfaces like wire mesh or grid walls. This effect is considered a dopaminergic behavioral response. If a test drug reduces or abolishes this behavior, it suggests that the drug has dopamine receptor antagonistic properties.

5.3.3.2 Dopaminergic Stimulation Leads to Climbing in Mice

Upon administration of apomorphine, mice exhibit repetitive climbing, often rising on their hind legs and grasping cage walls or suspended wires. This climbing is not exploratory but rather stereotyped and repetitive, lasting several minutes. The response is dose-dependent, with higher doses inducing quicker onset and more intense climbing behavior. The model is typically conducted in male albino mice to ensure uniformity.

5.3.3.3 Procedure

- Apomorphine Administration: Mice are injected subcutaneously with apomorphine, usually at a dose of 1–2 mg/kg.
- Observation Period: Animals are placed individually in cylindrical wire mesh cages, and their behavior is monitored for 30 minutes.
- Measured Parameters:

  ○ Latency to climbing (time from drug injection to first climbing response),
  ○ Duration of climbing (total time spent climbing),
  ○ Intensity or frequency of climbing episodes.

- Co-administration: The test drug is administered 30–60 minutes before apomorphine, and its ability to suppress climbing behavior is assessed. A significant reduction in climbing indicates antagonism of dopaminergic pathways.

5.3.3.4 Antidepressants or Antipsychotics Block Dopamine Response

- Typical antipsychotics (e.g., haloperidol) block dopamine receptors and thus inhibit apomorphine-induced climbing, confirming their D_2 antagonistic activity.
- Some antidepressants, especially those with antipsychotic profiles or dopamine receptor modulation, also attenuate climbing behavior, although classical monoaminergic antidepressants may not significantly affect this model.
- Therefore, suppression of climbing suggests the test compound interferes with dopaminergic neurotransmission, making this test relevant for screening antipsychotic or atypical antidepressant agents.

5.3.3.5 Differentiates Dopaminergic Activity of Test Agents
This model is particularly useful for distinguishing:

- Dopamine agonists (which increase climbing),
- Dopamine antagonists (which block climbing), and
- Non-dopaminergic agents (which do not influence climbing behavior significantly).

It helps researchers determine whether a compound's mechanism of action involves the dopaminergic system, thus guiding further testing in CNS pharmacology.

5.4 Summary of CNS Screening Methods

Screening methods for central nervous system (CNS) drugs play a vital role in the early identification of pharmacologically active compounds, helping researchers predict potential therapeutic value before clinical trials. The various animal models discussed in this chapter—such as amphetamine-induced hyperactivity, conditioned avoidance response, forced swim test, tail suspension test, and apomorphine-induced climbing behavior—offer valuable mechanistic insights into the drug's effects on dopaminergic, serotonergic, or noradrenergic pathways.

5.4.1 Comparison of Models (Specificity, Sensitivity, Practicality)

Each model has its **own strengths and limitations** based on its specificity to neurotransmitter systems, sensitivity to drug classes, and ease of use:

- **Amphetamine-induced hyperactivity** is highly **sensitive for dopamine antagonists** and suitable for detecting **typical antipsychotic** effects. It is simple, quick, and requires minimal training.
- **Conditioned avoidance response** offers high **predictive value for antipsychotic drugs** and helps **differentiate typical from atypical agents**, but it demands trained animals and sophisticated apparatus (shuttle box).
- **Forced swim test** and **tail suspension test** are **sensitive to a wide range of antidepressants** and provide **quick, quantitative measures**. However, TST is limited to mice, while FST can be used in both rats and mice.
- **Apomorphine-induced climbing** is highly specific for **dopaminergic mechanisms**, allowing classification of agents based on **agonistic or antagonistic profiles**.

In terms of practicality for academic laboratories, **FST and TST** are among the most feasible due to **low cost, limited space requirements, and short duration.**

5.4.2 Limitations and Ethical Concerns

Despite their utility, these models carry certain **scientific and ethical limitations**:

- **Species differences** in behavior and neurochemistry may limit the **translational accuracy** of results to humans.
- Some models, particularly those inducing **despair or aversive stimuli**, may cause **stress or discomfort** to animals, raising concerns over **animal welfare and ethical compliance**.
- The **risk of false positives or false negatives** exists, especially with drugs acting through **non-monoaminergic or novel mechanisms**, which may not produce measurable effects in these classical models.

These limitations highlight the importance of **3Rs principles (Replacement, Reduction, Refinement)** in CNS screening.

5.4.3 Selection Criteria for Models in Academic Settings

When selecting models in academic institutions, several factors must be considered:

- **Availability of equipment** (e.g., actophotometer, shuttle box, swim tanks),
- **Species accessibility** and familiarity with animal handling,
- **Regulatory approvals and ethical clearance** from Institutional Animal Ethics Committees (IAEC),
- **Training and expertise of personnel** to minimize procedural errors,
- **Cost-effectiveness and reproducibility** of the method.

Focusing on **models that are simple, standardized, and ethically justifiable** ensures that students gain practical skills in pharmacological screening while adhering to CPCSEA and institutional guidelines.

Short answer questions

1. What is the basic principle of the catalepsy test in rodents?
2. Name a commonly used antipsychotic drug that induces catalepsy in rodents.
3. What behavioral sign is used to assess catalepsy in rats or mice?
4. How is the bar test conducted for catalepsy?
5. What is the usual cut-off time used in catalepsy tests?

6. Which type of antipsychotic drugs generally induce strong cataleptic responses?
7. What is stereotypy in animal behavior studies?
8. Name two behaviors indicative of stereotypy.
9. Which dopamine agonist is commonly used to induce stereotypy in rodents?
10. What kind of stereotypy is observed after apomorphine administration?
11. How does haloperidol affect apomorphine-induced behaviors?
12. What is the main purpose of using the apomorphine-induced rotation model?
13. What does a contralateral rotation indicate in a 6-OHDA lesioned rat model?
14. How does apomorphine induce yawning in rats?
15. Which dopamine receptor subtype is mainly responsible for yawning behavior?
16. What is the significance of the tail suspension test in antidepressant screening?
17. Which animal is commonly used for the tail suspension test?
18. What is measured in the tail suspension test?
19. How is immobility interpreted in the tail suspension test?
20. Name a standard antidepressant that reduces immobility time in the tail suspension test.
21. What is the forced swim test (FST) used for?
22. How is the FST performed in rodents?
23. What behaviors are observed in the forced swim test?
24. How do antidepressant drugs affect the outcome of the FST?
25. Which neurotransmitter systems are typically targeted by antidepressants?
26. What is the difference in action between typical and atypical antipsychotics in catalepsy tests?
27. How is drug-induced motor impairment ruled out during antipsychotic screening?
28. What is the mechanism of action of haloperidol?
29. What is the main difference in side effect profiles between haloperidol and clozapine?
30. What is the purpose of using models of dopamine supersensitivity in antipsychotic screening?

31. Name an antipsychotic drug with a lower risk of inducing extrapyramidal side effects.
32. What is a major advantage of using the apomorphine-induced rotation model?
33. What is the standard dose of apomorphine for inducing rotations in lesioned rats?
34. How is the number of rotations quantified in rotation behavior tests?
35. What role does the mesolimbic pathway play in antipsychotic drug action?
36. What behavioral endpoint is used to indicate antidepressant efficacy in rodents?
37. Why is a quiet and low-stress environment necessary for behavioral tests?
38. What class of drugs does fluoxetine belong to?
39. What is the primary mechanism of tricyclic antidepressants?
40. Why is it important to perform behavioral assays at consistent times of the day?
41. What is the relevance of using positive controls in CNS screening models?
42. Why is video tracking software often used in modern behavioral assays?
43. What is the major confounding factor in evaluating open-field locomotor activity?
44. What precautions should be taken when testing CNS depressants in catalepsy models?
45. What kind of model is the tail suspension test—acute or chronic?
46. What is a limitation of using the FST in antidepressant screening?
47. Which behavioral test can differentiate between sedative and anxiolytic effects?
48. What happens if an animal shows decreased locomotor activity after drug administration in a test designed to detect antidepressant activity?
49. What are extrapyramidal symptoms and why are they important in screening antipsychotics?
50. How do dopamine antagonists affect locomotor behavior?

MCQs

Which behavioral model is used to evaluate **catalepsy** in rodents?

- a) Bar test
- b) Hole board test
- c) Grip strength test
- d) Tail immersion test
  Answer: a

2. The **bar test** measures:

- a) Exploratory behavior
- b) Seizure activity
- c) Motor rigidity
- d) Learning ability
  Answer: c

3. Apomorphine-induced yawning is mainly mediated through:

- a) D1 receptors
- b) Serotonin receptors
- c) D2 receptors
- d) GABA receptors
  Answer: c

4. In **6-OHDA lesioned rats**, apomorphine causes:

- a) Lateral movement
- b) Contralateral rotation
- c) Vertical climbing
- d) Stereotypy suppression
  Answer: b

5. Apomorphine acts as a:

- a) Selective D2 antagonist
- b) Non-selective dopamine agonist

- ◦ c) GABA enhancer
- ◦ d) Cholinergic blocker
  Answer: b

6. The elevated plus maze is used to assess:

- ◦ a) Memory
- ◦ b) Anxiety
- ◦ c) Seizures
- ◦ d) Sedation
  Answer: b

7. Which parameter increases after anxiolytic treatment in the EPM test?

- ◦ a) Time in closed arms
- ◦ b) Rearing frequency
- ◦ c) Time in open arms
- ◦ d) Latency to fall
  Answer: c

8. Forced swim test is commonly used to screen:

- ◦ a) Antipsychotics
- ◦ b) Antidepressants
- ◦ c) Hypnotics
- ◦ d) Anxiolytics
  Answer: b

9. Increased immobility time in the **forced swim test** indicates:

- ◦ a) Stimulation
- ◦ b) Depression-like behavior
- ◦ c) Seizure threshold
- ◦ d) Cognitive enhancement
  Answer: b

10. The **tail suspension test** is performed in:

- a) Guinea pigs
- b) Dogs
- c) Mice
- d) Rabbits
  Answer: c

1. **Locomotor activity test** primarily measures:

- a) Dopamine levels
- b) Reflex time
- c) Exploratory behavior
- d) Neurotoxicity
  Answer: c

12. A CNS stimulant like **amphetamine** causes:

- a) Reduced activity
- b) Catalepsy
- c) Increased locomotion
- d) Sedation
  Answer: c

13. CNS depressants can be evaluated by:

- a) Conditioned place preference
- b) Rotarod test
- c) Pentobarbital sleep time
- d) Forced swim test
  Answer: c

14. In **pentobarbital sleep time test**, the parameter measured is:

- a) Memory index
- b) Locomotion index
- c) Onset and duration of sleep
- d) Yawning frequency
  Answer: c

15. An agent that **increases sleep time** in pentobarbital assay is likely:

- a) Stimulant
- b) Antidepressant
- c) Sedative
- d) Anticonvulsant
  Answer: c

16. Catalepsy is commonly induced using:

- a) Clozapine
- b) Diazepam
- c) Haloperidol
- d) Sertraline
  Answer: c

17. Which model uses a **horizontal bar** to assess motor rigidity?

- a) Rotarod test
- b) Bar test
- c) Swim test
- d) Open field test
  Answer: b

18. Stereotypy includes all EXCEPT:

- a) Gnawing
- b) Sniffing
- c) Yawning
- d) Grooming
  Answer: c

19. The **grip strength test** is used to assess:

- a) Depression
- b) Muscle tone
- c) Reflex latency

- d) Anxiety
  Answer: b

20. Open field test measures:

- a) Convulsions
- b) Neurotoxicity
- c) Locomotion
- d) Memory
  Answer: c

21. One feature of CNS stimulant overdose is:

- a) Bradycardia
- b) Catalepsy
- c) Seizures
- d) Hypotension
  Answer: c

22. Which assay is used to evaluate **motor coordination**?

- a) EPM
- b) Rotarod
- c) Hole board
- d) Bar test
  Answer: b

23. CNS stimulants often act by increasing:

- a) Histamine
- b) Dopamine and norepinephrine
- c) Acetylcholine
- d) GABA
  Answer: b

24. CNS depressants like benzodiazepines act by enhancing:

- a) NMDA receptors

- b) Glutamate
- c) GABA-A receptors
- d) D2 receptors
  Answer: c

25. Which test uses **rearing and center time** as parameters?

- a) Tail suspension
- b) Rotarod
- c) Open field
- d) Forced swim
  Answer: c

26. The **conditioned avoidance response (CAR)** test differentiates:

- a) Sedatives from antidepressants
- b) Typical from atypical antipsychotics
- c) CNS stimulants from opioids
- d) SSRIs from MAO inhibitors
  Answer: b

27. In CAR test, the shock is used to:

- a) Induce seizure
- b) Train the animal to escape
- c) Measure catalepsy
- d) Assess sleep time
  Answer: b

28. Atypical antipsychotics are preferred due to:

- a) Increased catalepsy
- b) No CNS penetration
- c) Fewer extrapyramidal effects
- d) Faster onset of sedation
  Answer: c

29. The neurotransmitter most associated with **antipsychotic activity** is:

- a) Acetylcholine
- b) Serotonin
- c) Dopamine
- d) Glutamate
Answer: c

30. An **increase in climbing behavior** in mice after apomorphine suggests:

- a) Dopamine antagonism
- b) Serotonin depletion
- c) Dopamine receptor stimulation
- d) GABAergic inhibition
Answer: c

31. Which of the following tests is used for **positive symptom screening in schizophrenia?**

- a) Tail suspension
- b) Rotarod
- c) Amphetamine-induced hyperactivity
- d) Open field test
Answer: c

32. Which antipsychotic is known for causing **less catalepsy?**

- a) Haloperidol
- b) Risperidone
- c) Clozapine
- d) Chlorpromazine
Answer: c

33. An example of a centrally acting antidepressant is:

- a) Metformin
- b) Sertraline
- c) Atropine
- d) Propranolol
Answer: b

34. The **immobility time** in forced swim test is reduced by:

- a) CNS stimulants
- b) Anticonvulsants
- c) Antidepressants
- d) Anticholinergics
Answer: c

35. Apomorphine-induced climbing test is especially sensitive to:

- a) SSRIs
- b) MAO inhibitors
- c) Dopaminergic antagonists
- d) Antihistamines
Answer: c

36. One major limitation of behavioral despair models is:

- a) High reproducibility
- b) Unreliable in rodents
- c) Inability to mimic chronic depression
- d) Requirement of anesthetics
Answer: c

37. Which of the following tests is **not used** for screening antidepressants?

- a) Tail suspension
- b) Forced swim
- c) Bar test
- d) Apomorphine-induced climbing
Answer: c

38. Which behavior is suppressed in conditioned avoidance test?

- a) Grooming
- b) Eating
- c) Learned avoidance

- d) Seizure threshold

  Answer: c

39. **Catalepsy** can be defined as:

- a) Hyperactive reflexes
- b) Sleep induction
- c) Lack of movement with muscle rigidity
- d) Muscle flaccidity

  Answer: c

40. **Haloperidol** is classified as a:

- a) Typical antipsychotic
- b) Tricyclic antidepressant
- c) MAO inhibitor
- d) SSRI

  Answer: a

41. The **latency to fall** in rotarod test is used to assess:

- a) Memory
- b) Motor coordination
- c) Blood pressure
- d) Depression

  Answer: b

42. A test animal shows **increased open-arm entries** in EPM. This indicates:

- a) Aggression
- b) Depression
- c) Anxiolytic effect
- d) Memory enhancement

  Answer: c

43. CNS-active drugs must be evaluated for:

- a) Food intake

- b) Gastrointestinal motility
- c) Behavioral and motor effects
- d) Serum cholesterol
  Answer: c

44. Which of the following is a **dopamine receptor agonist?**

- a) Chlorpromazine
- b) Apomorphine
- c) Diazepam
- d) Imipramine
  Answer: b

45. Drug-induced **stereotypy** is a hallmark of:

- a) GABA inhibition
- b) Serotonin depletion
- c) Excess dopaminergic activity
- d) NMDA antagonism
  Answer: c

46. Forced swim test is also known as:

- a) Porsolt test
- b) Pentylenetetrazole test
- c) EPM
- d) Tail flick test
  Answer: a

47. The tail suspension test is **sensitive to:**

- a) GABAergic agents
- b) SSRIs and TCAs
- c) NMDA blockers
- d) Opioids
  Answer: b

48. SSRIs like fluoxetine act by:

- a) Inhibiting MAO enzyme
- b) Blocking norepinephrine reuptake
- c) Increasing GABA
- d) Inhibiting serotonin reuptake

Answer: d

49. Which test measures **learned escape behavior?**

- a) Apomorphine test
- b) Tail suspension
- c) Conditioned avoidance
- d) Catalepsy bar test

Answer: c

50. In **CNS pharmacology**, drug screening must balance:

- a) Onset only
- b) Potency and ethics
- c) Speed and color
- d) Cost and flavor

Answer: b

Fill-in-the-Blanks

1. The **Open Field Test** is used to evaluate ___________ and anxiety in rodents.
2. In the **Hole Board Test**, the number of ___________ into holes indicates exploratory behavior.
3. The **Rotarod Test** measures ___________ and balance.
4. The **Grip Strength Test** is used to assess ___________ strength in rodents.
5. CNS stimulants like amphetamine increase activity by acting on ___________ neurotransmission.
6. The Elevated Plus Maze is primarily used to screen ___________ drugs.
7. **Pentobarbital-induced sleep time** is increased by ___________ drugs.
8. The **MES test** is used to screen drugs effective against ___________ seizures.
9. **PTZ-induced seizures** are used to screen drugs for ___________ seizure activity.
10. **Scopolamine-induced amnesia** is a model used to study ___________ disease.
11. **MPTP** is a neurotoxin that models ___________ disease in mice.
12. In the Open Field Test, increased time spent in the center indicates reduced ___________.
13. **Conditioned Place Preference (CPP)** is commonly used to assess ___________ potential.
14. CNS depressants act by enhancing ___________ activity in the brain.
15. The **Tail Flick Test** measures ___________ response to thermal stimulus.
16. **Apomorphine-induced rotation** is a model used for ___________ disease.
17. **EAE model** is used to study ___________ ___________ (write full disease name).
18. CNS stimulants are commonly used to treat disorders like ADHD and ___________.
19. The **blood-brain barrier** limits the entry of many drugs into the ___________.
20. **Rotarod latency to fall** is reduced in animals with impaired ___________ coordination.

Fill-in-the-Blanks – Answer Key

1. locomotor activity
2. head dips
3. motor coordination
4. muscle
5. dopaminergic
6. anxiolytic
7. sedative-hypnotic
8. tonic-clonic
9. absence
10. Alzheimer's
11. Parkinson's
12. anxiety
13. addiction
14. GABAergic
15. nociceptive
16. Parkinson's
17. Multiple Sclerosis
18. narcolepsy
19. central nervous system
20. neuromuscular

True/False

1. CNS stimulants always decrease locomotor activity.
2. The Elevated Plus Maze is a test to assess memory in rodents.
3. The Rotarod test helps assess skeletal muscle strength.
4. PTZ-induced seizures model absence seizures.
5. Pentobarbital is used in screening CNS stimulant drugs.
6. Open Field Test is useful in assessing anxiolytic drugs.
7. CNS depressants increase dopamine release in the brain
8. Kindling model is used to study chronic epilepsy.
9. The Grip Strength Test measures anxiety-like behavior.
10. MES test is used to evaluate tonic seizures.
11. Apomorphine is a dopamine antagonist.
12. CPP measures preference or aversion to a specific environment.
13. Mice and rats are commonly used in CNS screening.
14. The Morris Water Maze is used to study seizure threshold.
15. The locomotor activity test can evaluate the sedative effects of drugs.
16. CNS drugs must be evaluated for abuse potential during preclinical studies.
17. Alzheimer's disease models include scopolamine-induced memory loss.
18. The EPM test uses light-dark transition boxes.
19. Anxiolytic drugs increase time spent in closed arms in EPM.
20. CNS stimulants suppress glutamate signaling.

True/False – Answer Key

1. False
2. False
3. True
4. True
5. False
6. True
7. False
8. True
9. False
10. True
11. False
12. True

13. **True**
14. **False**
15. **True**
16. **True**
17. **True**
18. **False**
19. **False**
20. **False**

CHAPTER SIX

Screening for CNS Activity – II (Antiepileptics and Sedatives)

6.1 Introduction

Disorders related to **neuronal excitability and central nervous system depression**, such as **epilepsy, insomnia, and muscle spasticity**, represent major clinical challenges that require long-term and often complex pharmacological treatment. A wide variety of CNS-active drugs—including **antiepileptics, sedative-hypnotics, and muscle relaxants**—have been developed to modulate neuronal activity through various mechanisms like **GABAergic enhancement, ion channel modulation, or glutamate inhibition**. Preclinical screening of these agents in animal models remains essential for evaluating **efficacy, onset of action, duration**, and **selectivity for CNS pathways**, before human testing.

6.1.1 Overview of CNS Disorders: Epilepsy, Insomnia, Muscle Spasticity

- **Epilepsy** is a neurological disorder marked by **recurrent, unprovoked seizures**, caused by abnormal electrical activity in the brain. It affects over **50 million people worldwide** and is classified into **generalized** and **partial seizures.**

- **Insomnia** and other sleep disorders are prevalent, particularly in the elderly, and involve **difficulty initiating or maintaining sleep**. Pharmacological intervention often involves **sedative-hypnotic agents** acting on **GABA-A receptors**.

- **Muscle spasticity**, commonly observed in **multiple sclerosis, cerebral palsy, or spinal cord injuries**, involves **increased muscle tone and exaggerated reflexes**, requiring agents that depress **spinal or supraspinal reflexes**.

These disorders differ in pathophysiology but share a common target—**altered CNS excitability**, which can be measured reliably using animal models.

6.1.2 Need for Animal Models in Evaluating Seizure Threshold, Sedation, and Motor Coordination

Animal models are indispensable for the early-stage evaluation of CNS depressant drugs. These models enable researchers to:

- **Quantify seizure thresholds** using chemically or electrically induced seizure paradigms.
- **Assess sedative and hypnotic properties**, including **sleep latency** and **duration** using behavioral assays.
- Evaluate **motor coordination and muscle relaxation** to determine CNS selectivity and avoid undesirable side effects like **ataxia or sedation**.

Without such models, it would be difficult to **predict the therapeutic index, neurotoxicity**, or **functional selectivity** of investigational drugs.

6.1.3 General Goals of CNS Depressant Screening: Onset, Duration, and CNS Selectivity

In screening CNS depressant agents, researchers focus on several key pharmacological aspects:

- **Onset of action**: How quickly the drug produces observable effects after administration (e.g., time to induce sleep or prevent seizure onset).
- **Duration of action**: The **length of therapeutic activity**, important for determining dosing frequency and risk of residual sedation or rebound excitation.
- **CNS selectivity**: Ability of the drug to selectively depress abnormal neuronal activity without impairing **motor function, cognition, or respiration**. For example, an ideal antiepileptic drug should control seizures without causing excessive sedation or motor incoordination.

These screening endpoints help in shortlisting drug candidates with optimal **efficacy and safety profiles** for further development.

6.2 Screening Methods for Antiepileptic Drugs

Screening for **antiepileptic activity** involves animal models that simulate human seizure types—primarily **generalized tonic-clonic seizures and absence seizures**. Among these, the **Maximal Electroshock (MES) model** is one of the most validated and widely accepted models for identifying compounds that prevent or attenuate **generalized seizures.** It is particularly useful in predicting the clinical efficacy of drugs like **phenytoin, valproic acid**, and **carbamazepine.**

6.2.1 Maximal Electroshock (MES)-Induced Seizure Model

6.2.1.1 Principle: Electrical Induction of Generalized Tonic-Clonic Seizures

In the MES model, **generalized seizures** are induced by delivering a calibrated electric shock through the animal's **head or cornea.** The resulting seizure sequence closely mimics human **tonic-clonic seizures.** Drugs that **block or reduce the tonic phase**, particularly **hind limb tonic extension (HLTE)**, are considered to possess **antiepileptic potential** against generalized seizures. The test is useful for screening **sodium channel blockers and broad-spectrum antiepileptics.**

6.2.1.2 Model: Rats or Mice

The model is typically performed on **adult male Wistar rats (150–200 g)** or **Swiss albino mice (25–30 g).** Animals are selected based on **weight uniformity and good health,** and are housed under standard laboratory conditions. Fasting may be required prior to the test, depending on institutional protocols.

6.2.1.3 Procedure

- **Electrode Placement**: Two electrodes are used—either **corneal electrodes** with saline-moistened pads or **ear clip electrodes**—to ensure effective current delivery. Corneal application is often preferred in mice, while ear electrodes are more common in rats.
- **Stimulation Parameters:**

  - **Current**: ~50 mA (mice), 150 mA (rats)
  - **Duration**: 0.2 seconds

- ◦ **Frequency**: 50–60 Hz
- ◦ Delivered using a **convulsiometer** or electroshock generator

- **Seizure Phases**:

  - ◦ **Tonic flexion**: Initial phase involving forelimb contraction
  - ◦ **Tonic extension**: Characteristic hind limb extension beyond 90°
  - ◦ **Clonus**: Rhythmic jerking of limbs
  - ◦ **Stupor or Recovery**: Followed by spontaneous recovery or death (in absence of treatment)

6.2.1.4 Endpoint: Abolition of Hind Limb Tonic Extension (HLTE)

The **key observation** is the presence or absence of **HLTE**, which is considered the most reliable marker of seizure severity. If a test compound **abolishes or significantly reduces HLTE**, it is interpreted as having **anticonvulsant activity**. The **percentage of animals protected** from HLTE in a group is often used as a quantitative measure of efficacy.

For example:

- In control mice, HLTE is observed in **100% of animals** after MES.
- After administration of **phenytoin (25 mg/kg i.p.)**, HLTE may be abolished in **80–100% of treated animals**.

6.2.1.5 Drug Prediction: Efficacy Against Generalized Seizures

The MES model is highly predictive for drugs that are effective in treating **generalized tonic-clonic and partial seizures** in humans. Drugs identified using this model include:

- **Phenytoin**
- **Valproic acid**
- **Carbamazepine**
- **Lamotrigine**

These drugs typically act by **stabilizing voltage-gated sodium channels**, thereby reducing the spread of seizure activity in the brain.

6.3 Screening Methods for Sedative and Hypnotic Agents

Screening sedative and hypnotic agents involves evaluating their **ability to suppress CNS activity**, particularly through **GABA-A receptor potentiation**. These drugs are often prescribed for **insomnia, anxiety, and preoperative sedation**. The **pentobarbital-induced sleep test** is a classical pharmacological model used to measure the **sedative-hypnotic potential** of new compounds in **preclinical studies**, based on their **effect on sleep induction and maintenance**.

6.3.1 Pentobarbital-Induced Sleep Test

6.3.1.1 Principle: CNS Depressants Enhance GABAergic Inhibition, Prolong Sleep

Pentobarbital sodium, a **barbiturate**, acts by **potentiating GABAergic neurotransmission** at the GABA-A receptor, leading to sedation and sleep. When administered to animals, it induces **loss of righting reflex**, which is considered a behavioral indicator of sleep. **Test compounds with sedative or hypnotic activity**, especially those that enhance GABAergic inhibition (e.g., benzodiazepines, barbiturates, or non-benzodiazepine hypnotics), **reduce the latency to sleep and increase the duration of sleep** induced by pentobarbital.

6.3.1.2 Model: Mice or Rats

Both **Swiss albino mice (20–30 g)** and **Wistar rats (150–250 g)** are used in this model. Mice are generally preferred due to their **rapid and uniform behavioral responses**. Animals should be healthy, age-matched, and maintained under standard lab conditions. Testing is typically performed during **light hours**, when animals are less active.

6.3.1.3 Procedure

- Pre-treatment: The test compound or reference drug (e.g., diazepam, zolpidem) is administered intraperitoneally (i.p.), usually 30–60 minutes before the induction of sleep.
- Induction of Sleep: Pentobarbital sodium (35–40 mg/kg i.p.) is injected as the sleep-inducing agent. This dose is sub-hypnotic and allows evaluation of potentiation or suppression of sleep by the test drug.
- Observations Recorded:

  ○ Sleep latency: The time interval between pentobarbital injection and the loss of righting reflex (animal placed on its back fails to return to normal posture).

- Sleep duration: The time between loss and recovery of righting reflex, indicating how long the animal remains sedated.

Multiple animals (n = 6–8 per group) are tested to allow statistical comparison with control and standard-treated groups.

6.3.1.4 Drug Prediction: Diazepam, Zolpidem, Phenobarbitone Prolong Sleep Time

- **Benzodiazepines** (e.g., diazepam) and **non-benzodiazepine hypnotics** (e.g., zolpidem) **increase sleep duration** and **reduce latency** in this model, reflecting **sedative-hypnotic efficacy**.
- **Phenobarbitone**, a long-acting barbiturate, also prolongs sleep, serving as a positive control.
- A drug that significantly **increases sleep duration compared to control** is considered to have **CNS depressant activity**, and its effect may be dose-dependent.

This model is particularly useful in identifying **sleep-inducing agents** and determining their **potency, onset, and duration of action**, while also helping to differentiate **GABAergic drugs** from those acting through other CNS pathways.

6.3.2 Open Field Test

The **Open Field Test (OFT)** is a widely used behavioral assay designed to assess the **locomotor and exploratory activity** of rodents in a novel environment. It serves as a **general screen for CNS depressants, anxiolytics**, and **stimulants**, based on changes in spontaneous movement. It is one of the simplest and most reproducible models for evaluating **sedative-hypnotic activity**, especially in combination with other CNS parameters like anxiety and stress responsiveness.

6.3.2.1 Principle: Measures Exploratory Behavior and Locomotor Activity

When placed in a new environment, rodents typically display **exploratory behavior**, such as moving around, rearing, sniffing, and grooming. These behaviors are modulated by **neurochemical systems** (dopaminergic, serotonergic, and GABAergic). **Sedative agents or CNS depressants** reduce these activities, while **stimulants enhance them**. The OFT provides quantitative data on the **degree of central inhibition or stimulation**, making it valuable for detecting pharmacological effects on the

CNS.

6.3.2.2 Setup: Open Box with Grid Markings

The apparatus consists of a **square or circular open field arena**, usually made of **wood, Plexiglas, or plastic**, with the floor marked into equal-sized grids (e.g., 10 × 10 cm squares). The standard dimensions are:

- For mice: ~40 × 40 × 40 cm
- For rats: ~60 × 60 × 50 cm

The setup should be well-lit and free from external noise. The animal is placed at the center of the arena and observed for a **standard time period (commonly 5–10 minutes)**.

6.3.2.3 Parameters

Key behaviors recorded during the test include:

- **Number of squares crossed**: Indicates **horizontal locomotor activity;** higher numbers mean more activity.
- **Rearing frequency**: Number of times the animal stands on its hind legs, representing **vertical exploratory behavior.**
- **Grooming**: Reflects **self-soothing** or anxiety-related behavior.
- **Defecation and urination**: Often considered indirect markers of **emotionality or stress.**

Data may be collected manually or using **video tracking systems** for higher accuracy.

6.3.2.4 Sedatives Reduce Locomotor Activity

CNS depressants such as **diazepam, phenobarbitone, and chlorpromazine** cause a **dose-dependent reduction in locomotor and exploratory behavior**. This is characterized by:

- Fewer grid crossings
- Reduced rearing
- Longer periods of immobility

Conversely, **psychostimulants (e.g., amphetamines)** produce the opposite effect, increasing movement and rearing frequency.

6.3.2.5 Useful for Screening Anxiolytics and CNS Depressants

The OFT is a **versatile screening tool:**

- For **sedatives and hypnotics**, it confirms central inhibitory effects.
- For **anxiolytics**, changes in rearing and central area exploration help identify **anxiety-reducing potential**.
- It is also useful for assessing **motor impairments**, thereby differentiating sedative effects from motor dysfunction.

Overall, the Open Field Test is a **non-invasive, sensitive, and low-cost method** for initial behavioral screening of CNS-active agents.

6.4 Screening of Skeletal Muscle Relaxants

The evaluation of **skeletal muscle relaxant activity** is crucial for identifying compounds that can reduce **muscle tone, spasms, or involuntary contractions**, often used in conditions like **spinal cord injury, multiple sclerosis, or muscle strain**. The most reliable animal model for assessing **motor coordination and muscle relaxation** is the **Rotarod Performance Test**, which quantifies the **ability of an animal to maintain balance on a rotating rod**.

6.4.1 Rotarod Performance Test

6.4.1.1 Principle: Muscle Relaxants Impair Motor Coordination

Skeletal muscle relaxants act on **spinal or supraspinal pathways**, often modulating **GABAergic or glutamatergic transmission** to reduce voluntary motor output. This leads to **reduced coordination and increased likelihood of falls** when animals are placed on a rotating rod. The **rotarod test** quantitatively measures **motor impairment**, making it a standard tool for screening **muscle relaxants, sedatives, and CNS depressants**.

6.4.1.2 Setup: Rotating Rod (2–3 rpm)

The **rotarod apparatus** consists of a **horizontal rotating rod (3 cm diameter)** elevated above a platform, divided into separate lanes to test multiple animals simultaneously. The rod typically rotates at a **constant speed of 2–3 revolutions per minute (rpm)**, but some models allow acceleration. A soft pad is placed below the apparatus to prevent injury when animals fall.

6.4.1.3 Procedure

- **Training Phase**: Animals (mice or rats) are first trained to stay on the rotating rod for a **minimum duration (e.g., 180 seconds)**. Those that fail to learn are excluded.

- **Drug Administration**: The test compound or reference drug (e.g., **diazepam, baclofen**) is administered via intraperitoneal injection. The dose and time to testing are based on pharmacokinetics (e.g., 30 minutes post-injection).
- **Testing Phase**:

  ○ Animals are placed back on the rotating rod.
  ○ **Fall-off time** or **latency to fall** is recorded for each animal.
  ○ Multiple trials may be conducted to ensure consistency.

Control animals typically stay on the rod for the full cutoff time (e.g., 180 seconds), whereas **treated animals** with impaired motor coordination fall earlier.

6.4.1.4 Drugs Like Diazepam or Baclofen Reduce Fall-Off Time

- **Diazepam**, a benzodiazepine, enhances **GABA-A mediated inhibition** and causes **muscle relaxation** along with sedation.
- **Baclofen**, a **GABA-B agonist**, acts predominantly on spinal cord neurons and is effective in reducing **spasticity**.

Both drugs **reduce the fall-off time**, indicating their **muscle relaxant properties**. The model can distinguish between **central vs peripheral muscle relaxants** and is sensitive to dose-dependent effects.

The Rotarod test is therefore **a validated, quantitative, and easy-to-standardize model** for screening new agents with potential **muscle relaxant or motor-impairing properties**.

6.4.2 Chimney Test

The **Chimney Test** is a simple and effective behavioral model used to evaluate the **skeletal muscle relaxant activity** of test compounds, particularly in mice. It is based on the animal's **innate ability to climb backward** out of a narrow vertical tube. The test primarily assesses **motor coordination and muscular strength**, and is highly sensitive to agents that cause **central muscle relaxation or sedation**.

6.4.2.1 Principle: Measures the Animal's Ability to Climb Backwards in a Narrow Tube

Mice naturally attempt to **escape when placed in a confined space**, such as a vertical tube. This climbing behavior requires proper **motor coordination, muscle strength, and balance**. Administration of a **muscle**

relaxant impairs these functions, resulting in **increased escape latency or complete failure to climb.** Thus, the test directly correlates **muscular weakness** or **sedation** with the animal's **inability to perform escape behavior.**

6.4.2.2 Loss of Motor Strength = Failure to Escape

If the mouse **fails to climb out of the tube within a predefined cutoff time** (e.g., 30 seconds), it is considered to exhibit **muscle relaxation or motor incoordination.** The **degree of impairment** can be compared across treatment groups to evaluate the **potency of the test compound.** Unlike the rotarod test, the chimney test is less affected by the animal's initial training and requires minimal equipment.

6.4.2.3 Procedure

- **Apparatus:** A **glass or plastic tube,** approximately **30 cm in length and 3 cm in diameter,** open at both ends and positioned vertically.
- **Step-by-Step Method:**

  - Place the mouse **gently at the bottom** of the vertical tube with the head facing downward.
  - The mouse will instinctively attempt to **escape by climbing backward** toward the open top.
  - **Time is recorded** from placement to complete emergence from the tube.
  - A **cutoff time (usually 30 seconds)** is set. If the mouse fails to escape within this time, it is scored as a **positive result** for muscle relaxation.

The test may be repeated for each mouse after administering different doses of the **test drug or reference compound.**

Muscle relaxants such as **diazepam, baclofen,** and **chlorpromazine** cause a **significant increase in escape time or complete failure to climb,** confirming their **central depressant or muscle relaxant effect.** The chimney test is thus a **quick, cost-effective,** and **low-stress alternative** to the rotarod, especially in undergraduate teaching labs and primary screening programs.

6.5 Interpretation and Application

The interpretation of screening results from **antiepileptic, sedative, and muscle relaxant models** is crucial for understanding a test compound's **CNS activity spectrum**. Different models target distinct aspects of CNS pharmacology—**electrical excitability, behavioral suppression, or motor coordination**—and thus help to **classify the drug pharmacologically**, identify **therapeutic potential**, and detect **unwanted side effects**. Appropriate model selection enhances the translational relevance of preclinical testing and ensures efficient identification of promising lead compounds.

6.5.1 Choice of Test Depends on the Pharmacological Class Being Screened

Each **screening model** is optimized to evaluate a **specific pharmacological class:**

- The **MES model** is ideal for screening drugs with potential **anti-generalized seizure activity**, such as **phenytoin or valproate**.
- The **PTZ model** helps detect drugs effective against **absence seizures**, such as **ethosuximide**.
- **Pentobarbital-induced sleep** and the **open field test** are tailored to assess **sedative-hypnotic or anxiolytic activity**, suitable for compounds like **benzodiazepines, zolpidem**, and **barbiturates**.
- **Rotarod and chimney tests** are specific for detecting **skeletal muscle relaxant activity** and differentiating **central vs peripheral actions**.

Thus, the choice of the model must align with the **mechanism of action and therapeutic target** of the test compound.

6.5.2 Some Drugs Show Both Sedative and Antiepileptic Actions (e.g., Benzodiazepines)

Certain drugs exhibit **overlapping effects** across different CNS models. For example:

- **Diazepam**, a classical benzodiazepine, shows **anticonvulsant activity in the MES model, sedative effects in the pentobarbital sleep test**, and **muscle relaxation in rotarod and chimney tests**.
- These multiple effects arise from its action on **GABA-A receptors**, which regulate both **neuronal excitability and muscle tone**.

This pharmacological overlap requires careful interpretation to distinguish **therapeutic efficacy** from **side effects**, such as unwanted sedation during antiepileptic therapy.

6.5.3 Importance of Combining Multiple Models for Comprehensive CNS Profiling

A single model rarely provides a **complete picture** of a compound's action on the CNS. Therefore, **a battery of tests** is often employed:

- **Antiepileptic drugs** are tested in **both MES and PTZ models** to assess broad-spectrum efficacy.
- **Sedatives and hypnotics** are evaluated using both **behavioral and electrophysiological models** to confirm onset, duration, and depth of sedation.
- **Muscle relaxant activity** is confirmed using both **rotarod and chimney tests**, which assess coordination and strength through different motor pathways.

Using **complementary models** allows researchers to **triangulate the pharmacological profile**, reduce false positives or negatives, and improve the **predictive validity** of preclinical screening.

Short Answer Questions

1. **What is the Maximal Electroshock (MES) test used for?**
   To screen drugs effective against tonic-clonic seizures.
2. **Which convulsion model is induced using pentylenetetrazole (PTZ)?**
   PTZ-induced seizure model for absence and myoclonic seizures.
3. **What is the primary endpoint in MES test?**
   Tonic hindlimb extension (THE).
4. **Name one standard drug used in the MES model.**
   Phenytoin.
5. **What type of seizure does PTZ induce in rodents?**
   Clonic seizures.
6. **What is the standard drug used in the PTZ model?**
   Ethosuximide.
7. **Define kindling in epilepsy screening.**
   Repeated sub-threshold stimulation leading to permanent seizure susceptibility.
8. **Which chemical is used for electrical kindling in rats?**
   Pentylenetetrazole (in subconvulsive doses).
9. **What is the significance of latency in seizure models?**
   It indicates the time taken for seizure onset after induction.
10. **Which behavioral test is used to screen sedative activity?**
    Pentobarbital-induced sleeping time test.
11. **Which parameter indicates sedative efficacy in sleep time test?**
    Duration of loss of righting reflex.
12. **Which neurotransmitter system is most targeted in sedative screening?**
    GABAergic system.
13. **Which sedative class acts by enhancing GABA-A receptor activity?**
    Benzodiazepines.
14. **Name one standard sedative used in animal models.**
    Diazepam.
15. **How is the open field test useful in CNS depression studies?**
    It assesses reduced locomotor activity indicating sedation.
16. **What is the effect of CNS depressants on the rotarod test?**
    Reduced motor coordination and endurance.
17. **Which animal species is most commonly used in epilepsy screening?**
    Mice and rats.

18. **What is the route of PTZ administration in animal models?**
    Intraperitoneal (i.p.).
19. **What is the common voltage range used in MES test?**
    150–180 V for 0.2 seconds.
20. **What is the role of the kindling model in epilepsy research?**
    To mimic chronic epilepsy and study neuroplasticity.
21. **What is a hypnotic drug?**
    A drug that induces sleep.
22. **What type of seizures are better modeled by PTZ than MES?**
    Absence seizures.
23. **Name two benzodiazepines used in sedative studies.**
    Diazepam and lorazepam.
24. **Which test evaluates the sedative-induced muscle relaxation?**
    Rotarod test.
25. **Which receptor do barbiturates act on?**
    GABA-A receptor (positive allosteric modulator).
26. **What is the effect of phenobarbital in MES test?**
    Prevents tonic hindlimb extension.
27. **Why is the PTZ test called a chemoconvulsant model?**
    Because seizures are induced by chemical injection.
28. **What is the significance of latency in PTZ test?**
    Longer latency indicates better anticonvulsant effect.
29. **What type of drug is valproic acid classified as?**
    Broad-spectrum antiepileptic.
30. **How is drug efficacy in sedative tests generally interpreted?**
    By prolongation of sleep time and reduction in activity.
31. **What is the function of the righting reflex in sedative tests?**
    It indicates recovery from drug-induced sleep.
32. **What is the standard duration of observation in MES test?**
    20 seconds post-shock for tonic phase.
33. **What is the role of the EEG in advanced epilepsy screening?**
    To confirm electrographic seizure activity.
34. **Why is dose titration important in antiepileptic screening?**
    To establish ED50 and safety margin.
35. **Which test is used to evaluate both hypnotic and sedative action?**
    Pentobarbital-induced sleeping time test.
36. **What kind of control is required in CNS screening studies?**
    Positive (e.g., diazepam) and negative (vehicle) controls.

37. **What does the term 'anti-seizure latency' refer to?**
Time between PTZ injection and onset of convulsions.

38. **Which animal behavior indicates sedation in open field test?**
Decreased ambulation and exploration.

39. **What are the limitations of PTZ test?**
Poor modeling of partial seizures.

40. **Name a drug that shows efficacy in both MES and PTZ models.**
Valproic acid.

41. **What is the impact of high dose barbiturates?**
CNS depression, respiratory arrest, and coma.

42. **Which assay is considered most predictive of hypnotic effect?**
Pentobarbital-induced sleeping time.

43. **Which structure is often implanted for electrical kindling?**
Amygdala.

44. **What is used to measure seizure severity?**
Scoring scales (e.g., Racine scale).

45. **Why are rodents preferred in CNS screening?**
Easy handling, well-characterized models, and genetic uniformity.

46. **What is the difference between hypnotic and sedative doses?**
Hypnotics induce sleep; sedatives calm without sleep.

47. **Which ion channel is targeted by phenytoin?**
Voltage-gated sodium channels.

48. **Which non-benzodiazepine hypnotic acts on GABA-A receptor?**
Zolpidem.

49. **What happens if the dose in MES test is too high?**
Excessive mortality and false-negative results.

50. **What are the key observations in sedative screening?**
Sleep onset, duration, loss and regain of righting reflex.

Fill-in-the-Blanks

1. The MES model is used to screen drugs against ___________ seizures.
2. PTZ-induced seizures are used to model ___________ seizures in animals.
3. In the MES test, the key observation is prevention of ___________.
4. ___________ is a standard drug used in PTZ-induced seizure screening.
5. The chemical name of PTZ is ___________.
6. Diazepam enhances ___________ neurotransmission in the CNS.
7. Pentobarbital-induced sleep test is used to evaluate ___________ activity.
8. A drug that induces sleep is called a ___________.
9. Loss of ___________ reflex is an indicator of sleep in sedative tests.
10. The open field test measures ___________ activity and anxiety-like behavior.
11. ___________ test is used to evaluate motor coordination and muscle relaxation.
12. A commonly used muscle relaxant in the rotarod test is ___________.
13. Valproic acid is a ___________-spectrum antiepileptic drug.
14. The rotarod apparatus rotates at a speed of approximately ___________ rpm.
15. In PTZ test, latency to seizure is measured in ___________.
16. ___________ is the endpoint for tonic-clonic seizure in MES.
17. Sedative drugs typically ___________ locomotor activity in rodents.
18. Kindling leads to permanent changes in ___________ excitability.
19. Zolpidem is a non-benzodiazepine drug acting on ___________ receptors.
20. In pentobarbital test, longer sleep time indicates ___________ sedative effect.

Answer Key

1. **tonic-clonic**
2. **absence**
3. **hind limb tonic extension**
4. **Ethosuximide**
5. **Pentylenetetrazole**
6. **GABAergic**
7. **sedative or hypnotic**

8. hypnotic
9. righting
10. locomotor
11. Rotarod
12. Diazepam
13. broad
14. 2–3
15. seconds
16. abolition of tonic hind limb extension
17. decrease
18. neuronal
19. GABA-A
20. greater

MCQs

1. The MES model is primarily used to evaluate:

- a) Anti-inflammatory drugs
- b) Antiepileptic drugs
- c) Sedatives
- d) Antipsychotics
  Ans: b

1. In the MES model, seizures are induced by:

- a) Sound stimulation
- b) Electric shock
- c) PTZ injection
- d) Thermal stimulation
  Ans: b

3. Which is a standard drug for MES test?

- a) Aspirin
- b) Diazepam
- c) Phenytoin
- d) Paracetamol
  Ans: c

4. The endpoint in the MES model is:

- a) Clonic spasms
- b) Tonic flexion
- c) Hind limb tonic extension
- d) Loss of consciousness
  Ans: c

5. PTZ stands for:

- a) Phenylthiourea
- b) Pentylenetetrazole

- c) Pentazocine
- d) Phenobarbitone
Ans: b

6. PTZ-induced seizures are used to model:

- a) Generalized tonic seizures
- b) Absence seizures
- c) Localized pain
- d) Hyperactivity
Ans: b

7. Standard drug for PTZ test is:

- a) Ibuprofen
- b) Ethosuximide
- c) Morphine
- d) Sucralfate
Ans: b

8. Diazepam acts by enhancing:

- a) Serotonin transmission
- b) Dopaminergic inhibition
- c) GABAergic activity
- d) Noradrenaline synthesis
Ans: c

9. Pentobarbital-induced sleeping time test is used to screen:

- a) Antipyretics
- b) Antidiabetics
- c) Sedatives
- d) Antihypertensives
Ans: c

10. Which is a common sedative used in animal studies?

- a) Atorvastatin
- b) Diazepam
- c) Ranitidine
- d) Enalapril
  Ans: b

11. Righting reflex is lost in:

- a) Active behavior
- b) Hypnotic sleep
- c) Convulsions
- d) Climbing test
  Ans: b

12. Open field test measures:

- a) Bleeding time
- b) Gastric motility
- c) Exploratory behavior
- d) Pain threshold
  Ans: c

13. Which CNS parameter is assessed in open field test?

- a) Memory
- b) Locomotor activity
- c) Inflammation
- d) Fever
  Ans: b

14. Rotarod test is used to evaluate:

- a) Liver function
- b) Pain threshold
- c) Motor coordination
- d) Heart rate
  Ans: c

15. In the rotarod test, muscle relaxants cause:

- a) Increased reflexes
- b) Improved performance
- c) Reduced fall-off time
- d) Faster breathing
  Ans: c

16. Which model is used for screening hypnotics?

- a) Tail flick test
- b) Writhing test
- c) MES model
- d) Pentobarbital sleep test
  Ans: d

17. A drug that prolongs sleep in pentobarbital test likely has:

- a) Analgesic activity
- b) CNS depressant action
- c) Antihistaminic property
- d) Antipyretic activity
  Ans: b

18. Zolpidem is classified as a:

- a) Barbiturate
- b) Muscle relaxant
- c) Non-benzodiazepine hypnotic
- d) Diuretic
  Ans: c

19. In PTZ test, the longer the seizure latency:

- a) The weaker the drug
- b) The stronger the convulsion
- c) The better the anticonvulsant effect

- d) The higher the sedation

Ans: c

20. MES-induced seizures mimic:

- a) Psychosis
- b) Inflammatory responses
- c) Tonic-clonic seizures
- d) Anxiety

Ans: c

21. The rotarod rotates at approximately:

- a) 10 rpm
- b) 1 rpm
- c) 2–3 rpm
- d) 100 rpm

Ans: c

22. Standard CNS depressant for rotarod test:

- a) Acetaminophen
- b) Diazepam
- c) Furosemide
- d) Salbutamol

Ans: b

23. The principle of the chimney test is based on:

- a) Forward motion
- b) Water escape
- c) Backward climbing
- d) Food reward

Ans: c

24. The PTZ model is useful for drugs treating:

- a) Fever

- b) Absence seizures
- c) Bacterial infections
- d) Pain
  Ans: b

25. GABA is an example of:

- a) Excitatory neurotransmitter
- b) Hormone
- c) Inhibitory neurotransmitter
- d) Ion channel
  Ans: c

26. Which test detects reduced locomotion?

- a) Open field test
- b) Tail immersion test
- c) Writhing test
- d) Langendorff's test
  Ans: a

27. Barbiturates act primarily on:

- a) NMDA receptors
- b) Muscarinic receptors
- c) GABA-A receptors
- d) Dopamine transporters
  Ans: c

28. Kindling leads to:

- a) Pain suppression
- b) Motor coordination
- c) Increased seizure susceptibility
- d) Gastric motility
  Ans: c

29. Antiepileptics generally:

- a) Enhance CNS stimulation
- b) Block sodium channels
- c) Reduce diuresis
- d) Increase heart rate
  Ans: b

30. A hypnotic drug:

- a) Raises blood glucose
- b) Reduces fever
- c) Induces sleep
- d) Enhances immunity
  Ans: c

31. MES-induced seizures are triggered by:

- a) Acetic acid
- b) Electrical shock
- c) PTZ
- d) Ethanol
  Ans: b

32. Pentylenetetrazole causes:

- a) Myocardial infarction
- b) Febrile seizures
- c) Clonic convulsions
- d) Skeletal pain
  Ans: c

33. Which phase is assessed in MES?

- a) Sedation
- b) Climbing
- c) Tonic extension
- d) Tail flick
  Ans: c

34. The chimney test is used for:

- a) Pain testing
- b) Muscle relaxation
- c) Fever induction
- d) Blood glucose estimation
  Ans: b

35. The primary endpoint in pentobarbital test:

- a) Tail flick
- b) Sleep latency
- c) Grip strength
- d) Muscle weight
  Ans: b

36. Drugs with sedative properties will:

- a) Increase exploratory behavior
- b) Decrease motor activity
- c) Raise heart rate
- d) Improve balance
  Ans: b

37. Which animal is commonly used for CNS screening?

- a) Dog
- b) Cow
- c) Rat
- d) Monkey
  Ans: c

38. PTZ-induced seizures can be prevented by:

- a) Diuretics
- b) CNS stimulants
- c) Anticonvulsants

- d) Antipyretics
  Ans: c

39. Righting reflex is an indicator of:

- a) Antioxidant effect
- b) Neuromuscular strength
- c) Sleep recovery
- d) Spinal cord injury
  Ans: c

40. Barbiturates prolong:

- a) Wakefulness
- b) Anxiety
- c) Inflammatory response
- d) Sleep duration
  Ans: d

41. Which of the following is NOT a sedative-hypnotic?

- a) Phenobarbital
- b) Diazepam
- c) Zolpidem
- d) Lisinopril
  Ans: d

42. Loss of coordination in rotarod test indicates:

- a) Strength gain
- b) CNS depression
- c) Hyperactivity
- d) Reflex arc blockage
  Ans: b

43. Chimney test assesses:

- a) Thermoregulation

- b) Airflow
- c) Skeletal muscle strength
- d) Nociceptive response
  Ans: c

44. CNS stimulants would cause:

- a) Increased open field activity
- b) Prolonged sleep
- c) Reduced motor activity
- d) Loss of righting reflex
  Ans: a

45. Benzodiazepines exert their action through:

- a) Dopamine blockade
- b) Alpha-adrenergic stimulation
- c) GABA-A receptor facilitation
- d) Serotonin antagonism
  Ans: c

46. Which drug reduces fall-off time in rotarod?

- a) Diazepam
- b) Omeprazole
- c) Zolpidem
- d) Chlorpheniramine
  Ans: a

47. Which test is not used for epilepsy screening?

- a) PTZ model
- b) MES model
- c) Chimney test
- d) Kindling model
  Ans: c

48. Which is a commonly used hypnotic in animal screening?

- a) Paracetamol
- b) Phenobarbitone
- c) Ibuprofen
- d) Ranitidine
  Ans: b

49. PTZ-induced seizures begin with:

- a) Muscle paralysis
- b) Sudden death
- c) Myoclonic jerks
- d) High fever
  Ans: c

50. Open field test typically lasts for:

- a) 1 minute
- b) 5–10 minutes
- c) 1 hour
- d) 24 hours
  Ans: b

True / False

1. The MES model is used to evaluate sedative activity.
False
2. Diazepam is effective in both MES and PTZ models.
True
3. PTZ induces seizures by GABA receptor antagonism.
True
4. The endpoint in MES is observation of paw licking.
False
5. Pentobarbital-induced sleep test is used to screen sedatives.
True
6. In the rotarod test, longer fall-off time indicates stronger sedation.
False
7. Open field test measures exploratory behavior in animals.
True
8. The chimney test is used to evaluate cardiovascular function.
False
9. PTZ is commonly used to induce absence-type seizures.
True
10. Sedatives increase locomotor activity in open field test.
False
11. GABA is an excitatory neurotransmitter.
False
12. Diazepam enhances GABAergic inhibition in the brain.
True
13. Hind limb tonic extension is a key sign in the MES model.
True
14. MES-induced seizures are primarily clonic in nature.
False
15. Phenobarbitone is a barbiturate with sedative and antiepileptic effects.
True
16. Chimney test evaluates memory in rodents.
False
17. Loss of righting reflex is observed in pentobarbital-induced sleep.
True

18. PTZ model is inappropriate for screening GABAergic drugs.
False
19. Zolpidem acts on benzodiazepine sites on GABA-A receptors.
True
20. In MES, phenytoin is used as the reference antiepileptic.
True
21. Open field test is used to measure ulcer healing in rats.
False
22. Shorter latency in rotarod test indicates motor coordination.
False
23. Pentobarbital shortens sleep duration in the presence of a sedative.
False
24. In the chimney test, failure to climb indicates muscle relaxation.
True
25. Electrical stimulation in MES is applied to the tail of animals.
False
26. PTZ-induced seizures start with clonic jerks.
True
27. Sedatives prolong the sleeping time in pentobarbital test.
True
28. Rotarod test requires trained animals.
True
29. Chlorpromazine is a standard sedative drug.
False
30. Benzodiazepines bind at NMDA receptors.
False
31. The chimney test involves vertical climbing by mice.
True
32. PTZ increases the seizure threshold in treated animals.
False
33. The rotarod rotates at a speed of 2–3 rpm during tests.
True
34. Animals are fasted before the pentobarbital sleep test.
False
35. Sedative screening often includes observation of grooming behavior.
True
36. MES seizures are induced using chemical agents.
False

37. Open field squares crossed indicates activity level.
True
38. Muscle relaxants decrease the fall-off time in rotarod.
True
39. Diazepam has both sedative and anxiolytic effects.
True
40. GABA-A receptors are ionotropic chloride channels.
True
41. MES model evaluates partial seizures effectively.
False
42. PTZ can induce myoclonic seizures in rodents.
True
43. The chimney test is performed on rats.
False
44. Ethosuximide is effective in MES model.
False
45. Sleep latency increases after sedative administration.
False
46. Antiepileptic drugs increase the severity of seizures.
False
47. Sedatives cause hyperactivity in open field test.
False
48. Rotarod is suitable for measuring grip strength.
False
49. Open field test may record defecation frequency.
True
50. Longer sleeping time indicates CNS stimulant activity.
False

CHAPTER SEVEN

Screening for Cardiovascular and Diuretic Agents

7.1 Introduction

Cardiovascular diseases continue to be a major cause of morbidity and mortality globally, which makes cardiovascular pharmacology a key area in drug development. Drug discovery programs targeting the heart and vascular system aim to produce new agents that can control cardiac contractility, correct arrhythmias, reduce blood pressure, or regulate fluid-electrolyte balance. To ensure safety and therapeutic efficacy, various screening models are used at the preclinical level before human studies. These models are essential for identifying the pharmacodynamic effects of investigational drugs on parameters such as heart rate, contractility, blood pressure, vascular resistance, and renal excretion of electrolytes.

Evaluation of cardiovascular drugs requires a combination of in vivo and in vitro techniques. In vivo models involve intact animals where parameters like blood pressure or electrocardiograms are recorded using instruments such as pressure transducers, polygraphs, or telemetry systems. In vitro models allow the study of isolated organs like the frog heart or guinea pig atria to assess direct cardiac effects under controlled conditions. Both approaches help in understanding drug actions on contractile force, conduction system, and vascular tone.

Cardiotonic agents are used to improve the force of cardiac contraction, especially in congestive heart failure. These include digitalis glycosides and newer inotropes. Antihypertensives are used to reduce elevated blood pressure and act through mechanisms like vasodilation, sympatholytic activity, or inhibition of the renin-angiotensin system. Antiarrhythmic drugs are employed to restore normal heart rhythm by targeting ion channels or conduction pathways. Diuretics promote fluid and electrolyte excretion through the kidneys and are used in hypertension, edema, and heart failure. Each of these drug categories has unique mechanisms of action, requiring specific models for their evaluation in laboratory animals.

7.2 Screening Methods for Cardiotonic Agents

7.2.1 Isolated Frog Heart Preparation (Digitoxin Model)

7.2.1.1 Principle: Cardiotonic Drugs Increase Force of Contraction (Positive Inotropy)

Cardiotonic agents are pharmacological substances that enhance the force of myocardial contraction without significantly increasing oxygen consumption. These drugs exhibit positive inotropic effects by increasing intracellular calcium availability or sensitization of the contractile machinery to calcium ions. The isolated frog heart model is a classical ex vivo preparation widely used for the primary screening of cardiotonic activity. It provides a controlled environment for observing the direct effects of test substances on cardiac contractility and rhythm, making it suitable for identifying drugs similar in action to cardiac glycosides like digitoxin and digoxin.

7.2.1.2 Animal Model: Isolated Frog Heart (Ex Vivo)

The model involves the heart of an adult frog, generally *Rana tigrina* or *Rana hexadactyla*, which is excised and maintained in a functional state by perfusion with physiological saline such as Ringer's solution. This amphibian model is particularly advantageous in undergraduate pharmacology education due to ease of availability, clear visualization of cardiac movements, and minimal ethical concerns compared to mammalian models. The frog heart is naturally resistant to anoxia, which allows prolonged observation even outside the body.

7.2.1.3 Procedure

The frog is first immobilized by pithing to abolish central nervous system activity and eliminate pain perception. The thoracic cavity is opened to expose the beating heart, and a small cut is made in the sinus venosus to insert a fine cannula. The heart is then perfused continuously with Ringer's solution at room temperature to maintain viability and rhythmic contractions. A force transducer is connected to the apex of the ventricle through a thread to record contractile strength on a kymograph or digital data acquisition system.

Once a baseline recording is established, the test compound or standard drug such as digitoxin is administered directly through the cannula in graded concentrations. The following parameters are closely monitored:

- Heart rate (chronotropic effect): A decrease or increase in beats per minute is noted.
- Force of contraction (inotropic effect): Observed as increased amplitude of contraction waves on the recording.

Digitoxin, when introduced in appropriate doses, produces a marked increase in contractile force with a gradual slowing of heart rate. At higher concentrations, toxic effects such as arrhythmias or cardiac arrest may be observed, which helps determine therapeutic and toxic thresholds. This preparation is highly useful for evaluating the potency, onset of action, and cardiac specificity of investigational cardiotonic agents.

7.2.1.4 Advantages: Simple, Cost-Effective

The isolated frog heart preparation offers several practical advantages, particularly for preliminary screening in academic and research laboratories. It is technically simple and does not require advanced surgical or instrumentation skills. The setup is cost-effective, involving minimal reagents such as Ringer's solution and basic laboratory tools like a kymograph or force transducer. The heart remains viable for extended durations under continuous perfusion, allowing the recording of stable baseline and drug-induced responses. The clear visibility of atrial and ventricular movements enables direct observation of cardiac effects. Additionally, this model helps demonstrate fundamental concepts of inotropy and chronotropy to students in a hands-on manner.

7.2.1.5 Limitations: Does Not Mimic Mammalian Cardiovascular System

Despite its educational and screening utility, the frog heart model presents important physiological limitations. Amphibian cardiac physiology differs significantly from that of mammals in aspects such as the three-chambered heart structure, slower heart rate, and different ion channel kinetics. The absence of coronary circulation and complex regulatory pathways limits its relevance for evaluating the systemic effects of cardiotonic drugs in humans. Furthermore, the pharmacokinetics and receptor sensitivities in amphibians do not reflect those of higher vertebrates, making it unsuitable for advanced pharmacodynamic or toxicological studies. Therefore, results obtained in this model must be validated using mammalian preparations or in vivo models for reliable drug development decisions.

7.2.2 Isolated Guinea Pig or Rabbit Heart (Langendorff's Apparatus)

7.2.2.1 Heart is Perfused with Oxygenated Solution

The Langendorff preparation is an ex vivo model where the heart of a small mammal, typically a guinea pig or rabbit, is excised and perfused retrogradely via the aorta with a continuously oxygenated physiological solution, such as Krebs-Henseleit buffer. This technique allows the heart to beat in a controlled environment without systemic influences, making it ideal for studying the direct effects of cardiotonic agents on myocardial performance. The perfusion is maintained at constant pressure or constant flow, and the solution is kept at 37°C with continuous oxygenation using a carbogen mixture containing 95 percent oxygen and 5 percent carbon dioxide. The retrograde perfusion causes the aortic valve to close and forces the solution into the coronary arteries, thus maintaining cardiac viability for extended experimental periods.

7.2.2.2 Measures

This setup permits real-time recording of several cardiovascular parameters:

- **Coronary flow**: This is measured by collecting the perfusate exiting the heart via the right atrium or coronary sinus. Changes in coronary flow reflect the vascular effects of test drugs on coronary arteries. Vasodilators increase flow, while vasoconstrictors reduce it.
- **Left ventricular pressure**: A fluid-filled balloon is inserted into the left ventricle and connected to a pressure transducer. This enables the measurement of ventricular pressure changes during systole and diastole, giving insight into the inotropic activity of the test compound.
- **Heart rate**: The number of contractions per minute is recorded using an electrocardiogram or by analyzing the pressure tracings. Any bradycardia or tachycardia induced by the drug provides information about its chronotropic effects.

The Langendorff heart model closely mimics mammalian cardiac physiology and is therefore used extensively in pharmacological research for testing the cardiac safety and efficacy of new drug molecules. The ability to isolate the heart from systemic influences allows the detection of subtle drug effects on myocardial tissue, conduction system, and vascular tone. It also enables the assessment of cardiac arrhythmogenic potential, making it a gold standard for in vitro cardiac evaluation.

7.2.2.3 Used for Assessing Both Efficacy and Cardiac Toxicity

The Langendorff's isolated heart preparation is a highly versatile model that allows simultaneous evaluation of the therapeutic efficacy and cardiac toxicity of investigational compounds. By measuring parameters such as left ventricular developed pressure, coronary flow, and heart rate, researchers can determine whether a compound has positive inotropic effects beneficial for heart failure treatment. At the same time, the model can detect adverse effects such as arrhythmias, conduction blocks, or coronary vasoconstriction, which may indicate potential cardiotoxicity. Because the setup is devoid of systemic influences, any observed effect can be directly attributed to the test compound, making it ideal for mechanistic studies. This model is also useful in safety pharmacology as mandated by regulatory guidelines, where early identification of cardiac liabilities is crucial for drug candidate selection and development.

7.3 Screening Methods for Antihypertensive Drugs

7.3.1 Two Kidney One Clip (2K1C) Goldblatt Model

7.3.1.1 Principle: Partial Constriction of Renal Artery Induces Secondary Hypertension

The Two Kidney One Clip (2K1C) Goldblatt model is a well-established and widely used method for inducing renovascular hypertension in rats. It mimics human secondary hypertension caused by renal artery stenosis. The partial constriction of one renal artery leads to reduced perfusion of the clipped kidney, which stimulates excessive renin release from the juxtaglomerular apparatus. This activates the renin-angiotensin-aldosterone system (RAAS), resulting in systemic vasoconstriction, sodium retention, and a progressive rise in blood pressure. The contralateral non-clipped kidney serves to balance fluid and electrolyte excretion, allowing sustained hypertension to develop over a period of weeks.

7.3.1.2 Animal: Rat

Adult male Wistar or Sprague-Dawley rats, typically weighing 180 to 250 grams, are preferred for this model due to their well-characterized cardiovascular physiology and high reproducibility of hypertension following renal artery clipping. The animals are maintained under standard environmental conditions with free access to food and water. Blood pressure monitoring is initiated before and after surgical intervention to confirm the development of hypertension.

7.3.1.3 Procedure

The rat is anaesthetized using agents such as ketamine and xylazine or sodium pentobarbital. A midline abdominal incision is made to expose the left renal artery. A **U-shaped silver or stainless steel clip with an internal gap of 0.2 mm** is placed around the artery, partially occluding blood flow. Care is taken to avoid complete obstruction. The incision is sutured, and the animal is allowed to recover. Hypertension typically develops over **3 to 4 weeks**.

Blood pressure is measured using either a **non-invasive tail-cuff system**, which records systolic BP in conscious animals using volume-pressure plethysmography, or by **direct intra-arterial catheterization** under anesthesia for more precise readings. Following confirmation of stable hypertension, test drugs are administered orally or intraperitoneally. The blood pressure is then recorded at regular intervals to assess the **antihypertensive efficacy** of the compound.

This model is suitable for screening **angiotensin-converting enzyme (ACE) inhibitors, angiotensin receptor blockers**, and **vasodilators**. The gradual and sustained elevation in blood pressure closely resembles the human condition, making it a valuable model for preclinical antihypertensive drug evaluation.

7.3.2 DOCA-Salt Hypertension Model

7.3.2.1 Principle: Desoxycorticosterone Acetate with High Salt Intake Causes Volume-Dependent Hypertension

The DOCA-salt model of hypertension is a classic method to induce volume-dependent hypertension in laboratory animals, particularly rats. It involves the administration of desoxycorticosterone acetate (DOCA), a mineralocorticoid hormone analogue, combined with a high-salt diet and drinking water supplemented with saline. DOCA promotes sodium and water retention by acting on renal tubular epithelium, while the excess dietary salt further increases extracellular fluid volume. The cumulative effect leads to increased cardiac preload, elevated systemic vascular resistance, and arterial pressure, thereby creating a reliable model of mineralocorticoid-induced hypertension. This model does not rely on the renin-angiotensin system and is thus particularly useful for evaluating drugs that act independently of RAAS.

7.3.2.2 Endpoint: Systolic BP Rise, Cardiac Hypertrophy

Hypertension in this model is assessed by a progressive rise in systolic blood pressure, which is generally measurable within two weeks of starting treatment and becomes significantly elevated by the fourth week. Blood pressure is usually measured using the tail-cuff method or intra-arterial catheterization in anesthetized rats. In addition to increased BP, animals typically exhibit cardiac hypertrophy, particularly left ventricular enlargement, due to the chronic volume overload and increased afterload. Histological evaluation often shows fibrosis, vascular wall thickening, and glomerular injury, mimicking features seen in hypertensive heart disease and nephropathy in humans.

7.3.2.3 Useful for Mineralocorticoid Antagonists and Diuretics

This model is highly suitable for screening **mineralocorticoid receptor antagonists** such as **spironolactone and eplerenone**, as well as **thiazide and loop diuretics**, which counteract sodium and water retention. It is also useful for assessing the **cardioprotective** and **renoprotective effects** of test compounds beyond blood pressure reduction. Since the model exhibits low plasma renin activity, it is not suitable for evaluating ACE inhibitors or angiotensin receptor blockers. However, its reproducibility, pathophysiological relevance, and sensitivity to volume-regulating agents make it a powerful tool for preclinical antihypertensive research.

7.4 Screening Methods for Antiarrhythmic Drugs

7.4.1 Aconitine-Induced Arrhythmia in Rats

7.4.1.1 Principle: Aconitine Causes Arrhythmias via Na^+ Channel Activation

Aconitine, an alkaloid derived from Aconitum species, induces arrhythmias by acting as a **voltage-gated sodium channel activator**. It causes persistent opening of sodium channels, leading to **prolonged depolarization**, disturbed action potential propagation, and ultimately **ventricular ectopic activity and fibrillation**. This uncontrolled influx of sodium ions disrupts normal cardiac rhythm, making aconitine a potent and reliable agent for generating experimental arrhythmias. This model is used to screen **Class I antiarrhythmic drugs**, particularly sodium channel blockers, which can restore normal rhythm by stabilizing the inactivated state of sodium channels.

7.4.1.2 ECG Monitoring of Induced Arrhythmia

The procedure is carried out in adult rats under light anesthesia using agents such as urethane or ketamine to avoid suppression of arrhythmic responses. Aconitine is administered intravenously through the femoral or tail vein at a dose that induces arrhythmia without causing immediate death, commonly around **10 to 20 µg/kg**. Simultaneous **electrocardiogram (ECG) monitoring** is performed using subcutaneous needle electrodes or limb lead placement. The ECG is recorded continuously before, during, and after drug administration.

Typical arrhythmic patterns include **ventricular premature beats, ventricular tachycardia,** and **fibrillation**. The onset, frequency, and severity of these arrhythmias are carefully noted. The ECG allows real-time visualization of **QRS complex widening, T wave abnormalities,** and **P-R interval changes**, providing direct evidence of the electrophysiological effects of aconitine and the test drug.

7.4.1.3 Reduction in Arrhythmia Episodes After Drug = Positive Result

To evaluate the antiarrhythmic potential, test compounds are administered intravenously or orally prior to or shortly after aconitine challenge. A **positive result** is indicated by a **delay in onset, reduction in frequency,** or **complete suppression of arrhythmic episodes** compared to the untreated control group. Some studies also calculate the **arrhythmia score, incidence,** and **survival time** as quantitative endpoints.

Standard reference drugs such as **lidocaine, procainamide,** or **quinidine** are used as comparators. A significant reduction in arrhythmia severity or improvement in survival suggests that the test compound possesses useful antiarrhythmic activity. This model is highly specific for drugs that target sodium channel kinetics and is suitable for preliminary as well as mechanistic screening of antiarrhythmic agents.

7.4.2 Electrically Induced Arrhythmia (Ventricular Fibrillation Threshold)

7.4.2.1 Principle: Evaluates Ability of Drug to Prevent VF Under Electrical Stimulation

The ventricular fibrillation threshold (VFT) model is a well-validated method used to assess the **antiarrhythmic potential** of investigational drugs by determining their ability to **prevent electrically induced ventricular fibrillation**. In this model, **progressively increasing electrical stimuli** are delivered directly to the heart to provoke fibrillation. Ventricular fibrillation is a life-threatening arrhythmia characterized by **rapid, uncoordinated**

contractions of the ventricles, resulting in an immediate loss of cardiac output. A higher threshold for fibrillation, after drug treatment, implies that the heart becomes more resistant to electrical disturbances, indicating **stabilization of cardiac electrophysiology.**

7.4.2.2 Endpoint: Increase in VF Threshold Suggests Antiarrhythmic Action

This model is commonly performed in anesthetized rats, guinea pigs, or dogs. A thoracotomy is carried out to expose the heart, and a pair of platinum electrodes is placed on the epicardial surface of the ventricle. A stimulator is used to deliver a train of electrical pulses at increasing voltage or current. The **lowest intensity of stimulus** required to induce **sustained ventricular fibrillation** is recorded as the **ventricular fibrillation threshold.**

The test drug is administered prior to stimulation. If the **VF threshold increases significantly** in the treated group compared to the control, it indicates **antiarrhythmic activity.** Drugs such as **amiodarone, lidocaine,** and **propranolol** are known to increase VFT and serve as reference standards. The model is sensitive to agents acting on **sodium, potassium, or calcium channels**, as well as **beta-adrenergic antagonists.** This method is particularly useful in evaluating the **prophylactic effect** of drugs against electrically triggered arrhythmias and offers insights into their **electrophysiological safety profile.**

7.5 Screening for Diuretic Activity

7.5.1 Saluretic and Natriuretic Activity Test in Rats

7.5.1.1 Principle: Diuretics Increase Urine Output and Sodium/ Potassium Excretion

Diuretics are agents that promote the excretion of water and electrolytes, particularly sodium and chloride, from the body through urine. The saluretic and natriuretic activity test is designed to evaluate the **ability of test compounds to enhance urinary excretion of electrolytes**, mainly **sodium and potassium,** over a specified period. This test helps classify drugs based on their site and mechanism of action in the nephron and differentiates between **loop diuretics, thiazides, and potassium-sparing agents.** A high sodium excretion with moderate potassium loss is characteristic of loop or thiazide diuretics, whereas selective potassium retention suggests potassium-sparing activity.

7.5.1.2 Animal Model: Normal Rats (Fasted and Hydrated)

Healthy adult male Wistar rats, typically weighing between 180 to 220 grams, are used for this test. The animals are fasted overnight, but free access to drinking water is allowed to ensure hydration. This helps minimize the variability in urine output due to feeding and maintains renal perfusion. The animals are housed individually in **metabolic cages** that allow separate collection of urine, feces, and food residues, preventing contamination and ensuring accuracy in urine volume measurement.

7.5.1.3 Procedure

The test compound or standard drug (e.g., **furosemide or hydrochlorothiazide**) is administered orally or intraperitoneally at doses ranging from **5 to 50 mg/kg,** depending on the drug's potency and class. Control animals receive the same volume of vehicle. Immediately after dosing, the animals are placed in metabolic cages for **urine collection over a 5-hour period.** During this time, no food or additional water is provided.

At the end of 5 hours, total urine volume is measured using a graduated cylinder. A portion of the urine is then subjected to **electrolyte analysis** using **flame photometry** or **ion-selective electrodes** to determine the concentrations of **sodium (Na^+), potassium (K^+),** and **chloride (Cl^-).** The values are expressed in mEq/L and used to calculate excretion rates. Additionally, **natriuretic index (Na^+/K^+ ratio)** and **diuretic index (test group urine volume/control group urine volume)** are calculated to compare efficacy.

Drugs that produce a significant increase in urine volume and sodium excretion, compared to the control, are considered to have strong **diuretic and natriuretic effects.** This model serves as a basic yet reliable tool for screening new diuretics and understanding their electrolyte-modulating profiles.

7.5.1.4 Saluretic Index: Na^+ + Cl^- Excretion

The saluretic index is calculated by summing the amounts of **sodium (Na^+)** and **chloride (Cl^-)** excreted in urine during the observation period. These two ions represent the primary contributors to extracellular fluid volume, and their excretion reflects the **ability of a diuretic to promote salt loss.** Saluretic index is particularly useful when comparing the activity of loop and thiazide diuretics, as both typically enhance Na^+ and Cl^- elimination. It is expressed in milliequivalents per kilogram or per rat and serves as a marker for overall **salt-wasting efficacy** of the test compound.

7.5.1.5 Natriuretic Index: Na^+/K^+ Ratio

The natriuretic index is a ratio that provides insight into the **selectivity of sodium over potassium excretion**. It is calculated by dividing the concentration of Na^+ by the concentration of K^+ in the collected urine sample. A **higher Na^+/K^+ ratio** indicates a favorable **natriuretic profile**, where sodium is excreted more prominently than potassium. This is desirable because excessive potassium loss can lead to **hypokalemia**, a common side effect of many diuretics. **Potassium-sparing diuretics**, like amiloride or spironolactone, typically show a **high natriuretic index**, while loop and thiazide diuretics often display lower ratios.

7.5.1.6 Diuretic Index: Total Urine Volume Compared to Control

The diuretic index quantifies the relative increase in urine volume in the treated group compared to the control group. It is calculated as the ratio of urine volume excreted by the drug-treated animal to that excreted by the control animal during the same period. A value greater than one indicates a diuretic effect, and the magnitude of this index reflects the potency of the compound under investigation. This parameter is helpful in distinguishing between high-ceiling diuretics like furosemide and mild diuretics like xanthine derivatives or herbal formulations.

7.5.2 Lipchitz Test

7.5.2.1 Rats Given Drug + Normal Saline Orally

The Lipchitz test is a classical in vivo method used for preliminary screening of diuretic agents. It evaluates the compound's ability to increase urine output following oral administration in a saline-loaded state. In this model, adult rats are given a **measured oral dose of the test drug**, immediately followed by a fixed volume of **normal saline (commonly 25 mL/kg)** to provide a uniform water load that stimulates diuresis. This controlled hydration ensures that the renal system is primed for urine formation, and any observed increase in urine volume can be confidently attributed to the action of the drug being tested.

7.5.2.2 Urine Collected for 5 Hours and Measured

After dosing, the rats are placed in individual metabolic cages that allow clean and separate collection of urine without contamination. The urine is collected over a 5-hour period, a duration sufficient to capture the diuretic action of most agents. The total urine volume is recorded using graduated cylinders or measuring tubes, and comparisons are made with a control group that receives saline alone without the test drug. Additional parameters such as urine pH, conductivity, and specific gravity may also be recorded if extended analysis is required. The test is simple and suitable for comparing multiple samples simultaneously in a consistent and reproducible manner.

7.5.2.3 Standard Drug: Furosemide or Hydrochlorothiazide

Well-known diuretics such as furosemide (loop diuretic) and hydrochlorothiazide (thiazide diuretic) are used as reference standards in the Lipchitz test. These drugs produce a marked increase in urine output within the 5-hour window, serving as a benchmark for evaluating the potency and efficacy of test compounds. The diuretic activity index is often calculated as the ratio of urine volume produced by the test group to that of the control group. A value significantly higher than one indicates effective diuretic action. This model is particularly useful for screening herbal extracts, novel formulations, and synthetic compounds in the early stages of drug discovery.

7.6 Interpretation and Significance

7.6.1 Need to Combine Multiple Endpoints for Proper Cardiovascular Profiling

In cardiovascular pharmacology, relying on a single endpoint often provides an incomplete picture of a drug's action. Comprehensive profiling requires integrating data from hemodynamic parameters, electrolyte balance, cardiac contractility, arrhythmia susceptibility, and vascular effects. For instance, a compound that reduces blood pressure might also depress cardiac output or alter renal perfusion. Similarly, an antiarrhythmic agent may exert unwanted inotropic or chronotropic effects. Therefore, using multiple validated models—such as isolated heart assays, renal excretion studies, and in vivo blood pressure monitoring—allows a well-rounded evaluation of therapeutic potential, mechanism of action, and systemic implications. These combinations enhance the translational relevance of preclinical findings and guide clinical development.

7.6.2 Importance of Both Efficacy and Safety Evaluation (e.g., QT Prolongation Risk)

Efficacy alone is insufficient in cardiovascular screening, as many promising compounds fail due to cardiac safety liabilities. One major concern is QT interval prolongation, which increases the risk of torsades de pointes and sudden cardiac death. This phenomenon often results from unintended interactions with hERG potassium channels. Preclinical studies must therefore include electrocardiographic analysis and arrhythmia scoring systems to identify such risks early. Tools like Langendorff heart preparation and in vivo telemetry can detect proarrhythmic tendencies while simultaneously assessing the intended pharmacodynamic effects. Such dual assessments help balance efficacy with safety, improving the selection of viable drug candidates for further development.

7.6.3 Role of Telemetry and Digital Systems in Advanced Cardiovascular Research

Advancements in technology have transformed cardiovascular screening through the use of telemetry-based systems, which enable continuous, real-time recording of parameters such as blood pressure, heart rate, ECG, and body temperature in conscious, freely moving animals. This eliminates the confounding influence of anesthesia and stress associated with restraint. Digital systems equipped with data acquisition software allow precise analysis of beat-to-beat variability, arrhythmia detection, and circadian rhythms, providing a robust platform for both acute and chronic studies. These methods are also highly compliant with Good Laboratory Practice (GLP) and regulatory requirements. As a result, modern cardiovascular research increasingly relies on such tools for non-invasive, high-throughput, and ethical pharmacological testing.

Short Answer Questions (with Answers)

1. **What is the primary function of cardiotonic drugs?**
   Increase the force of cardiac contraction (positive inotropy).
2. **Which species is commonly used in the isolated frog heart preparation?**
   Frog.
3. **What is the principle behind the Langendorff's apparatus?**
   Isolated heart is perfused with oxygenated solution to study cardiac function.
4. **What parameters are measured in the Langendorff heart model?**
   Heart rate, coronary flow, and ventricular pressure.
5. **What does 2K1C model stand for?**
   Two Kidney One Clip (Goldblatt hypertension model).
6. **How is hypertension induced in the 2K1C model?**
   By partial constriction of one renal artery using a clip.
7. **Which model uses desoxycorticosterone acetate and salt to induce hypertension?**
   DOCA-Salt model.
8. **Name one endpoint measured in the DOCA-Salt model.**
   Systolic blood pressure or cardiac hypertrophy.
9. **What does the aconitine-induced arrhythmia model test for?**
   Antiarrhythmic drug activity.
10. **What is measured in ventricular fibrillation threshold testing?**
    The minimum current required to induce ventricular fibrillation.
11. **Which drug is commonly used as a standard in cardiotonic screening?**
    Digitoxin.
12. **What does an increase in VF threshold indicate?**
    Positive antiarrhythmic activity.
13. **What is the principle of the saluretic activity test?**
    Increased excretion of sodium and chloride in urine.
14. **Which ions are measured to assess diuretic activity?**
    Sodium (Na^+), Potassium (K^+), Chloride (Cl^-).
15. **Which equipment is used to measure ion concentrations in urine?**
    Flame photometer or ion-selective electrodes.
16. **What is the diuretic index?**
    Ratio of urine volume in test vs control.

17. **What does a natriuretic index indicate?**
Ratio of Na^+ to K^+ excretion.

18. **What is the saluretic index?**
Sum of Na^+ and Cl^- excreted.

19. **What is the endpoint of the Lipchitz test?**
Urine volume measured over 5 hours.

20. **Which animals are preferred for diuretic studies?**
Rats.

21. **Name one standard diuretic used in screening.**
Furosemide or hydrochlorothiazide.

22. **Why are animals hydrated before diuretic tests?**
To ensure consistent baseline urine output.

23. **What is the purpose of using a control group in diuretic studies?**
To compare and calculate diuretic indices.

24. **How is blood pressure monitored in hypertensive models?**
Tail-cuff method or carotid artery catheterization.

25. **What is an advantage of the isolated frog heart model?**
Simple, cost-effective setup.

26. **What is one limitation of the frog heart model?**
It does not mimic mammalian cardiovascular physiology.

27. **What is a common symptom of cardiac toxicity?**
Arrhythmia or reduced ventricular contraction.

28. **What is telemetry used for in cardiovascular research?**
To monitor heart rate and ECG in conscious animals.

29. **What is a common anesthetic used in heart perfusion models?**
Urethane or pentobarbital.

30. **What is the ideal observation period for urine collection in rats?**
Up to 5 hours.

31. **What is a common marker for renal toxicity?**
Elevated blood urea nitrogen or creatinine.

32. **What is the role of the plethysmograph in cardiovascular studies?**
To measure paw edema or blood flow.

33. **Which model is suitable for testing ACE inhibitors?**
DOCA-salt or 2K1C models.

34. **What is digitoxin's mechanism of action?**
Inhibits Na^+/K^+-ATPase, increasing intracellular Ca^{2+}.

35. **What is the main disadvantage of DOCA-salt model?**
Takes several weeks to develop hypertension.

36. **What parameter indicates diuretic potency?**
Volume of urine and ion excretion.
37. **Why are metabolic cages used in diuretic studies?**
To separately collect urine and feces.
38. **What is the purpose of using a reference drug in pharmacological screening?**
To validate the test procedure.
39. **How is cardiac hypertrophy assessed in DOCA model?**
Heart weight/body weight ratio.
40. **What type of arrhythmia does aconitine induce?**
Ventricular arrhythmia.
41. **What does ECG stand for?**
Electrocardiogram.
42. **What is a common sign of diuretic-induced potassium loss?**
Hypokalemia.
43. **What is the primary outcome in natriuretic activity?**
Sodium excretion.
44. **What animal is commonly used in the Langendorff setup?**
Guinea pig or rabbit.
45. **What is the physiological role of aldosterone?**
Sodium retention and potassium excretion.
46. **Which model mimics renovascular hypertension?**
2K1C model.
47. **What is used to induce cardiac failure in animal models?**
Isoproterenol or doxorubicin.
48. **Which part of the ECG is most altered during arrhythmia?**
QRS complex or QT interval.
49. **What method assesses kidney function alongside diuretic action?**
Creatinine clearance test.
50. **Which software or digital tools are used for ECG analysis in research?**
LabChart, ECG Auto, Biopac.

Multiple Choice Questions (MCQs)

1. **Which of the following is used in the DOCA-salt induced hypertension model?**
   a) Propranolol
   b) Deoxycorticosterone acetate
   c) Streptozotocin
   d) Alloxan
   Answer: b) Deoxycorticosterone acetate

2. **Which standard drug is used as a potassium-sparing diuretic in screening tests?**
   a) Furosemide
   b) Hydrochlorothiazide
   c) Amiloride
   d) Acetazolamide
   Answer: c) Amiloride

3. **Which of the following models is used to study arrhythmias?**
   a) Tail-cuff method
   b) Langendorff heart preparation
   c) ECG Monitoring
   d) Elevated plus maze
   Answer: c) ECG Monitoring

4. **Telemetry in cardiovascular screening is used to record:**
   a) Liver enzymes
   b) Intraocular pressure
   c) ECG and BP
   d) Reflex activity
   Answer: c) ECG and BP

5. **The Langendorff preparation involves perfusion of the heart via the:**
   a) Pulmonary vein
   b) Coronary artery
   c) Aorta
   d) Vena cava
   Answer: c) Aorta

6. **Which electrolyte's excessive loss can indicate a potassium-wasting diuretic?**
   a) Sodium

b) Chloride

c) Potassium

d) Calcium

Answer: c) Potassium

7. **Saluretic effect is determined by measuring the excretion of:**

a) Na^+ only

b) K^+ only

c) Na^+ and Cl^-

d) Cl^- and K^+

Answer: c) Na^+ and Cl^-

8. **Which of the following is a non-invasive blood pressure measurement technique in rats?**

a) Intra-arterial cannulation

b) Tail-cuff method

c) ECG telemetry

d) Baroreflex test

Answer: b) Tail-cuff method

9. **Furosemide acts mainly on:**

a) Proximal tubule

b) Loop of Henle

c) Distal tubule

d) Collecting duct

Answer: b) Loop of Henle

10. **Which of the following is considered a loop diuretic?**

a) Amiloride

b) Hydrochlorothiazide

c) Spironolactone

d) Furosemide

Answer: d) Furosemide

11. **In cardiovascular pharmacology, atropine is used to block:**

a) Alpha receptors

b) Beta receptors

c) Muscarinic receptors

d) Dopamine receptors

Answer: c) Muscarinic receptors

12. **Increased heart rate and decreased blood pressure are typically caused by:**

a) Phenylephrine

b) Isoproterenol

c) Atropine

d) Norepinephrine

Answer: b) Isoproterenol

13. **Which preparation is best for studying vasodilatory drugs without systemic interference?**
a) Telemetry

b) Langendorff preparation

c) ECG monitoring

d) Tail-cuff method

Answer: b) Langendorff preparation

14. **A test showing significant Na^+/K^+ excretion ratio indicates:**
a) Potassium-sparing effect

b) Natriuretic effect

c) CNS stimulation

d) Sedative action

Answer: b) Natriuretic effect

15. **Chronic models of hypertension are useful for evaluating:**
a) Acute toxicity

b) Reflex cardiac responses

c) Long-term antihypertensive effects

d) CNS depressants

Answer: c) Long-term antihypertensive effects

16. **Which method is used for continuous monitoring of cardiovascular parameters in freely moving animals?**
a) Tail-cuff method

b) Intra-arterial cannulation

c) ECG telemetry

d) Langendorff model

Answer: c) ECG telemetry

17. **Which of the following is a hallmark of DOCA-salt hypertension?**
a) Hypotension

b) Low sodium levels

c) Fluid retention and vascular resistance

d) Bradycardia

Answer: c) Fluid retention and vascular resistance

18. **Which parameter is not measured in saluretic and natriuretic tests?**
a) Na^+

b) Cl^-

c) Glucose

d) K^+

Answer: c) Glucose

19. **Baroreflex sensitivity is tested using:**

a) Propranolol

b) Phenylephrine or sodium nitroprusside

c) Furosemide

d) Spironolactone

Answer: b) Phenylephrine or sodium nitroprusside

20. **Which drug increases heart rate by blocking vagal tone?**

a) Isoproterenol

b) Phenylephrine

c) Atropine

d) Verapamil

Answer: c) Atropine

Fill-in-the-Blanks (20)

1. The Langendorff's apparatus is used to study the __________ function in isolated heart preparations.
   Answer: cardiac
2. DOCA-salt model is used to induce __________ in rats.
   Answer: hypertension
3. Diuretics promote the excretion of __________ and water from the body.
   Answer: sodium
4. The saluretic index is calculated based on __________ and __________ excretion.
   Answer: sodium, chloride
5. In the 2K1C model, one __________ artery is clipped to induce hypertension.
   Answer: renal
6. The frog heart preparation is an example of an __________ model.
   Answer: ex vivo
7. Furosemide acts on the __________ of Henle.
   Answer: loop
8. The natriuretic index is expressed as the __________ to __________ ratio.
   Answer: sodium, potassium
9. The standard drug used in the Lipchitz test is __________.
   Answer: furosemide
10. Ventricular fibrillation threshold is a test used for __________ drug screening.
    Answer: antiarrhythmic
11. Spironolactone is an example of a __________-**sparing** diuretic.
    Answer: potassium
12. __________ monitoring is used for real-time ECG and BP recording in conscious animals.
    Answer: Telemetry
13. Digitoxin is a commonly used standard drug in __________ screening.
    Answer: cardiotonic
14. In the DOCA-salt model, animals are given a __________-rich diet.
    Answer: salt

15. Antiarrhythmic drugs act on ion channels like __________, __________, and __________.
    Answer: sodium, potassium, calcium
16. The tail-cuff method measures __________ in rodents.
    Answer: blood pressure
17. Aconitine-induced arrhythmia is mediated by increased __________ channel activation.
    Answer: sodium
18. __________ is used to assess left ventricular pressure in isolated heart setups.
    Answer: Langendorff's method
19. Excessive potassium loss can cause __________.
    Answer: hypokalemia
20. Digitoxin exerts a __________ **inotropic** effect on the heart.
    Answer: positive

True or False (20)

1. The 2K1C model is used to induce diabetes.
   False
2. Langendorff apparatus requires oxygenated perfusion fluid.
   True
3. Furosemide is a loop diuretic.
   True
4. Saluretic index involves the calculation of glucose and sodium levels.
   False
5. The Lipchitz test is used to evaluate antiulcer activity.
   False
6. Spironolactone conserves potassium during diuresis.
   True
7. DOCA-salt model involves subcutaneous implantation of DOCA and salt supplementation.
   True
8. Aconitine induces seizures in rodents.
   False
9. Antiarrhythmic drugs can increase the ventricular fibrillation threshold.
   True

10. The digitoxin model uses rabbits in in vivo setups.
False (frog heart ex vivo)
11. Sodium and potassium excretion are key to evaluating diuretic activity.
True
12. ECG telemetry is not useful in drug screening studies.
False
13. Diuretics are used to increase urine output.
True
14. Langendorff heart model measures liver enzyme activity.
False
15. The natriuretic index is calculated using sodium and potassium levels.
True
16. Carrageenan is used in screening cardiovascular drugs.
False
17. Tail-cuff method is a non-invasive technique to measure BP in rodents.
True
18. DOCA-salt model is suitable for testing mineralocorticoid receptor antagonists.
True
19. Diuretics have no effect on electrolyte balance.
False
20. The diuretic index is based on urine volume compared to control.
True

CHAPTER EIGHT

Screening for Metabolic Disorders

8.1 Introduction

8.1.1 Overview of Metabolic Disorders in Pharmacology: Diabetes, Obesity, Hyperlipidemia

Metabolic disorders such as diabetes mellitus, obesity, and hyperlipidemia are among the most prevalent chronic health conditions worldwide. They are characterized by disruptions in glucose, lipid, and energy homeostasis and are major contributors to cardiovascular diseases, renal dysfunction, and neurological complications. Diabetes is primarily marked by hyperglycemia resulting from insulin deficiency or resistance, while obesity is associated with excessive fat accumulation and metabolic imbalance. Hyperlipidemia involves elevated levels of cholesterol, triglycerides, or both in plasma. Together, these disorders pose a considerable burden on healthcare systems, making the development of effective pharmacological interventions a high priority in drug discovery programs.

8.1.2 Need for Reliable In Vivo Screening Models

The complex pathophysiology of metabolic disorders necessitates the use of well-characterized animal models that closely replicate human disease mechanisms. In vivo models allow the assessment of pharmacodynamic effects in a systemic and integrated manner, including interactions with endocrine, hepatic, renal, and cardiovascular systems. For example, chemically-induced diabetic models like alloxan- or streptozotocin-treated rats provide insight into insulin-dependent glucose regulation, while diet-induced obesity models are used to investigate fat metabolism and appetite control. These models are essential for studying drug efficacy, onset of action, and side effects, and they provide the foundation for selecting candidates for clinical trials.

8.1.3 Role of Biochemical Markers in Efficacy Evaluation

Biochemical parameters serve as critical indicators of therapeutic efficacy and metabolic regulation. In diabetes models, fasting blood glucose, oral glucose tolerance test (OGTT), plasma insulin, and glycosylated hemoglobin (HbA1c) levels are commonly evaluated. For lipid metabolism, serum levels of total cholesterol, low-density lipoprotein (LDL), high-density lipoprotein (HDL), and triglycerides are used to assess anti-hyperlipidemic effects. In obesity studies, body weight changes, adipose tissue mass, leptin, and adiponectin levels are often monitored. These markers provide quantifiable endpoints for determining the dose-response relationship, duration of effect, and mechanism of action of test compounds.

8.2 Screening Methods for Antidiabetic Agents

8.2.1 Alloxan-Induced Diabetes Model

8.2.1.1 Principle: Alloxan Selectively Destroys Pancreatic β-Cells

The alloxan-induced diabetes model is a classical and widely used in vivo method to study type 1 diabetes mellitus. Alloxan is a cytotoxic glucose analogue that selectively targets and destroys the insulin-producing β-cells of the pancreatic islets of Langerhans. This destruction occurs due to the generation of reactive oxygen species (ROS) and hydroxyl free radicals, which damage DNA and cellular membranes of β-cells, leading to insulin deficiency. As a result, animals develop a condition of persistent hyperglycemia, mimicking insulin-dependent diabetes. The simplicity and reliability of this model make it an excellent tool for evaluating the efficacy of insulin-mimetic drugs, β-cell protectants, and insulin-replacement therapies.

8.2.1.2 Animal Model: Rats or Mice

Adult Wistar rats or Swiss albino mice are commonly used for this model due to their well-characterized metabolic profile and sensitivity to alloxan. The animals are fasted overnight (12–16 hours) to ensure low baseline glucose levels, which enhances the diabetogenic effect of alloxan. Alloxan monohydrate is freshly prepared in normal saline or citrate buffer (pH 4.5) and administered intraperitoneally or intravenously at a dose of

120–150 mg/kg for rats or 80–100 mg/kg for mice. To prevent immediate hypoglycemia caused by sudden insulin release, glucose solution (5–10%) is provided orally for the next 24 hours.

After 72 hours of administration, blood glucose levels are measured using tail vein blood and a glucometer. Animals showing fasting blood glucose levels above 200 mg/dL are considered diabetic and selected for drug testing. The test compound is then administered orally or parenterally for 7 to 21 days, and changes in blood glucose, body weight, and urine glucose are monitored. Serum insulin levels may also be assessed using ELISA to evaluate the β-cell regeneration potential of the drug.

This model is particularly useful for studying drugs like sulfonylureas (e.g., glibenclamide), herbal formulations, and insulin analogues, which can restore normoglycemia either by stimulating residual β-cells or providing exogenous insulin activity.

8.2.1.3 Procedure

To begin the experiment, rats are fasted overnight but allowed access to water. Alloxan monohydrate is dissolved in cold normal saline or citrate buffer immediately before use to ensure chemical stability. A single intraperitoneal (IP) dose of 120–150 mg/kg is administered to each rat. Following injection, animals are given 5% glucose solution orally or added to their drinking water for the next 24 hours to prevent fatal hypoglycemia due to initial insulin surge caused by partial β-cell stimulation. After 72 hours, fasting blood glucose is measured using a glucometer or a biochemical auto-analyzer. Only animals with fasting glucose levels exceeding 200 mg/dL are selected as diabetic models. The test compound is then administered either orally or intraperitoneally for a duration of 7 to 14 days, depending on the design and expected time of action.

8.2.1.4 Observation

During the treatment period, blood glucose levels are recorded at regular intervals (e.g., day 3, day 7, and day 14) to evaluate the hypoglycemic effect of the test compound. Simultaneously, body weight is monitored because diabetic rats typically exhibit progressive weight loss due to glucose wasting and protein catabolism. Any reversal of weight loss during drug treatment suggests a positive therapeutic outcome. In some protocols, urine sugar, serum insulin, and lipid profile may also be assessed to gain additional insights into the metabolic correction offered by the compound.

8.2.1.5 Standard Drug: Glibenclamide or Metformin

Glibenclamide, a sulfonylurea, is commonly used as a reference drug in this model due to its β-cell stimulating properties. It enhances endogenous insulin secretion and effectively lowers blood glucose in models with residual β-cell function. Alternatively, **metformin**, a biguanide, may be used when studying drugs with **insulin-sensitizing** or **hepatic glucose-lowering** mechanisms. These standard drugs help in **benchmarking the efficacy** of the test compound and validate the experimental design.

8.2.2 Streptozotocin (STZ)-Induced Diabetes Model

8.2.2.1 Principle: STZ Causes DNA Alkylation in β-Cells, Leading to Insulin Deficiency

Streptozotocin (STZ) is a naturally occurring nitrosourea compound that is selectively toxic to pancreatic β-cells due to its high affinity for the glucose transporter-2 (GLUT2), which is abundantly expressed in these cells. Upon cellular uptake, STZ causes DNA alkylation, nitrosourea-induced free radical generation, and oxidative stress, leading to β-cell necrosis and insulin deficiency. This results in persistent hyperglycemia, mimicking diabetes mellitus. Depending on the dose and administration protocol, STZ can be used to model type 1 or type 2 diabetes, making it one of the most versatile and widely accepted tools for antidiabetic drug screening.

8.2.2.2 Doses

- Type 1 Diabetes Model: A single high dose of STZ, typically 60 mg/kg intraperitoneally (IP) in rats or 100–150 mg/kg IP in mice, is used to induce rapid and near-complete destruction of β-cells, leading to insulin-dependent diabetes. Animals must be fasted for 12–16 hours before injection. STZ is freshly dissolved in cold citrate buffer (pH 4.5) and administered within 15 minutes due to its instability.

- Type 2 Diabetes Model: To mimic the partial β-cell dysfunction and insulin resistance characteristic of type 2 diabetes, a low-dose STZ regimen is combined with nicotinamide (120 mg/kg IP) administered 15 minutes before STZ. A common STZ dose in this setting is 35–45 mg/kg IP, which induces moderate hyperglycemia without total β-cell ablation. This model better reflects the metabolic and insulin dynamics of type 2 diabetes.

8.2.2.3 Test Drug Given for 7–28 Days

Following confirmation of diabetes (usually 72 hours after STZ administration), animals with **fasting blood glucose levels above 200–250 mg/dL** are selected. The test compound is administered either **orally or IP** for a treatment period ranging from **7 to 28 days**, depending on the desired pharmacological outcome and the chronicity of the model. Daily or alternate-day monitoring of glucose levels is performed to assess the drug's hypoglycemic effect over time.

8.2.2.4 Biochemical Endpoints

To assess therapeutic efficacy, several **biochemical markers** are measured:

- Fasting Blood Glucose: Indicates the primary antidiabetic effect.
- Serum Insulin: Assessed via ELISA to evaluate insulin secretion or sensitivity.
- Glycated Hemoglobin (HbA1c): Reflects long-term glycemic control over 2–3 weeks.
- Lipid Profile: Includes serum cholesterol, triglycerides, LDL, and HDL levels.
- Liver Function Tests (LFT): AST, ALT, ALP levels to monitor hepatic toxicity or protection.
- Kidney Function Tests (KFT): Serum creatinine, urea, and BUN for renal safety profiling.

These endpoints provide a comprehensive overview of the compound's antidiabetic activity, safety, and metabolic impact.

8.2.2.5 Standard Drugs: Insulin, Pioglitazone, Metformin

In insulin-deficient models, **human insulin** is used as a positive control to restore normoglycemia. For type 2 models, **pioglitazone**, a PPAR-γ agonist that improves insulin sensitivity, and **metformin**, a biguanide that reduces hepatic glucose output and increases peripheral glucose uptake, are standard reference drugs. Their inclusion helps validate the model and provides a benchmark for assessing the test compound's efficacy.

8.3 Screening Methods for Anti-Obesity Agents

8.3.1 High-Fat Diet (HFD)-Induced Obesity Model
8.3.1.1 Diet Composition: 45–60% kcal from Fat

The high-fat diet (HFD)-induced obesity model is a widely accepted and reproducible in vivo method to study dietary obesity and evaluate the efficacy of anti-obesity agents. In this model, animals—typically rats or mice—are fed a customized diet in which 45% to 60% of total calories are derived from fats, as opposed to the 10–15% fat content found in standard laboratory chow. The high caloric density leads to a positive energy balance, promoting adipogenesis, lipid accumulation, and body weight gain, closely mimicking the pathophysiological features of human obesity. The fats used in the diet are usually a mix of lard, butter, or vegetable oil, and the rest of the macronutrient content consists of moderate protein and reduced carbohydrates.

8.3.1.2 Duration: 4–8 Weeks

To establish a stable obese phenotype, animals are maintained on the HFD for a period of **4 to 8 weeks**. During this period, progressive increases in **body weight, adipose tissue mass**, and **plasma lipid levels** are observed. The chronic duration of feeding is essential to induce **metabolic dysregulation**, including **leptin resistance**, **insulin resistance**, and **systemic inflammation**, which together provide a suitable background for testing pharmacological interventions aimed at reversing or preventing obesity.

8.3.1.3 Evaluation Parameters

- **Body Weight Gain:** This is the most basic and direct measure of diet-induced obesity. Weekly weight recordings help track the pattern of weight gain and the impact of the test drug in treated animals.
- **Food Intake:** Measuring daily or cumulative food intake ensures that weight loss is not merely due to reduced appetite or anorexia. It helps differentiate between drugs with **anorectic effects** versus those acting on **metabolism** or **fat absorption**.
- **Lee Index:** A commonly used obesity index in rodents, calculated as:

$$\text{Lee Index} = \left\{ \frac{(\text{Body Weight})^{1/3}(g)}{\text{Naso-anal Length (cm)}} \right\} \times 1000$$

Lee Index formula

A Lee index value **greater than 300** is indicative of obesity in rats. It is a useful parameter for evaluating **body shape and adiposity.**

- **Fat Pad Weight:** At the end of the study, animals are sacrificed, and specific fat depots such as **epididymal, retroperitoneal,** and **mesenteric fat pads** are dissected and weighed. These values provide a direct estimate of **visceral adiposity** and are highly correlated with metabolic risk.

Additional parameters such as **plasma leptin, adiponectin, lipid profile, glucose tolerance test (GTT),** and **insulin tolerance test (ITT)** may also be used to evaluate the metabolic effects of the test drug beyond weight reduction.

8.3.2 Monosodium Glutamate (MSG)-Induced Obesity in Neonatal Mice

8.3.2.1 SC Injection of MSG in Neonatal Period

The monosodium glutamate (MSG)-induced obesity model involves subcutaneous (SC) administration of MSG to neonatal mice during their early postnatal days, typically from day 2 to day 10 of life. The MSG is administered at a dose of 2 to 4 mg/g body weight, once daily, in a small volume of sterile saline. The neonatal period is particularly sensitive to MSG because the blood-brain barrier is not yet fully developed, allowing MSG to enter the central nervous system and exert its neurotoxic effects. The treatment results in the targeted degeneration of arcuate nucleus neurons in the hypothalamus, a brain region responsible for appetite regulation and energy balance.

8.3.2.2 Induces Hypothalamic Obesity Due to Neurotoxicity

The damage to hypothalamic neurons impairs leptin signaling and satiety regulation, leading to persistent hyperphagia, reduced energy expenditure, and eventual obesity. Affected animals show a gradual but significant increase in body weight, even when fed a normal diet. They also develop endocrine imbalances, including elevated insulin levels, impaired glucose tolerance, and altered lipid metabolism, closely mimicking the neuroendocrine form of obesity seen in certain human metabolic disorders. This model does not rely on dietary manipulation, making it ideal for studying central mechanisms of obesity and for evaluating centrally acting anti-obesity drugs.

8.3.2.3 Long-Term Model for Evaluating Anti-Obesity Agents Acting Centrally

The MSG model is used as a **long-term pharmacological model**, with evaluations typically starting from **8 to 10 weeks of age** and continuing for several weeks. During this period, animals are monitored for **body weight changes, food and water intake**, and **metabolic parameters** such as **glucose, insulin, leptin, and lipid profile**. Test drugs are usually administered orally or intraperitoneally and are evaluated for their ability to **modulate central appetite control, restore hypothalamic neuropeptide balance,** or **enhance thermogenesis**. The model is particularly useful for studying **hypothalamic regulators, neuropeptide antagonists**, and **sympathomimetic agents** targeting central appetite pathways.

8.4 Screening Methods for Antihyperlipidemic Agents

8.4.1 Triton WR-1339-Induced Hyperlipidemia Model

8.4.1.1 Principle: Triton Inhibits Lipoprotein Lipase, Increasing Serum Cholesterol and Triglycerides

The Triton WR-1339-induced hyperlipidemia model is a well-established **acute in vivo method** used to evaluate the lipid-lowering potential of antihyperlipidemic agents. Triton WR-1339 (also known as Tyloxapol) is a nonionic surfactant that blocks the action of **lipoprotein lipase**, an enzyme responsible for the breakdown of **chylomicrons and very-low-density lipoproteins (VLDL)** into free fatty acids. As a result, it leads to **accumulation of circulating lipoproteins**, causing an artificial elevation in **serum cholesterol and triglyceride levels**. This hyperlipidemic state mimics certain aspects of human dyslipidemia and is particularly useful for **short-term screening of statins, fibrates, and herbal lipid-lowering compounds**.

8.4.1.2 Procedure

The experiment is typically carried out in **overnight-fasted albino rats** weighing between 150 and 200 grams. Triton WR-1339 is freshly prepared in **0.9% saline** or **phosphate-buffered saline** and administered via a **single intraperitoneal (IP) injection at a dose of 400 mg/kg body weight.** Immediately or shortly after the induction, the test drug is administered orally in a suitable vehicle (such as 0.5% CMC or distilled water) at the desired dose. The treatment continues either as a **single dose** or **repeated daily administration**, depending on the study design. Blood samples are collected from the **retro-orbital plexus** or **tail vein** after **24 to 48 hours**, when lipid levels are at their peak.

8.4.1.3 Parameters

The collected blood is centrifuged at **3000 rpm for 10 minutes** to separate serum. The following lipid profile parameters are measured using commercial kits:

- **Total Cholesterol (TC):** Indicates the overall level of cholesterol in the bloodstream.
- **Triglycerides (TG):** Elevated in hyperlipidemia; reduction suggests effectiveness of lipolysis or inhibition of lipid synthesis.
- **High-Density Lipoprotein (HDL):** Protective lipoprotein; increase is a positive outcome.
- **Low-Density Lipoprotein (LDL):** Atherogenic lipoprotein; reduction is a key goal in therapy.

These parameters are typically expressed in **mg/dL**, and changes are calculated relative to both the hyperlipidemic control and normal baseline.

8.4.1.4 Standard Drugs: Atorvastatin, Fenofibrate

Atorvastatin, an HMG-CoA reductase inhibitor, is used as the **standard statin drug** for comparison. It acts by inhibiting cholesterol biosynthesis in the liver and enhancing LDL clearance. **Fenofibrate**, a PPAR-α agonist, serves as a **standard fibrate** and is particularly effective in reducing serum triglycerides and improving HDL levels. These reference drugs help validate the model and enable quantification of the test compound's lipid-lowering potency in a standardized manner.

8.4.2 High-Fat Diet-Induced Hyperlipidemia

8.4.2.1 Diet Rich in Fat and Cholesterol for 4–6 Weeks

The high-fat diet (HFD)-induced hyperlipidemia model is a chronic in vivo screening method used to study lipid abnormalities similar to those found in human metabolic syndrome and atherosclerosis. Animals, typically Wistar rats or Swiss albino mice, are fed a specially formulated diet enriched with fat (30–40%) and cholesterol (1–2%) for a duration of 4 to 6 weeks. The diet may also include cholic acid (0.5%) to facilitate cholesterol absorption. The excessive intake of fat and cholesterol leads to a gradual rise in serum lipid levels, resulting in hypercholesterolemia, hypertriglyceridemia, and low HDL levels—mimicking the lipid profile of individuals at risk of cardiovascular disease.

During this induction period, **body weight, food intake**, and **clinical signs** are monitored regularly. At the end of the induction phase, animals are confirmed to be hyperlipidemic through blood analysis and are then randomized into different treatment groups. The **test drug is administered orally**, usually for **2 to 4 weeks**, while the animals continue receiving the high-fat diet.

8.4.2.2 Monitors Changes in Lipid Parameters and Atherogenic Index

To evaluate the antihyperlipidemic activity of the test compound, several **biochemical markers** are assessed from serum samples obtained by retro-orbital bleeding or tail vein puncture:

- **Total Cholesterol (TC)**
- **Triglycerides (TG)**
- **Low-Density Lipoprotein (LDL)**
- **High-Density Lipoprotein (HDL)**

In addition to these values, the **atherogenic index (AI)** is calculated as:

$$\text{Atherogenic Index (AI)} = \frac{\text{Total Cholesterol} - \text{HDL}}{\text{HDL}}$$

An elevated AI reflects **increased cardiovascular risk**, and a **reduction in AI after drug treatment** is indicative of therapeutic potential in preventing atherosclerosis.

This model is especially useful for evaluating drugs that affect **lipid metabolism, cholesterol biosynthesis, or LDL receptor modulation**, such as **statins, fibrates, niacin derivatives**, and various **herbal or nutraceutical** formulations. It also allows for **histopathological examination of liver and aortic tissues**, offering insight into **fatty liver changes** and **early plaque formation**.

8.5 Biochemical Parameters and Assay Techniques

8.5.1 Blood Glucose Measurement

8.5.1.1 Methods: Glucometer (Finger Prick), Glucose Oxidase-Peroxidase Assay

Blood glucose measurement is one of the most essential biochemical parameters in metabolic disorder research, especially in evaluating **antidiabetic agents**. The two common methods used are the **glucometer-based finger prick method** and the **glucose oxidase-peroxidase (GOD-POD) enzymatic assay**.

The **glucometer method** involves collecting a small drop of blood from the tail vein of rats or mice using a sterile lancet or needle. The sample is placed on a test strip inserted into the glucometer, which provides an instant reading in **mg/dL**. This method is rapid, minimally invasive, and suitable for **frequent monitoring** during long-term studies.

The **GOD-POD method** is a laboratory-based, colorimetric assay. In this technique, glucose in the serum reacts with the **glucose oxidase enzyme**, forming **gluconic acid** and **hydrogen peroxide**. The hydrogen peroxide then reacts with a chromogenic substrate in the presence of **peroxidase enzyme** to produce a **colored compound**, typically read at **505–520 nm** using a spectrophotometer. The intensity of color is directly proportional to the glucose concentration in the sample.

8.5.1.2 Sample: Fasting vs Postprandial Glucose

Glucose levels are measured under two physiological states: **fasting** and **postprandial**. Fasting glucose is measured after a **12–16 hour food deprivation period**, which provides baseline glycemic status without interference from recent meals. This is particularly important in diabetic screening to assess insulin-independent glucose regulation.

Postprandial glucose is measured **1 to 2 hours after feeding or glucose administration** (as in oral glucose tolerance tests). It reflects the body's **ability to manage glucose load** and the efficiency of insulin secretion and action. Both measurements are necessary to evaluate the **comprehensive glycemic profile** of the test animal and determine the mechanism of action of the antidiabetic drug being tested.

8.5.2 Serum Insulin Levels

8.5.2.1 ELISA or RIA (Radioimmunoassay)

Measurement of **serum insulin levels** is a critical parameter in evaluating the **endocrine function of pancreatic β-cells** and assessing the impact of test compounds on **insulin secretion** or **resistance**. The two most commonly used techniques for insulin estimation in preclinical research are **Enzyme-Linked Immunosorbent Assay (ELISA)** and **Radioimmunoassay (RIA)**.

In the **ELISA method**, insulin in the serum sample binds to specific **monoclonal or polyclonal anti-insulin antibodies** coated on the microtiter plate. A secondary antibody linked to an enzyme such as **horseradish peroxidase (HRP)** is then added, which binds to the insulin-antibody complex. After adding a suitable substrate like **TMB (tetramethylbenzidine)**, a color change occurs that is proportional to the insulin concentration. The absorbance is measured using a plate reader at **450 nm**, and insulin concentration is quantified using a standard curve.

Radioimmunoassay (RIA) uses a radioactively labeled insulin tracer, which competes with endogenous insulin in the sample for a limited number of antibody binding sites. The amount of radioactivity bound is inversely proportional to the insulin concentration. Although RIA is highly sensitive, it requires **radioisotope handling facilities** and is subject to **radiation safety regulations**, which limits its routine use in many laboratories.

8.5.2.2 Used in HOMA-IR and Insulin Sensitivity Index

Serum insulin levels are often used in conjunction with fasting glucose levels to calculate **insulin resistance** and **insulin sensitivity indices**, such as:

- **HOMA-IR (Homeostasis Model Assessment of Insulin Resistance):**

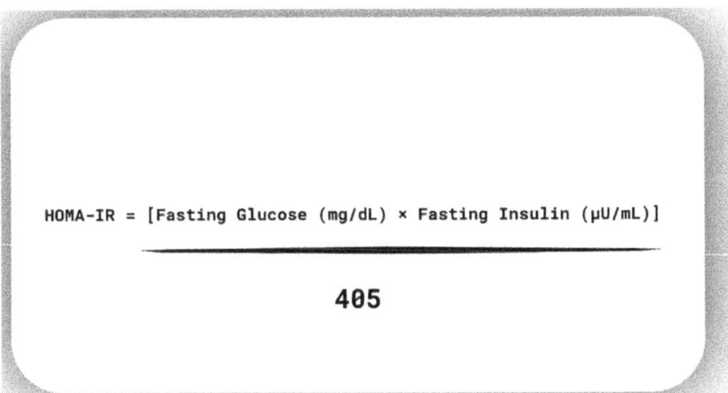

HOMA-IR Equation

Higher values indicate greater insulin resistance.
QUICKI (Quantitative Insulin Sensitivity Check Index):

$$\frac{1}{[\log(\text{Fasting Insulin}) + \log(\text{Fasting Glucose})]}$$

QUICKI Formula

These calculations are crucial for identifying the mechanism of action of test compounds, distinguishing whether they enhance insulin secretion, improve peripheral sensitivity, or reduce insulin resistance. These indices are particularly important in models of type 2 diabetes, where hyperinsulinemia with normoglycemia may indicate compensatory pancreatic function.

8.5.3 Lipid Profile Measurement

8.5.3.1 Parameters: TC, TG, HDL-C, LDL-C, VLDL

Lipid profile analysis is essential in evaluating drugs targeting **hyperlipidemia, obesity,** and **metabolic syndrome.** The standard parameters include:

- **Total Cholesterol (TC):** Represents the sum of all cholesterol fractions.

- **Triglycerides (TG):** Reflect circulating fat levels and are elevated in dyslipidemia and insulin resistance.
- **High-Density Lipoprotein Cholesterol (HDL-C):** Known as "good cholesterol"; higher levels are protective.
- **Low-Density Lipoprotein Cholesterol (LDL-C):** Referred to as "bad cholesterol"; associated with atherogenic risk.
- **Very Low-Density Lipoprotein (VLDL):** Carries triglycerides; often estimated as TG/5 in mg/dL.

These parameters are typically evaluated using **serum samples collected after 12–16 hours of fasting** to avoid postprandial lipid variation. Blood is withdrawn, allowed to clot, and then centrifuged to obtain clear serum for biochemical analysis.

8.5.3.2 Atherogenic Index: (TC – HDL)/HDL

To assess the cardiovascular risk beyond individual lipid values, the **atherogenic index (AI)** is calculated. It is a useful ratio to estimate the **balance between atherogenic and anti-atherogenic lipoproteins**, given by:

$$\text{Atherogenic Index (AI)} = \frac{\text{(Total Cholesterol} - \text{HDL)}}{\text{HDL}}$$

Atherogenic Index

A higher AI indicates a **greater risk of atherosclerosis**, while a lower AI reflects **better lipid balance**. This index is especially valuable in experimental models of hyperlipidemia and in screening antihyperlipidemic agents.

8.5.3.3 Enzymatic Kits Used in Colorimetric Analysis

Lipid levels are measured using **enzymatic colorimetric kits**, which are widely available and validated for preclinical studies. These kits work based on enzyme-catalyzed reactions that generate a **colored end product**, measured by spectrophotometry at specific wavelengths:

- **Cholesterol Estimation:** Uses **cholesterol esterase and cholesterol oxidase**, generating hydrogen peroxide which reacts with a chromogen.

- **Triglyceride Estimation:** Involves **lipase, glycerol kinase,** and **glycerol phosphate oxidase.**
- **HDL-C Estimation:** Precipitation of LDL and VLDL, followed by enzymatic measurement of HDL.
- **LDL and VLDL:** Either calculated using the **Friedewald formula** or measured directly using specific assay kits.

These assays offer **rapid, accurate, and reproducible** results, and their use ensures compliance with **Good Laboratory Practice (GLP)** standards. The lipid profile is a cornerstone in the evaluation of cardiometabolic interventions in experimental pharmacology.

8.6 Significance and Limitations

8.6.1 Advantages: Simple Models, Reproducible Endpoints, Cost-Effective

The in vivo and in vitro screening models used for studying metabolic disorders such as diabetes, obesity, and hyperlipidemia offer several significant advantages in pharmaceutical research. These models are **relatively simple to establish and maintain**, especially in rodent species, and provide **reproducible physiological endpoints** such as blood glucose levels, lipid profiles, insulin response, and body weight changes. Standardization of procedures, dosing, and assay kits across laboratories contributes to **reliable inter-laboratory comparisons**. Additionally, these models are **cost-effective**, as they typically require minimal infrastructure and short study durations, especially for acute models like Triton WR-1339-induced hyperlipidemia or alloxan-induced diabetes. Their affordability and adaptability make them widely used in academic institutions and early-stage drug discovery.

8.6.2 Limitations: Do Not Fully Mimic Human Pathophysiology

Despite their utility, these animal models **do not completely replicate the complexity of human metabolic diseases.** For example, streptozotocin-induced diabetes produces rapid β-cell destruction, resembling type 1 diabetes, but fails to model **progressive insulin resistance** seen in human type 2 diabetes. Similarly, Triton-induced hyperlipidemia is an **acute model**, lacking chronic inflammatory and vascular changes associated with human dyslipidemia. Differences in **metabolism, drug absorption, and endocrine responses** between rodents and humans may result in variable drug efficacy and safety profiles. Furthermore, long-term complications such as **retinopathy, nephropathy,** and **macrovascular disease** are rarely seen in short-duration animal studies.

8.6.3 Ethical Considerations and Need for Proper Controls

All experimental procedures involving animals must strictly adhere to **ethical guidelines** laid down by regulatory authorities such as **CPCSEA** in India and **OECD** internationally. The **3Rs principle**—Replacement, Reduction, and Refinement—must guide all study designs. Proper **control groups**, such as vehicle-treated and standard drug-treated animals, are essential for valid interpretation of results. Adequate attention must be given to **animal welfare**, including proper housing, humane handling, and timely euthanasia where necessary. Regular ethical review, veterinary oversight, and trained personnel are crucial to maintain the **scientific validity and moral responsibility** of preclinical pharmacological research.

Short Answer Type Questions

1. **What is the mechanism of action of streptozotocin in inducing diabetes?**
   It selectively destroys pancreatic β-cells through DNA alkylation and nitric oxide generation.

2. **Which animal species is most commonly used for antidiabetic screening models?**
   Wistar rats or Swiss albino mice.

3. **What dose of streptozotocin is typically used to induce Type 1 diabetes in rats?**
   A single dose of 50–60 mg/kg intraperitoneally.

4. **How does alloxan induce diabetes?**
   It generates reactive oxygen species that destroy pancreatic β-cells.

5. **What is the preferred route of administration for alloxan in rodents?**
   Intraperitoneal or intravenous.

6. **What is the fasting period before inducing diabetes with alloxan?**
   12–16 hours.

7. **What is the purpose of glucose tolerance tests in diabetic models?**
   To evaluate how effectively the body clears glucose from the bloodstream.

8. **What parameter is used to confirm diabetes in rats?**
   Fasting blood glucose level above 250 mg/dL.

9. **Which biochemical marker is used to assess long-term glycemic control?**
   Glycated hemoglobin (HbA1c).

10. **What is OGTT?**
    Oral Glucose Tolerance Test.

11. **Name one oral antidiabetic drug used as a standard in preclinical models.**
    Metformin.

12. **What is the principle of the high-fat diet model for obesity?**
    Induces weight gain and insulin resistance due to increased fat intake.

13. **Which enzyme's activity increases in obesity models?**
    Lipoprotein lipase.

14. **What is the normal range of fasting blood glucose in rats?**
    70–110 mg/dL.

15. **What method is used to estimate plasma insulin levels?**
    ELISA (Enzyme-linked Immunosorbent Assay).

16. **What is the Atherogenic Index formula?**
   log(TG/HDL-C).
17. **What is the purpose of Triton WR-1339 in lipid studies?**
   It induces hyperlipidemia by inhibiting lipoprotein lipase.
18. **What is the standard drug for anti-hyperlipidemic activity in rats?**
   Atorvastatin.
19. **What does VLDL-C stand for?**
   Very Low-Density Lipoprotein Cholesterol.
20. **What is the formula to calculate VLDL-C?**
   TG/5 (in mg/dL).
21. **What is the role of HDL-C in lipid metabolism?**
   It facilitates reverse cholesterol transport.
22. **Which lipoprotein is considered 'bad' cholesterol?**
   LDL (Low-Density Lipoprotein).
23. **Which organ is primarily affected in diet-induced obesity models?**
   Liver (fatty liver).
24. **What dietary component is used in high-cholesterol diet models?**
   Cholesterol (1–2%) with saturated fats.
25. **Name one method to measure serum total cholesterol.**
   Enzymatic colorimetric assay.
26. **What is the full form of HbA1c?**
   Hemoglobin A1c.
27. **Which parameter indicates insulin resistance?**
   Elevated fasting insulin and glucose.
28. **What is the major adverse effect of alloxan administration?**
   Hypoglycemia-induced death if not stabilized with glucose.
29. **Which biochemical test is used for triglyceride estimation?**
   Glycerol phosphate oxidase-peroxidase (GPO-POD) method.
30. **What is the function of insulin in glucose metabolism?**
   Facilitates cellular uptake of glucose.
31. **Which immunoassay is most sensitive for insulin detection?**
   Electrochemiluminescence (ECL).
32. **How long does it take for alloxan to induce diabetes?**
   Within 48–72 hours post-injection.
33. **Why is 10% glucose solution administered after alloxan injection?**
   To prevent fatal hypoglycemia.
34. **Which parameter is most affected in Triton WR-1339-induced hyperlipidemia?**

Serum triglycerides.

35. **What type of diabetes does streptozotocin model best simulate?**
Type 1 diabetes.

36. **Which test drug is used in oral glucose tolerance test (OGTT)?**
Standard hypoglycemic agents like glibenclamide.

37. **What is one advantage of ELISA over RIA in insulin measurement?**
No use of radioactive substances.

38. **Which lipid profile parameter increases in atherogenic state?**
LDL-C and total cholesterol.

39. **What is the significance of measuring HDL/LDL ratio?**
Indicator of cardiovascular risk.

40. **How is diabetes confirmed in STZ model?**
By fasting blood glucose >250 mg/dL.

41. **Which organ is targeted by streptozotocin?**
Pancreas (β-cells).

42. **How is insulin resistance evaluated in preclinical models?**
Using HOMA-IR (Homeostatic Model Assessment for Insulin Resistance).

43. **What is the role of cholic acid in high-fat diet models?**
Enhances intestinal lipid absorption.

44. **Which parameters are commonly used in glucose profile?**
Fasting glucose, postprandial glucose, OGTT values.

45. **What type of sampling is used for lipid profile analysis in rats?**
Retro-orbital or tail vein blood collection.

46. **Name a common standard anti-obesity agent.**
Orlistat.

47. **Which metabolic syndrome component is not tested in lipid profile?**
Insulin sensitivity.

48. **Why is serum separation important for biochemical tests?**
To remove cells and ensure accurate measurement of analytes.

49. **Which animal model can be used to study both obesity and diabetes together?**
High-fat diet + low-dose STZ combination.

50. **What is the main application of anti-hyperlipidemic drug screening?**
To evaluate cholesterol-lowering potential of test compounds.

Multiple Choice Questions (MCQs)

1. Which compound is commonly used to induce **Type 1 Diabetes** in animal models?
   a) Triton WR-1339
   b) Alloxan
   c) Nicotinamide
   d) Atorvastatin
   Ans: b) Alloxan

2. **Streptozotocin (STZ)** causes beta-cell destruction by:
   a) Inhibiting glucagon receptors
   b) DNA alkylation and oxidative stress
   c) Blocking insulin receptors
   d) Enhancing GLUT-4 translocation
   Ans: b) DNA alkylation and oxidative stress

3. The **OGTT** is used to assess:
   a) Insulin resistance
   b) Hypoglycemia
   c) Glucose tolerance
   d) Lipid metabolism
   Ans: c) Glucose tolerance

4. Which dose of STZ is typically used for **single-dose diabetes induction**?
   a) 10–20 mg/kg
   b) 25–35 mg/kg
   c) 50–65 mg/kg
   d) 75–100 mg/kg
   Ans: c) 50–65 mg/kg

5. **Triton WR-1339** model is used for:
   a) Anti-obesity screening
   b) Antidiabetic screening
   c) Hyperlipidemia screening
   d) Hypertension screening
   Ans: c) Hyperlipidemia screening

6. In diabetic models, a fasting blood glucose level >200 mg/dL is considered:
   a) Normal
   b) Hypoglycemia
   c) Pre-diabetes
   d) Diabetic
   Ans: d) Diabetic

7. The enzyme used in GOD-POD glucose estimation is:
   a) Glutathione oxidase
   b) Glucose oxidase
   c) Peroxidase kinase
   d) None of the above
   Ans: b) Glucose oxidase

8. **High-fat diets** are often combined with STZ to simulate:
   a) Type 1 diabetes
   b) Hypertension
   c) Type 2 diabetes
   d) Anemia
   Ans: c) Type 2 diabetes

9. Which of the following is a **lipid profile parameter?**
   a) HbA1c
   b) CK-MB
   c) LDL
   d) ALT
   Ans: c) LDL

10. **Fenofibrate** is commonly used as a:
    a) Standard antidiabetic
    b) Standard antihypertensive
    c) Lipid-lowering agent
    d) Antipsychotic control
    Ans: c) Lipid-lowering agent

11. The oral glucose dose in OGTT for rodents is typically:
    a) 1 g/kg
    b) 2 g/kg
    c) 4 g/kg
    d) 5 g/kg
    Ans: b) 2 g/kg

12. Which biochemical marker best reflects long-term glucose control?
    a) HDL
    b) HbA1c
    c) TG
    d) Insulin
    Ans: b) HbA1c

13. What is a hallmark feature of type 2 diabetes in animal models?
    a) Severe ketosis

     b) Insulin resistance

     c) Beta-cell hyperplasia

     d) Hypoglycemia

     Ans: b) Insulin resistance

14. **Cholic acid** is added to high-fat diets to:

     a) Reduce liver toxicity

     b) Induce insulin sensitivity

     c) Enhance lipid absorption

     d) Decrease triglycerides

     Ans: c) Enhance lipid absorption

15. **Alloxan** induces diabetes by:

     a) Blocking glucagon

     b) Increasing hepatic glucose output

     c) Causing beta-cell necrosis

     d) Enhancing insulin secretion

     Ans: c) Causing beta-cell necrosis

16. Which of the following is an **anti-obesity** drug model endpoint?

     a) OGTT

     b) Food intake

     c) Serum calcium

     d) ECG interval

     Ans: b) Food intake

17. The formula for **VLDL** estimation is:

     a) TG/3

     b) TG/5

     c) HDL/2

     d) LDL/5

     Ans: b) TG/5

18. A common endpoint in obesity models is:

     a) Heart rate

     b) BMI change

     c) Platelet count

     d) Muscle tone

     Ans: b) BMI change

19. An **atherogenic index** is calculated from:

     a) HbA1c/TG

     b) TG/HDL

     c) FBG/LDL

d) HDL/LDL

Ans: b) TG/HDL

20. **Simvastatin** primarily reduces:

    a) Glucose

    b) Cholesterol

    c) Sodium

    d) Protein

    Ans: b) Cholesterol

21. Which of the following is **not** a common endpoint in antidiabetic studies?

    a) Blood glucose

    b) Body temperature

    c) HbA1c

    d) Insulin level

    Ans: b) Body temperature

22. The **Lee index** is primarily used in:

    a) Hyperlipidemia models

    b) Hypertension studies

    c) Obesity models

    d) Hepatotoxicity studies

    Ans: c) Obesity models

23. MSG-induced obesity affects the:

    a) Thyroid gland

    b) Adrenal cortex

    c) Hypothalamus

    d) Pancreas

    Ans: c) Hypothalamus

24. Which route is commonly used to administer alloxan?

    a) Oral

    b) Subcutaneous

    c) Intravenous

    d) Intraperitoneal

    Ans: d) Intraperitoneal

25. A test drug's ability to **restore insulin sensitivity** is best measured by:

    a) OGTT

    b) HOMA-IR

    c) LDL assay

    d) Liver enzyme test

Ans: b) HOMA-IR

26. The **duration of high-fat diet feeding** to induce obesity is usually:
    a) 2–3 days
    b) 7–10 days
    c) 4–8 weeks
    d) 12 hours
    Ans: c) 4–8 weeks

27. In Triton model, lipoprotein lipase inhibition results in:
    a) Weight gain
    b) Hypoglycemia
    c) Hyperlipidemia
    d) Hypertension
    Ans: c) Hyperlipidemia

28. A key marker for insulin resistance is:
    a) Fasting insulin
    b) Serum urea
    c) Platelet count
    d) Alanine transferase
    Ans: a) Fasting insulin

29. One sign of uncontrolled diabetes in animals is:
    a) Hypothermia
    b) Polyuria
    c) Muscle hypertrophy
    d) Weight gain
    Ans: b) Polyuria

30. Which method is used to estimate insulin in pharmacological studies?
    a) Spectrophotometry
    b) ELISA
    c) SDS-PAGE
    d) Flame photometry
    Ans: b) ELISA

31. A **lipid-lowering effect** is shown by:
    a) Increased TG
    b) Increased HDL
    c) Increased VLDL
    d) Increased LDL
    Ans: b) Increased HDL

32. Which of the following is **not** used for inducing metabolic syndrome?
    a) Alloxan
    b) STZ
    c) Triton WR-1339
    d) Adrenaline
    Ans: d) Adrenaline

33. **Metformin** acts by:
    a) Enhancing insulin secretion
    b) Blocking glucagon
    c) Reducing hepatic glucose output
    d) Increasing appetite
    Ans: c) Reducing hepatic glucose output

34. A typical endpoint in **obesity studies** is:
    a) Platelet aggregation
    b) Weight of fat pads
    c) Heart rate
    d) ALT/AST
    Ans: b) Weight of fat pads

35. Type 2 diabetes models are **different from type 1** because:
    a) They involve beta-cell destruction
    b) They do not use glucose
    c) They involve insulin resistance
    d) They use viruses
    Ans: c) They involve insulin resistance

36. **Colorimetric estimation** of cholesterol uses:
    a) Biuret reagent
    b) Enzymatic kits
    c) Benedict's solution
    d) $FeCl_3$
    Ans: b) Enzymatic kits

37. **MSG-induced obesity** is initiated at:
    a) Adult stage
    b) Embryonic stage
    c) Neonatal stage
    d) Weaning stage
    Ans: c) Neonatal stage

38. Which hormone is **deficient in type 1 diabetes**?
    a) Glucagon

b) Insulin

c) Leptin

d) Ghrelin

Ans: b) Insulin

39. A high **atherogenic index** indicates:

a) Low cardiovascular risk

b) High lipid clearance

c) High cardiovascular risk

d) Normal metabolism

Ans: c) High cardiovascular risk

40. A **positive effect** of an anti-obesity drug is reflected by:

a) Increased LDL

b) Increased food intake

c) Reduced Lee index

d) Decreased insulin

Ans: c) Reduced Lee index

41. **Nicotinamide** is used along with STZ to mimic:

a) Type 1 diabetes

b) Type 2 diabetes

c) Pancreatitis

d) Glucagon resistance

Ans: b) Type 2 diabetes

42. An example of a **standard antidiabetic drug**:

a) Aspirin

b) Atorvastatin

c) Metformin

d) Diazepam

Ans: c) Metformin

43. In Triton-induced hyperlipidemia, test drugs are given:

a) 3 weeks after Triton

b) 10 days before Triton

c) Immediately after Triton

d) 48 hours after Triton

Ans: c) Immediately after Triton

44. **TG** stands for:

a) Total Glucose

b) Tri-glutamine

c) Triglycerides

d) Triglycine

Ans: c) Triglycerides

45. In blood glucose estimation, **GOD-POD** is:

    a) Glucose oxidase-peroxidase method

    b) Glycine oxidase method

    c) Glucagon-based digestion

    d) Glomerular output protocol

    Ans: a) Glucose oxidase-peroxidase method

46. **Pioglitazone** is classified under:

    a) Sulfonylureas

    b) Thiazolidinediones

    c) Meglitinides

    d) Biguanides

    Ans: b) Thiazolidinediones

47. The endpoint of **insulin sensitivity index** depends on:

    a) Insulin only

    b) Glucose only

    c) Both glucose and insulin

    d) TG levels

    Ans: c) Both glucose and insulin

48. Which organ is most affected in **hyperlipidemia studies**?

    a) Heart

    b) Kidney

    c) Liver

    d) Lung

    Ans: c) Liver

49. **Lipid-lowering drugs** are most effective in models with elevated:

    a) Glucose

    b) Insulin

    c) Cholesterol

    d) Urea

    Ans: c) Cholesterol

50. One method to measure lipid parameters involves:

    a) Gas chromatography

    b) Enzymatic colorimetry

    c) Spectrofluorometry

    d) Titration

    Ans: b) Enzymatic colorimetry

CHAPTER NINE

Screening for Gastrointestinal and Respiratory Drugs

9.1 Introduction

9.1.1 Importance of GI and Respiratory Disorders in Pharmacology

Gastrointestinal (GI) and respiratory disorders account for a substantial proportion of the global disease burden and have a major impact on public health, especially in developing nations. Conditions such as peptic ulcers, functional bowel disorders, asthma, and chronic obstructive pulmonary disease (COPD) affect millions worldwide and demand effective pharmacological intervention. These disorders often involve complex pathophysiological mechanisms, including inflammation, smooth muscle dysfunction, mucosal damage, and immune dysregulation, necessitating the development of multiple classes of drugs targeting diverse pathways. Therefore, robust pharmacological screening models are essential for evaluating the efficacy and mechanism of candidate drugs before human trials.

9.1.2 Need for Reliable and Reproducible In Vivo Models

To ensure the validity of pharmacological findings, in vivo experimental models must be sensitive, reproducible, and ethically acceptable. In GI pharmacology, reliable animal models allow the assessment of gastric secretion, mucosal protection, intestinal motility, and diarrhea inhibition, whereas respiratory models enable the evaluation of bronchoconstriction, inflammation, airway hyperresponsiveness, and mucus production. These models provide measurable endpoints that reflect clinical relevance, such as ulcer index, stool consistency, intestinal transit time, respiratory rate, and airway resistance. Standardized protocols improve reproducibility, enabling the comparison of test compounds with known standards like ranitidine, loperamide, and salbutamol.

9.1.3 Overview of Drugs Studied: Anti-Ulcer, Antidiarrheal, Prokinetic, Anti-Asthmatic

Pharmacological research in these domains primarily focuses on four major classes of drugs. Anti-ulcer agents include proton pump inhibitors and H2-blockers that reduce gastric acid secretion or enhance mucosal defense. Antidiarrheal drugs work by decreasing intestinal motility or improving fluid absorption. Prokinetic agents enhance gut motility and are used in treating gastric stasis and functional dyspepsia. Anti-asthmatic and bronchodilator drugs, including beta-2 agonists, corticosteroids, and leukotriene antagonists, are evaluated for their effects on airway caliber and inflammation. Each category has specific screening protocols and endpoints that guide their preclinical development.

9.2 Screening Methods for Anti-Ulcer Drugs

9.2.1 Pylorus Ligation Model (Shay Rat Model)

9.2.1.1 Principle: Accumulated Gastric Acid Causes Ulceration

The pylorus ligation model, also known as the Shay rat model, is one of the most widely used experimental methods to evaluate the anti-secretory and anti-ulcer activity of drugs. The model works on the principle that ligation of the pyloric end of the stomach causes accumulation of gastric acid and pepsin, which leads to auto-digestion of the gastric mucosa, resulting in the formation of ulcers. This model primarily assesses the acid-neutralizing, cytoprotective, or anti-secretory effects of test compounds.

9.2.1.2 Procedure

The experiment is typically conducted on healthy albino rats weighing between 150–200 grams. Animals are fasted for 24 hours prior to the procedure, with free access to water, to ensure an empty stomach and reduce variability in acid secretion.

Under light ether or ketamine anesthesia, a midline abdominal incision is made and the pyloric end of the stomach is ligated with care to avoid damage to blood vessels. The test drug is administered either pre-ligation (prophylactic) or post-ligation (therapeutic) via oral or intraperitoneal routes, depending on the study design. Animals are kept alive for 4–6 hours after the ligation and then sacrificed humanely.

The stomach is dissected out and opened along the greater curvature. Gastric contents are collected and analyzed for volume, pH, free acidity, and total acidity using titration with NaOH and phenolphthalein indicator. The ulcer index is calculated by visually examining the mucosal surface for number, severity, and area of ulcers under a dissecting microscope.

This model is ideal for screening H2 receptor antagonists (e.g., ranitidine), proton pump inhibitors (e.g., omeprazole), and mucosal protectants (e.g., sucralfate). It is simple, reproducible, and highly suitable for academic pharmacology labs.

9.2.1.3 Parameters

After the animal is sacrificed and the stomach is excised, several key parameters are measured to evaluate the anti-ulcer activity of the test drug:

- **Ulcer Index (UI):** The ulcer index reflects the severity of ulceration and is calculated based on the number and size of ulcers observed on the inner gastric lining. The scoring system generally follows this structure:

  - 0 = normal stomach
  - 1 = red coloration
  - 2 = spot ulcers
  - 3 = hemorrhagic streaks
  - 4 = deep ulcers
  - 5 = perforation

  final ulcer index is computed as the mean of individual scores per group. Alternatively, the formula used may be:

  Ulcer Index (UI) = (Number of ulcers + Severity score + Percentage of animals with ulcers) / 3

- Gastric Volume: After collection of the gastric contents, the volume is measured using a graduated cylinder. Increased volume may correlate with increased secretory activity.
- Free Acidity and Total Acidity: Free acidity is determined by titrating the gastric content with 0.01 N NaOH using Topfer's reagent as the indicator (red to yellow endpoint). Total acidity is then measured using phenolphthalein as the second indicator (pink endpoint). The titration result is expressed in mEq/L.

These measurements collectively help determine the **anti-secretory and cytoprotective potential** of the tested agent.

9.2.1.4 Standard Drugs: Omeprazole, Ranitidine, Sucralfate

The pylorus ligation model is often validated using **standard anti-ulcer drugs**:

- **Omeprazole** is a proton pump inhibitor that irreversibly blocks H^+ /K^+ ATPase, reducing gastric acid secretion.
- **Ranitidine** is a histamine H2 receptor antagonist that suppresses acid secretion by blocking histamine action on parietal cells.
- **Sucralfate** is a cytoprotective agent that forms a physical barrier over ulcers and stimulates prostaglandin and mucus production.

These reference drugs help to benchmark the efficacy of the test compound and confirm the responsiveness of the model.

9.2.1.4 Standard Drugs: Omeprazole, Ranitidine, Sucralfate

The pylorus ligation model is often validated using **standard anti-ulcer drugs**:

- **Omeprazole** is a proton pump inhibitor that irreversibly blocks H^+ /K^+ ATPase, reducing gastric acid secretion.
- **Ranitidine** is a histamine H2 receptor antagonist that suppresses acid secretion by blocking histamine action on parietal cells.
- **Sucralfate** is a cytoprotective agent that forms a physical barrier over ulcers and stimulates prostaglandin and mucus production.

These reference drugs help to benchmark the efficacy of the test compound and confirm the responsiveness of the model.

9.2.2 Ethanol-Induced Ulcer Model

9.2.2.1 Principle: Ethanol Causes Mucosal Damage and Oxidative Injury

The ethanol-induced ulcer model is a widely accepted method for evaluating cytoprotective activity of test drugs. Unlike the pylorus ligation model, which involves hyperacidity, the ethanol model produces ulcers primarily through direct mucosal injury, lipid peroxidation, and oxidative stress. Ethanol disrupts the mucus-bicarbonate barrier, penetrates epithelial cells, and generates reactive oxygen species (ROS), leading to capillary damage, cell necrosis, and ultimately hemorrhagic gastric lesions. This model is particularly useful for assessing drugs that strengthen mucosal defense mechanisms, stimulate prostaglandin synthesis, or exhibit antioxidant effects.

9.2.2.2 Procedure

Healthy adult albino rats weighing between **150–200 grams** are selected for the experiment. The animals are **fasted overnight** (16–18 hours) with access to water to ensure an empty stomach and uniform response to ethanol administration.

The **test drug is administered orally** or intraperitoneally **1 hour before ethanol challenge** to evaluate its protective effects. Ethanol is then administered at a dose of **1 mL per 200 g body weight**, typically using **absolute ethanol (99.5%)** or **70% ethanol**, depending on the severity desired. The ethanol is delivered via **oral gavage**.

After **1 hour**, the animals are **sacrificed humanely**, and the stomach is excised carefully and opened along the **greater curvature**. The mucosal surface is rinsed gently with saline and examined under a magnifying lens or dissecting microscope for the presence of **linear hemorrhagic bands, necrosis, or erosions**.

The **ulcer index** is calculated based on the number, size, and severity of lesions, using a scoring scale or planimetric method to assess total ulcerated area. The degree of **inhibition of ulcer formation** in the test group, when compared to control, is used to determine drug efficacy.

This model is commonly employed to screen drugs such as **sucralfate, misoprostol, rebamipide**, and **antioxidant-rich herbal extracts**. It also helps to study the **mechanisms of oxidative injury and gastroprotection**.

9.2.2.3 Parameters

The ethanol-induced ulcer model allows the evaluation of several quantitative and qualitative parameters to determine the **extent of mucosal injury** and the protective effect of the test compound:

- **Lesion Count and Size:** Each visible hemorrhagic lesion or erosion on the gastric mucosa is counted manually under magnification. The length and width of each lesion are measured using a millimeter scale or planimeter to estimate the **total lesion area**.
- Ulcer Index (UI): The ulcer index is calculated by considering the **number of ulcers, severity scores**, and **percentage of animals with ulcers**, similar to the pylorus ligation model. It reflects the **overall severity** of gastric damage. In some methods, ulcerated areas are traced

on transparent sheets and measured using graph paper to compute surface area involved.

- **Mucosal Thickness:** After dissection, the **gastric mucosal thickness** is measured using vernier calipers or a micrometer to assess the **integrity of mucosal protection.** Reduction in mucosal thickness indicates **epithelial erosion,** whereas preservation suggests effective cytoprotection by the test drug.

These parameters together help evaluate not only the **extent of damage** but also the **protective efficacy** of test substances in preserving gastric mucosal architecture.

9.2.2.4 Standard Drugs: Misoprostol, Pantoprazole

The ethanol ulcer model is validated using well-known **standard gastroprotective agents:**

- **Misoprostol** is a synthetic **prostaglandin E1 analogue** that enhances **mucus and bicarbonate secretion,** improves **mucosal blood flow,** and promotes **epithelial regeneration.**
- **Pantoprazole** is a **proton pump inhibitor** that blocks H^+ /K^+ ATPase, thereby suppressing gastric acid secretion and indirectly protecting mucosa from acid-mediated damage post-ethanol exposure.

Both these drugs serve as reference standards to benchmark the **efficacy of new cytoprotective or antioxidant agents** under investigation in preclinical GI pharmacology.

9.3.2 Charcoal Meal Transit Test (Prokinetic Model)

9.3.2.1 Principle: Measures Movement of Charcoal Through Intestine

The charcoal meal transit test is a standard experimental method used to evaluate the **effect of drugs on gastrointestinal motility.** It is commonly used for **screening both prokinetic and antimotility agents.** The test is based on tracking the movement of a charcoal suspension through the **small intestine.** Drugs that increase the speed of intestinal transit are identified as **prokinetic,** while those that slow it down exhibit **antidiarrheal or spasmolytic** properties.

9.3.2.2 Procedure

Healthy albino mice or rats, typically weighing **20–25 grams (mice)** or **150–200 grams (rats)**, are fasted for **12–18 hours** prior to the experiment to ensure empty intestines. The animals are divided into control, test, and standard groups. The **test compound** and **standard drug** are administered orally or intraperitoneally, followed by a charcoal meal after a pre-determined interval (usually **30 minutes**).

The **charcoal meal** is prepared using **activated charcoal (10%)** suspended in a **5% aqueous gum acacia** solution. Each animal receives a fixed volume orally using a gavage tube. After **30 minutes**, the animals are sacrificed humanely, and the entire **small intestine from pylorus to ileocecal junction** is carefully removed without stretching.

The **total length of the small intestine** and the **distance traveled by the charcoal** from the pylorus are measured using a ruler or thread and scale. The **percentage of intestinal transit** is calculated using the formula:

Percentage of Intestinal Transit = (Distance travelled by charcoal / Total length of small intestine) × 100

9.3.2.3 ↓ *Distance = Antidiarrheal Effect | ↑ Distance = Prokinetic Effect*

A decrease in the distance traveled by charcoal indicates reduced motility, which is interpreted as an antidiarrheal or spasmolytic effect. Conversely, an increase in the charcoal transit distance reflects enhanced peristalsis, indicating prokinetic activity.

This test is simple, rapid, and widely applicable in academic research to differentiate gut stimulants from relaxants.

9.3.2.4 *Standard Drugs: Metoclopramide (Prokinetic), Atropine (Antimotility)*

Two well-established standard drugs are used to validate the charcoal meal test:

- **Metoclopramide**, a dopamine D2 receptor antagonist, acts centrally and peripherally to **enhance gastric and intestinal motility**. It serves as the standard **prokinetic agent**.
- **Atropine**, a muscarinic receptor antagonist, reduces smooth muscle contraction in the GI tract and is the classical **antimotility reference drug** used for comparison.

These controls ensure that the model accurately reflects pharmacodynamic effects on GI motility and help in screening new compounds with potential therapeutic utility.

9.4 Screening Methods for Anti-Asthmatic and Bronchodilator Agents

9.4.1 Histamine or Acetylcholine-Induced Bronchospasm in Guinea Pigs

9.4.1.1 Principle

This method is based on the principle that inhalation of histamine or acetylcholine induces bronchoconstriction in guinea pigs, leading to signs of respiratory distress such as dyspnea (difficulty in breathing), convulsions, and potentially death. **Bronchodilator agents** are expected to delay or prevent the onset of bronchospasm, thus increasing the latency time and improving survival.

9.4.1.2 Procedure

Healthy guinea pigs weighing between 300–500 grams are selected for the study and acclimatized. The animals are then placed one at a time in an airtight **aerosol chamber** connected to a nebulizer or atomizer.

- A 0.2% solution of **histamine dihydrochloride** or **acetylcholine bromide** is nebulized using compressed air.
- The animal is exposed to the aerosol for a fixed time (usually 2–4 minutes), and the **time taken for the onset of dyspnea** (labored breathing), convulsions, or even death is recorded as **pre-drug control latency**.
- On a separate day, the same animal is **pre-treated with the test drug** (e.g., bronchodilator) via oral or intraperitoneal route.
- After 30–60 minutes, the animal is again exposed to the same concentration of bronchospastic agent in the aerosol chamber.
- The **post-treatment latency time** to onset of dyspnea is measured.

The **increase in latency time** after drug treatment, compared to control, indicates the **bronchodilatory potential** of the test substance.

9.4.1.3 Interpretation

An effective bronchodilator drug significantly **prolongs the latency to bronchospasm**, reduces the severity of symptoms, or completely prevents death. The **protection index** or **percentage protection** may be calculated by comparing pre- and post-treatment latency times.

9.4.1.4 Standard Drugs

- **Salbutamol** (a β_2 -agonist)
- **Theophylline** (a methylxanthine derivative)

These standard drugs serve as positive controls and are known to reduce histamine- or acetylcholine-induced bronchoconstriction in experimental models.

9.4.2 Egg Albumin-Induced Allergic Asthma Model

9.4.2.1 Immunization with Ovalbumin + Adjuvant

The egg albumin-induced allergic asthma model is one of the most widely used and well-characterized animal models for evaluating **anti-asthmatic drugs**, particularly those with anti-inflammatory and immunomodulatory effects. The model mimics key features of **human allergic asthma**, such as **airway inflammation, eosinophilia, mucus hypersecretion, and bronchial hyperresponsiveness**. It involves **sensitization** of the animal, usually mice or guinea pigs, using **ovalbumin (OVA)** as the antigen, mixed with an **adjuvant like aluminum hydroxide** to boost the immune response.

The typical sensitization schedule includes **two intraperitoneal injections** of OVA (10–20 µg per animal) mixed with alum on **day 0 and day 7**. This leads to the generation of **OVA-specific IgE antibodies** and primes the immune system to mount an allergic response upon subsequent inhalational exposure.

9.4.2.2 Aerosol Challenge Induces Inflammation and Airway Hyperresponsiveness

After sensitization, the animals are exposed to **aerosolized ovalbumin** (usually 1% OVA in saline) through a nebulizer for **20–30 minutes daily for 3–7 days**, beginning typically from day 14. This repeated airway exposure results in **localized allergic inflammation**, characterized by **infiltration of eosinophils, lymphocytes, and mast cells** in the bronchial walls and alveolar space.

Animals develop **airway hyperresponsiveness (AHR)**, which can be measured using non-invasive plethysmography or invasive methods to assess **airway resistance**. This bronchoconstriction and inflammation closely resemble features of human allergic asthma, making the model highly relevant.

9.4.2.3 Evaluation

Following the final allergen challenge, animals are sacrificed 24–48 hours later for assessment:

- **Lung Histopathology:** Lung tissues are fixed in formalin, embedded in paraffin, and sectioned for **hematoxylin and eosin (H&E)** staining. Inflammatory cell infiltration, goblet cell hyperplasia, and tissue remodeling are observed under the microscope.
- **Bronchoalveolar Lavage Fluid (BALF) Analysis:** BALF is collected by flushing the lungs with sterile saline via tracheal cannulation. The recovered fluid is centrifuged, and the **supernatant is analyzed for cytokines** like IL-4, IL-5, and IL-13 using ELISA, while the **pellet is used for total and differential cell counts** (eosinophils, macrophages, neutrophils, lymphocytes).
- **Inflammatory Cell Count:** The extent of airway inflammation is quantified by **counting inflammatory cells in BALF and lung sections,** providing a measurable index of allergic response severity.

These evaluations help determine the extent to which the test drug can **suppress allergic inflammation and restore normal lung function.**

9.4.2.4 Drugs Tested: Corticosteroids, Leukotriene Antagonists

This model is used to assess the efficacy of **anti-asthmatic drugs,** especially:

- **Corticosteroids** such as dexamethasone and budesonide, which exert potent anti-inflammatory effects by inhibiting cytokine production and immune cell infiltration.
- **Leukotriene receptor antagonists** like montelukast, which block leukotriene-mediated bronchoconstriction and eosinophil recruitment.

The OVA model serves as a benchmark system for preclinical screening of **novel anti-inflammatory, antiallergic, and immunosuppressive agents** intended for treating asthma and other respiratory allergic conditions.

9.5 Parameters and Evaluation Techniques

9.5.1 Ulcer Index = (Number × Severity Score) / Animal

In anti-ulcer screening models such as **pylorus ligation** and **ethanol-induced ulceration**, the **ulcer index** is a crucial quantitative measure. It takes into account the **number of ulcers** observed in the gastric mucosa and their **severity**, which is typically graded on a scale (e.g., 0 = no ulcer, 1 = superficial erosion, 2 = deep ulcer, 3 = perforation). The formula used is:

Ulcer Index = (Total number of ulcers × severity score) / number of animals.

This index allows comparison across groups and provides a numerical value for the protective effect of the test compound against ulcer formation.

9.5.2 Transit Index (%) = (Distance Travelled / Total Length) × 100

The **charcoal meal transit test** is used to evaluate **intestinal motility**. After administration of a charcoal meal, the **distance it travels through the small intestine** is measured and compared to the total intestinal length. The result is expressed as a percentage using the formula:

Transit Index (%) = (Distance travelled by charcoal / Total length of small intestine) × 100.

A **decrease** in the index indicates **antidiarrheal or antimotility** activity, whereas an **increase** suggests **prokinetic action**.

9.5.3 Bronchospasm Latency (in Seconds)

In respiratory models such as **histamine- or acetylcholine-induced bronchospasm**, the key parameter measured is the **latency period (in seconds)** from the administration of the bronchospasm-inducing agent to the onset of symptoms like labored breathing or convulsions. **Prolongation of latency** indicates the **bronchodilatory or anti-asthmatic effect** of the test drug. It is a sensitive indicator of **airway protection** conferred by therapeutic agents.

9.5.4 Stool Consistency and Count for Antidiarrheal Effect

In antidiarrheal models, the **number of stools** and their **consistency** (watery, semi-solid, or solid) are important indicators of drug efficacy. These parameters are observed over a defined period (e.g., 4–6 hours post-administration of castor oil or another diarrheagenic agent). A **reduction in stool frequency** and a **shift toward solid consistency** reflect a **positive antidiarrheal response**. This method provides a **simple, non-invasive** means of evaluating gastrointestinal drug activity.

9.5.5 Statistical Analysis Using Mean ± SEM and ANOVA

All experimental data are statistically analyzed to ensure reliability and reproducibility. Results are typically expressed as **Mean ± Standard Error** of Mean (SEM) for each group. When comparing multiple groups, **Analysis of Variance (ANOVA)** is used, followed by a suitable **post-hoc test** (such as Tukey's or Dunnett's) to determine statistical significance between individual pairs. A **p-value < 0.05** is usually considered significant. This approach helps confirm whether the observed effects are due to the test compound and not random variation.

9.6 Significance and Limitations

9.6.1 Significance of Selecting Appropriate Model Based on Drug Class

The selection of a suitable experimental model is crucial in **gastrointestinal and respiratory pharmacology**, as it determines the **relevance, accuracy, and predictive value** of the results. Each drug class—be it anti-ulcer, antidiarrheal, prokinetic, bronchodilator, or anti-asthmatic—has specific pharmacodynamic targets that must be tested in an **appropriate physiological context**. For instance, **pylorus ligation** is ideal for testing anti-secretory agents, while **ethanol-induced ulcer models** are better suited for cytoprotective drugs. Similarly, bronchodilators are best assessed in **histamine-induced bronchospasm models**, whereas **anti-inflammatory agents** used in asthma are validated using **egg albumin-induced asthma models**. The use of a wrong or non-specific model may yield misleading results, reduce reproducibility, and impair translational value. Therefore, **model selection must align with the mechanism of action and intended therapeutic use** of the drug under investigation.

9.6.2 Limitations

Despite their utility, experimental screening models in gastrointestinal and respiratory pharmacology come with several limitations that researchers must acknowledge and address.

- **Animal Stress:** Procedures such as oral gavage, anesthesia, invasive measurements, and forced restraint can lead to **physiological stress**, which may interfere with gastric secretions, motility, or airway responsiveness. Stress-induced variability can reduce the reliability of the data, necessitating **refined handling techniques** and minimal intervention strategies.
- **Species-Specific Responses:** Rodents and other laboratory animals exhibit **species-specific pharmacokinetics, immune responses, and receptor distribution**. As a result, the effects observed in animal models

may not always replicate those in humans. For example, airway responsiveness in guinea pigs may differ significantly from that in humans, and some ulcer-inducing agents act differently across species.

- **Ethical Concerns and Need for Humane Endpoints:** The use of animals in pharmacological research raises **ethical considerations** that require strict adherence to guidelines laid down by regulatory authorities such as **CPCSEA**. Procedures that cause severe pain, distress, or death must include **humane endpoints**, such as early euthanasia, to prevent unnecessary suffering. Additionally, the **3Rs principle (Replacement, Reduction, Refinement)** must be integrated into study design to ensure ethical and responsible research.

These limitations highlight the importance of **complementary in vitro and in silico approaches**, careful protocol design, and continual evaluation of model validity to enhance translational outcomes while maintaining ethical standards.

MCQs

1. **Which animal is most commonly used in the histamine-induced bronchospasm model?**
   A. Rat
   B. Mouse
   C. Guinea pig
   D. Rabbit
   Answer: C

2. **The main purpose of histamine-induced bronchospasm model is to screen:**
   A. Anti-inflammatory drugs
   B. Antihistaminics
   C. Antipyretics
   D. Antibiotics
   Answer: B

3. **Which receptor is targeted in histamine-induced bronchospasm?**
   A. H2
   B. H3
   C. H4
   D. H1
   Answer: D

4. **In acetylcholine-induced bronchospasm, what class of drugs is typically evaluated?**
   A. Antitussives
   B. Anticholinergics
   C. Corticosteroids
   D. Beta blockers
   Answer: B

5. **The protection index in respiratory models is calculated using:**
   A. Heart rate
   B. Respiratory rate
   C. Preconvulsive dyspnea time
   D. Bronchodilation index
   Answer: C

6. **Cigarette smoke-induced COPD model mimics which human condition?**
   A. Emphysema

B. Lung cancer

C. Bronchitis

D. Asthma

Answer: A

7. **What is used to induce emphysema in elastase-induced models?**

A. Trypsin

B. Papain

C. Pancreatic elastase

D. Albumin

Answer: C

8. **Which of the following is used to assess allergic response in anti-allergic models?**

A. PCA

B. Hot plate test

C. Tail immersion test

D. Y-maze test

Answer: A

9. **Aphrodisiac activity is commonly assessed by:**

A. Elevated plus maze

B. Mount latency and intromission frequency

C. Forced swim test

D. Preconvulsive time

Answer: B

10. **Which test is most relevant for antifertility screening?**

A. Rotarod test

B. Estrous cycle monitoring

C. Carrageenan paw edema

D. Acetic acid writhing

Answer: B

11. **Tail flick and hot plate tests are used for screening:**

A. Diuretics

B. Laxatives

C. Analgesics

D. Antacids

Answer: C

12. **NSAIDs show positive results in which analgesic model?**

A. Tail flick

B. Hot plate

C. Writhing test

D. All of the above

Answer: C

13. **Carrageenan-induced paw edema is a model for:**

A. Pyrexia

B. Diarrhea

C. Inflammation

D. Emesis

Answer: C

14. **In the Brewer's yeast-induced pyrexia model, the fever is induced by:**

A. Oral administration

B. Intravenous injection

C. Subcutaneous injection

D. Intramuscular injection

Answer: C

15. **Which ulcer model evaluates antisecretory activity?**

A. Pylorus ligation

B. Ethanol-induced

C. Cold restraint stress

D. Acetic acid ulcer

Answer: A

16. **The cold restraint stress model primarily evaluates:**

A. Anti-inflammatory drugs

B. Antidepressants

C. Anti-stress agents

D. Diuretics

Answer: C

17. **What is used as a standard drug in castor oil-induced diarrhea model?**

A. Atropine

B. Loperamide

C. Ibuprofen

D. Salbutamol

Answer: B

18. **Charcoal meal test is commonly used in:**

A. Analgesia screening

B. GI transit studies

C. Antidepressant models

D. Asthma models

Answer: B

19. **Which of the following shows decreased GI motility?**
    A. Castor oil
    B. Magnesium hydroxide
    C. Loperamide
    D. Aloe vera
    Answer: C

20. **A key parameter measured in laxative screening is:**
    A. Heart rate
    B. Stool consistency
    C. Pain threshold
    D. Convulsions
    Answer: B

21. **Which model is used to assess bronchodilator activity using histamine-induced bronchospasm?**
    A. Frog rectus abdominis test
    B. Rotarod test
    C. Preconvulsive dyspnea in guinea pigs
    D. Tail flick test
    Answer: C

22. **Which cytokine is primarily involved in yeast-induced pyrexia?**
    A. TNF-alpha
    B. IL-1
    C. IFN-gamma
    D. IL-4
    Answer: B

23. **What is the endpoint in pylorus ligation-induced ulcer model?**
    A. Temperature
    B. Ulcer index
    C. Salivation
    D. Diuresis
    Answer: B

24. **Ethanol-induced ulcer model works through:**
    A. Gastrin stimulation
    B. Oxidative stress and mucosal erosion
    C. Histamine release
    D. Sodium ion imbalance
    Answer: B

25. **The prokinetic effect is identified in charcoal meal transit test by:**
    A. Increase in food intake
    B. Increase in gastric pH
    C. Increased intestinal distance traveled by charcoal
    D. Increase in ulcer index
    Answer: C

26. **Which animal is used in the charcoal meal model?**
    A. Rabbit
    B. Rat
    C. Guinea pig
    D. Cat
    Answer: B

27. **Standard drug for antiulcer activity in pylorus ligation model:**
    A. Loperamide
    B. Omeprazole
    C. Ibuprofen
    D. Chlorpromazine
    Answer: B

28. **Which model mimics allergic asthma through ovalbumin sensitization?**
    A. Carrageenan-induced edema
    B. Histamine bronchospasm
    C. Egg albumin-induced asthma
    D. Charcoal meal test
    Answer: C

29. **BALF analysis in asthma models is used to evaluate:**
    A. Pain sensation
    B. Lung compliance
    C. Inflammatory cells
    D. Acid secretion
    Answer: C

30. **Which test evaluates antidiarrheal property by fecal count?**
    A. Castor oil-induced diarrhea
    B. Writhing test
    C. Paw edema test
    D. Tail suspension test
    Answer: A

31. **Which drug is used as standard in yeast-induced pyrexia?**
    A. Paracetamol
    B. Atenolol
    C. Omeprazole
    D. Salbutamol
    Answer: A

32. **Which organ is primarily assessed in ulcer models?**
    A. Heart
    B. Liver
    C. Stomach
    D. Lung
    Answer: C

33. **What is the purpose of using a plethysmometer in inflammation studies?**
    A. To measure ulcer index
    B. To calculate temperature
    C. To measure paw volume
    D. To assess muscle tone
    Answer: C

34. **What is the major factor in ethanol-induced ulcer?**
    A. Hyperacidity
    B. Histamine release
    C. Free radical generation
    D. Increased mucus
    Answer: C

35. **Standard drug for antidiarrheal screening is:**
    A. Metronidazole
    B. Loperamide
    C. Ranitidine
    D. Diclofenac
    Answer: B

36. **The atherogenic index is calculated in:**
    A. Antidiabetic models
    B. Hyperlipidemic models
    C. Antidiarrheal models
    D. Analgesic models
    Answer: B

37. **Charcoal travel distance is an indicator of:**
    A. Diuresis
    B. Prokinetic activity
    C. Ulcer formation
    D. Pyrexia
    Answer: B

38. **Which is not a parameter in antiulcer screening?**
    A. Ulcer index
    B. Gastric volume
    C. Hematocrit
    D. Free acidity
    Answer: C

39. **Which model evaluates protective effects of drugs in GI mucosa?**
    A. Pylorus ligation
    B. Rotarod
    C. Tail flick
    D. Rotating drum
    Answer: A

40. **Lesion scoring in antiulcer models involves:**
    A. Heart rate
    B. Number and severity of ulcers
    C. Liver enzyme activity
    D. Neuronal count
    Answer: B

41. **Respiratory distress in guinea pig models is caused by:**
    A. Histamine
    B. Dopamine
    C. Acetylcholine
    D. GABA
    Answer: A

42. **Eosinophil infiltration is a marker of:**
    A. Cardiac disease
    B. Neurological inflammation
    C. Allergic asthma
    D. Hepatotoxicity
    Answer: C

43. **Which index measures ulcer severity in rats?**
    A. Ulcer index

B. Inhibition ratio

C. Hematocrit

D. Intestinal transit

Answer: A

44. **Prokinetic activity is assessed by using:**

    A. Cold-restraint model

    B. Charcoal meal model

    C. Castor oil model

    D. Paw edema model

    Answer: B

45. **Which species is most sensitive in ulcer screening?**

    A. Dog

    B. Cat

    C. Rat

    D. Monkey

    Answer: C

46. **Which test drug shows bronchodilator effect in histamine model?**

    A. Atropine

    B. Salbutamol

    C. Aspirin

    D. Paracetamol

    Answer: B

47. **Ovalbumin challenge is conducted in:**

    A. Mice

    B. Rabbit

    C. Guinea pigs

    D. Frogs

    Answer: C

48. **Standard route for ethanol ulcer induction is:**

    A. IP

    B. IV

    C. Oral

    D. IM

    Answer: C

49. **Protective index is an indicator of:**

    A. Safety

    B. Mortality

    C. Bronchoprotection

D. Hepatoprotection

Answer: C

50. **Inflammation in asthma models is measured via:**

A. Gastric pH

B. Neutrophil count

C. Bronchoalveolar lavage

D. Rumen motility

Answer: C

Short Answer Questions

1. What is the principle behind the pylorus ligation ulcer model?
2. Name two standard drugs used in the ethanol-induced ulcer model.
3. How is the ulcer index calculated in experimental models?
4. Which substance is used to induce gastric ulcers in the ethanol-induced model?
5. What role does mucus play in gastric ulcer protection?
6. What is the standard fasting time before pylorus ligation in rats?
7. Name the common animal species used in anti-ulcer screening studies.
8. What is the use of the charcoal meal test in pharmacology?
9. How do you interpret increased charcoal transit in a charcoal meal test?
10. What is the principle behind the castor oil-induced diarrhea model?
11. Mention one drug that increases gastrointestinal motility.
12. Which standard drug is used as an antidiarrheal agent in castor oil-induced diarrhea?
13. Name a parameter used to evaluate the prokinetic effect of a drug.
14. How does ethanol damage the gastric mucosa?
15. What is the function of the mesenteric plexus in gastrointestinal activity?
16. Which nerve regulates intestinal motility?
17. What type of ulcers are formed in pylorus ligation?
18. What kind of inflammation is produced by egg albumin in asthma models?
19. What does BALF stand for?
20. How are inflammatory cells quantified in BALF?
21. What is the effect of histamine in the respiratory tract?
22. Which animals are commonly used in bronchospasm studies?
23. Name a leukotriene antagonist used in asthma studies.
24. What is the role of eosinophils in asthma?
25. What is the use of plethysmography in GI screening?
26. What is the unit of measurement for paw volume in rats?
27. Which model uses ulcer scoring based on severity?
28. Which cytokines are responsible for fever and inflammation?
29. What are the key symptoms of chemically induced asthma?
30. Name two drugs tested for anti-asthmatic activity.
31. What is the difference between antidiarrheal and prokinetic drugs?

32. What is the effect of atropine in the gastrointestinal tract?
33. Define the Transit Index in prokinetic screening.
34. How is stool consistency graded in animal models?
35. Name a natural stimulus for bronchoconstriction in guinea pigs.
36. What is the significance of the light/dark cycle in animal housing?
37. What are the advantages of the ethanol ulcer model?
38. What type of inflammation is produced by carrageenan?
39. How is the prokinetic activity quantified?
40. How do corticosteroids help in asthma?
41. Name a commonly used model for chronic gastric ulcer.
42. What is the source of the charcoal meal used in the transit test?
43. What is the standard volume of castor oil used in rats?
44. What effect does omeprazole have on gastric acid?
45. Which test helps differentiate central vs peripheral GI actions?
46. What kind of anesthesia is used for pylorus ligation?
47. What does a high ulcer index indicate?
48. Name two biochemical markers assessed in BALF.
49. What is the ideal observation period in charcoal transit test?
50. How are histological sections useful in ulcer studies?

Answers

1. Accumulated gastric secretions irritate the mucosa and lead to ulceration.
2. Misoprostol and pantoprazole.
3. Ulcer Index = (Number × Severity Score) / Animal.
4. Absolute ethanol (1 mL/200 g body weight).
5. Acts as a protective barrier against acid and enzymes.
6. 24 hours.
7. Wistar rats or albino mice.
8. To evaluate gastrointestinal motility.
9. Prokinetic effect.
10. It causes release of prostaglandins leading to increased motility and secretion.
11. Metoclopramide.
12. Loperamide.
13. Distance travelled by the charcoal meal.
14. Through oxidative stress and mucosal damage.
15. Regulates smooth muscle tone and motility.
16. Vagus nerve.
17. Peptic ulcers.
18. Allergic inflammation.
19. Bronchoalveolar lavage fluid.
20. Using differential cell count in stained smears.
21. Causes bronchoconstriction.
22. Guinea pigs and rats.
23. Montelukast.
24. They mediate allergic inflammation in lungs.
25. To measure changes in lung volume.
26. Millilitres (mL).
27. Ethanol-induced model.
28. IL-1, IL-6, and TNF-alpha.
29. Bronchoconstriction, wheezing, airway hyperresponsiveness.
30. Salbutamol and budesonide.
31. Antidiarrheals reduce motility; prokinetics enhance it.
32. Inhibits motility and secretions.
33. (Distance Travelled / Total Length) × 100.

34. By visual observation and scoring.
35. Histamine aerosol.
36. Maintains circadian rhythm and stress levels.
37. Quick induction of ulcers, reproducible.
38. Acute inflammation.
39. By calculating the Transit Index.
40. Reduce inflammation and eosinophil infiltration.
41. Acetic acid-induced ulcer model.
42. Activated charcoal suspended in water or gum acacia.
43. 1 mL per 100 g body weight.
44. Inhibits gastric proton pumps and reduces acidity.
45. Charcoal Meal Transit Test.
46. Ketamine/xylazine combination or ether.
47. Severe gastric mucosal damage.
48. Eosinophil count, total leukocyte count.
49. 30 minutes after charcoal meal administration.
50. To assess epithelial damage and inflammatory changes.

CHAPTER TEN

Screening for Analgesic, Anti-inflammatory, and Antipyretic Drugs

10.1 Introduction

Pain, inflammation, and fever are among the most common clinical symptoms encountered in medical practice, and they form the basis for the use of a large class of drugs collectively known as non-steroidal anti-inflammatory drugs (NSAIDs) and opioid analgesics. Understanding their pathophysiology and evaluating drug efficacy in preclinical studies require well-standardized animal models that can mimic the human condition. Pain serves as a protective mechanism, but in chronic conditions, it becomes pathological. Inflammation, an immune response to injury or infection, can lead to tissue damage if unresolved. Fever, or pyrexia, is a systemic response usually caused by infection or inflammation and is regulated by the hypothalamus via prostaglandin pathways.

Analgesics are broadly classified into centrally acting drugs, such as opioids that act on the central nervous system (e.g., morphine), and peripherally acting drugs, like NSAIDs, which reduce prostaglandin synthesis at the site of injury. To evaluate the effectiveness of these drugs, preclinical pharmacological screening methods must reliably simulate acute and chronic pain models, inflammatory responses, and fever induction mechanisms. This ensures that potential therapeutic compounds can be evaluated for their onset of action, duration, potency, and safety profile before entering clinical trials. Therefore, the use of validated animal models in analgesic, anti-inflammatory, and antipyretic screening is an essential step in early-phase drug development.

10.2 Screening Methods for Analgesic Activity

10.2.1 Tail-Flick Test

10.2.1.1 Principle: Measures Response to Thermal Nociceptive Stimulus

The tail-flick test is a widely accepted method for evaluating the central analgesic activity of drugs, particularly opioids. It is based on the principle that thermal pain stimulation to the tail induces a nociceptive reflex, and drugs that increase the time it takes for an animal to flick its tail away from the heat source are considered to possess analgesic properties. This model predominantly assesses the spinal reflex arc, which is modulated by supraspinal opioid pathways.

10.2.1.2 Model: Rats or Mice

The test is performed on healthy albino **rats or mice**, typically weighing **150–200 g (rats)** or **20–25 g (mice)**. Animals are acclimatized to the restraining apparatus for a few minutes prior to the test to reduce stress-related variability.

10.2.1.3 Procedure

In this procedure, the animal's tail is exposed to a **controlled thermal stimulus**, which can be applied by either placing the tail on a **heated nichrome wire** or immersing the tip (2–3 cm) of the tail in **hot water maintained at 55°C ± 0.5°C**. Care is taken to ensure uniform temperature and avoid tissue damage.

- The **latency period**, i.e., the **time taken (in seconds) for the animal to flick or withdraw its tail**, is recorded.
- A **cut-off time** (usually 10–12 seconds) is maintained to prevent burns or injury.
- The latency is measured **before (baseline)** and at fixed intervals **after drug administration**, typically at 15, 30, and 60 minutes.

10.2.1.4 Interpretation: ↑ Latency = Analgesic Activity (Centrally Acting)

An **increase in latency period** following drug administration indicates **suppression of pain sensation**, suggesting that the drug has **central**

analgesic activity. Centrally acting analgesics increase the pain threshold by modulating opioid receptors in the central nervous system. A statistically significant increase in tail-flick latency compared to the control group confirms the efficacy of the test compound.

10.2.1.5 Standard Drugs: Morphine, Tramadol

Standard reference drugs include:

- **Morphine**, a prototype μ-opioid receptor agonist known for its potent central analgesic action.
- **Tramadol**, a centrally acting synthetic opioid analgesic with dual-action (μ-opioid receptor agonist and serotonin/norepinephrine reuptake inhibition).

These drugs serve as positive controls for benchmarking the activity of test compounds. The tail-flick test remains one of the most reliable methods for evaluating **acute thermal nociception** in pharmacological research.

10.2.3 Acetic Acid-Induced Writhing Test

10.2.3.1 Principle: Acetic Acid Causes Pain via Prostaglandin Release

The acetic acid-induced writhing test is a sensitive and widely used method for screening peripherally acting analgesic agents. The underlying principle is that intraperitoneal injection of dilute acetic acid leads to the release of prostaglandins (especially PGE_2 and PGF_2 α) and cytokines in the peritoneal cavity, which in turn stimulate nociceptive neurons, resulting in a characteristic writhing response in mice. This test reflects the inflammatory component of pain and is particularly useful for evaluating NSAIDs and related drugs that inhibit cyclooxygenase enzymes and reduce prostaglandin synthesis.

10.2.3.2 Species: Mice

Healthy Swiss albino **mice**, weighing **20–25 grams**, are typically used. They are maintained under standard laboratory conditions and fasted for a few hours before the test. Animals are divided into groups receiving **test drugs, standard drugs, and control treatments**.

10.2.3.3 Procedure

The writhing response is induced as follows:

- A **1% v/v solution of acetic acid** is prepared in sterile distilled water.
- Each mouse receives an **intraperitoneal (IP) injection** of **0.1 mL/10 g body weight** of the acetic acid solution.

- The mice are immediately placed in individual transparent observation boxes.
- The number of **writhing movements** is counted for a period of **10 to 30 minutes** following injection. A writhe is characterized by **abdominal contraction, elongation of the body, and stretching of the hind limbs**.
- The **test drug or standard drug** is administered **30–60 minutes prior** to the acetic acid injection depending on the route and onset of action.

10.2.3.4 ↓ Number of Writhes = Peripheral Analgesic Activity

A **reduction in the number of writhes** compared to the control group indicates **analgesic activity**. Because the model primarily involves **peripheral pain pathways**, it is highly predictive for the efficacy of **non-opioid analgesics** such as NSAIDs. Results are typically expressed as **percentage inhibition of writhing**, using the formula:

Inhibition (%) = [(Mean writhes in control – Mean writhes in treated) / Mean writhes in control] × 10

10.2.3.5 Standard Drugs: Diclofenac, Aspirin

Commonly used **reference drugs** in this model include:

- **Diclofenac sodium**, a potent NSAID that inhibits both COX-1 and COX-2 enzymes.
- **Aspirin**, the classical NSAID with strong analgesic, anti-inflammatory, and antipyretic effects.

Both serve as **positive controls** to compare the efficacy of newly synthesized or plant-derived test compounds. The acetic acid writhing test remains a robust and economical method for **high-throughput screening of peripheral analgesics**.

10.3 Screening Methods for Anti-inflammatory Activity

10.3.1 Carrageenan-Induced Paw Edema Model

10.3.1.1 Principle: Carrageenan Injection Causes Acute Inflammation via Histamine, Kinins, and Prostaglandins

The carrageenan-induced paw edema model is a standard experimental method for evaluating acute anti-inflammatory effects of drugs. The principle is based on the fact that carrageenan, a sulfated polysaccharide derived from red algae, when injected into the subplantar region of the rat hind paw, induces a localized inflammatory response. This inflammation results from a cascade involving vasoactive mediators, including histamine, serotonin, bradykinin, and later prostaglandins, causing edema (swelling). Drugs that inhibit these mediators, particularly prostaglandin synthesis inhibitors like NSAIDs, significantly reduce paw swelling.

10.3.1.2 Species: Rats

This model is typically conducted on **adult Wistar rats** weighing between **150 and 200 grams**. The animals are acclimatized and grouped into **control, standard, and test groups**. They are fasted overnight with free access to water before the procedure to minimize variability in absorption and metabolism of the administered drug.

10.3.1.3 Procedure

- A **1% w/v suspension of carrageenan** is prepared freshly in sterile normal saline.
- Each rat receives a **subplantar injection of 0.1 mL carrageenan** in the right hind paw, using a 26G needle.
- The **test drug** or **standard anti-inflammatory agent** (e.g., indomethacin) is administered **orally or intraperitoneally, 30 to 60 minutes** before the carrageenan injection.
- **Paw volume** is measured at **0 (baseline), 1, 2, 3, and 4 hours** post-injection using a **plethysmometer**, an instrument that measures displacement caused by paw volume in a liquid column.
- The degree of inflammation is assessed by the **increase in paw volume**, and the **anti-inflammatory effect** is determined by comparing the test group with the control.

10.3.1.4 Inhibition % Calculated = (Control – Test) / Control × 100

The **percentage inhibition of edema** is calculated using the following formula:

Inhibition (%) = [(Paw volume in control – Paw volume in treated) / Paw volume in control] × 100

This quantifies the **anti-inflammatory efficacy** of the drug being tested.

10.3.1.5 Biphasic Inflammatory Response

The carrageenan model demonstrates a biphasic inflammatory response:

- First phase (0–1 hour): Dominated by the release of histamine and serotonin, which increase vascular permeability.

- Second phase (1–4 hours): Mediated by prostaglandins, particularly PGE_2 , and cytokines like IL-1β and TNF-α, contributing to the sustained swelling.

NSAIDs, which inhibit cyclooxygenase enzymes and thereby prostaglandin synthesis, are more effective in suppressing the second phase of the inflammation. This model is ideal for testing non-steroidal anti-inflammatory drugs and helps to determine onset, duration, and dose-response relationship of anti-inflammatory activity.

10.3.1.6 Standard Drugs: Indomethacin, Ibuprofen

In the carrageenan-induced paw edema model, indomethacin and ibuprofen are commonly used as standard reference drugs due to their well-established anti-inflammatory activity. These drugs are non-steroidal anti-inflammatory agents that inhibit cyclooxygenase (COX) enzymes, thereby suppressing prostaglandin synthesis, which plays a key role in the second phase of carrageenan-induced inflammation.

- Indomethacin is typically administered in a dose range of 10–20 mg/ kg orally in rats and shows a strong inhibitory effect on paw edema, especially during the prostaglandin-mediated second phase.
- Ibuprofen, often used at a dose of 30–40 mg/kg orally, also effectively reduces the swelling and serves as a benchmark for comparing the potency of new test compounds.

These standard drugs allow researchers to validate the experimental setup and quantitatively compare the efficacy of newly developed or herbal anti-inflammatory agents. The reproducibility and sensitivity of this model, especially when benchmarked against standard NSAIDs, make it an indispensable tool in preclinical anti-inflammatory drug research.

10.4 Screening Methods for Antipyretic Activity

10.4.1 Yeast-Induced Pyrexia Model

10.4.1.1 Principle: Brewer's Yeast Induces Pyrexia via Cytokines and PGE_2

The yeast-induced pyrexia model is a standard preclinical technique for evaluating the antipyretic activity of drugs. This model is based on the mechanism that Brewer's yeast, when injected subcutaneously, stimulates immune cells to produce pyrogenic cytokines such as interleukin-1 (IL-1), tumor necrosis factor-alpha (TNF-α), and interleukin-6 (IL-6). These cytokines in turn activate prostaglandin E_2 (PGE_2) synthesis in the hypothalamus, which raises the body's thermoregulatory set point, resulting in fever (pyrexia). Antipyretic agents reduce this elevated set point by inhibiting cyclooxygenase (COX) enzymes, thereby blocking PGE_2 synthesis.

10.4.1.2 Species: Rats

The model is usually performed on **adult Wistar rats**, weighing between **150 and 200 grams**. The rats are housed under standard conditions and allowed free access to water. Baseline **rectal temperature** is recorded using a digital or mercury thermometer before the experiment begins.

10.4.1.3 Procedure

- A 20% suspension of Brewer's yeast is freshly prepared in sterile normal saline.
- Each rat receives a subcutaneous injection of 10 mL/kg of the yeast suspension in the dorsal region of the back.
- Animals are kept under observation, and their rectal temperature is recorded at baseline (before yeast injection) and again at 18 hours post-injection to allow full development of fever.
- Only animals that show a minimum rise of 1°C or more from baseline are selected for further testing.
- The test drug or standard antipyretic is administered orally or intraperitoneally at this point.
- Rectal temperature is then recorded at 30-minute intervals for the next 3 hours to monitor the drug's effect on body temperature.

10.4.1.4 ↓ in Body Temperature = Antipyretic Effect

A reduction in rectal temperature compared to the pre-treatment value and control group is interpreted as a positive antipyretic effect. The magnitude and duration of the temperature drop provide insights into the onset and duration of action of the test compound. Results are often expressed as mean temperature change with statistical comparison to the control.

10.4.1.5 Standard Drugs: Paracetamol, Aspirin

Paracetamol (acetaminophen) and **aspirin** are widely used as standard drugs in this model. They are administered at doses of:

- **Paracetamol**: 100–150 mg/kg orally
- **Aspirin**: 300 mg/kg orally

These agents serve as positive controls due to their well-documented ability to inhibit hypothalamic PGE_2 synthesis, effectively reducing fever. The yeast-induced pyrexia model is particularly useful for screening non-opioid central antipyretics, especially during early drug development phases.

10.5 Evaluation and Parameters

10.5.1 Reaction Time (Seconds) in Tail-Flick and Hot Plate

In analgesic screening models such as the tail-flick and hot plate tests, the primary parameter evaluated is the reaction time, which is the latency period in seconds between the application of a thermal stimulus and the animal's nociceptive response. An increase in this latency following drug administration suggests central analgesic activity. A cut-off time is generally established (usually around 10–12 seconds) to avoid tissue damage, and the results are recorded as Mean ± SEM (Standard Error of Mean).

10.5.2 Number of Writhes in Acetic Acid Test

In the acetic acid-induced writhing test, the parameter of interest is the number of abdominal constrictions or writhes observed over a defined period (commonly 10 to 30 minutes). A significant reduction in the number of writhes compared to the control group indicates peripheral analgesic activity. Data are expressed as mean number of writhes ± SEM, and percentage inhibition is calculated for comparative analysis.

10.5.3 Paw Volume in mL in Carrageenan Test

In the carrageenan-induced paw edema model, inflammation is quantified by measuring the paw volume in milliliters (mL) using a plethysmometer at multiple time intervals (1, 2, 3, and 4 hours post-carrageenan injection). A decrease in paw volume in drug-treated animals indicates anti-inflammatory activity. The data are presented as Mean ± SEM, and the percentage inhibition of edema is computed relative to the control group.

10.5.4 Body Temperature in °C in Antipyretic Studies

In the yeast-induced pyrexia model, the rectal body temperature is measured in degrees Celsius (°C) at baseline, 18 hours after yeast injection, and at multiple time points post-treatment (typically every 30 minutes for 3 hours). A significant drop in temperature post-treatment signifies antipyretic activity. Data are expressed as Mean ± SEM, and results are compared to both control and standard drug groups.

10.5.5 Statistical Analysis: Mean ± SEM, t-Test or ANOVA

For all screening methods, results are typically expressed as Mean ± Standard Error of Mean (SEM). Statistical significance is evaluated using appropriate tests:

- Student's t-test for comparison between two groups (e.g., control vs test).
- One-way or two-way ANOVA followed by post-hoc tests (such as Dunnett's or Tukey's) for multiple group comparisons.

A p-value of less than 0.05 ($p < 0.05$) is generally considered statistically significant, supporting the pharmacological efficacy of the test compound. Proper statistical interpretation ensures scientific validity and reproducibility of the results, essential in preclinical pharmacological screening.

10.6 Significance and Limitations

10.6.1 Significance: Validated and Standardized Models

The screening models used for evaluating analgesic, anti-inflammatory, and antipyretic activity are among the most validated, reproducible, and widely accepted procedures in pharmacological research. These models, such as the tail-flick, hot plate, acetic acid-induced writhing, carrageenan-induced paw edema, and yeast-induced pyrexia tests, have been optimized over decades and are recognized by both regulatory agencies and scientific bodies for their predictive value. They provide a clear and quantifiable understanding of a compound's effect on pain pathways, inflammatory mediators, and thermoregulatory mechanisms.

These screening methods are not only essential for academic training and education, helping students understand fundamental pharmacological principles, but are also extensively used in the pharmaceutical industry to identify and characterize new chemical entities (NCEs) during preclinical development. Their ease of setup, low cost, and high sensitivity make them particularly suitable for early-stage drug discovery pipelines. Furthermore, results from these tests are often predictive of clinical efficacy, especially when combined with biochemical and histological analyses.

10.6.2 Limitations: Species Differences, Subjectivity, and Ethical Issues

Despite their widespread use and standardization, these screening models have certain limitations that must be carefully considered during experimental design and result interpretation. One major concern is species difference. The physiology and pharmacodynamics of laboratory animals, particularly rodents, may not fully mirror human responses. For example, drugs showing potent analgesic or antipyretic activity in rats may not exhibit similar efficacy in humans due to differences in pain perception, inflammatory mediator profiles, or drug metabolism.

Another limitation lies in the subjectivity of observational methods, particularly in tests like the writhing test or open field behaviors where subtle variations in handling, observer bias, or animal stress can lead to inconsistent data. Standardizing protocols and using automated systems when possible can help minimize these variances, but complete elimination of subjectivity is difficult.

A further concern involves ethical considerations, especially in models where animals are exposed to painful stimuli, such as thermal nociception or chemical-induced inflammation. There is increasing emphasis on following humane endpoints, minimizing distress, and incorporating refinement strategies like analgesia control, proper anesthesia, and training of personnel. Regulatory guidelines, including CPCSEA mandates, require justifications for using such models and promote alternatives when possible. Therefore, while these models remain essential in pharmacological screening, they must be applied with careful ethical oversight and scientific justification.

Review questions

1. What is the principle of the tail-flick test?
   Answer: It measures the latency of tail withdrawal to a heat stimulus as an indication of analgesic activity.
2. Name a standard drug used in the tail-flick test.
   Answer: Morphine.
3. What does increased latency in the hot plate test indicate?
   Answer: It suggests central analgesic activity.
4. What temperature is typically used in the hot plate test?
   Answer: Around 55°C.
5. Which animals are commonly used in analgesic screening tests?
   Answer: Rats and mice.
6. What test is used for evaluating peripherally acting analgesics?
   Answer: Acetic acid-induced writhing test.
7. What chemical is used to induce writhing in mice?
   Answer: Acetic acid.
8. What is recorded in the writhing test?
   Answer: The number of abdominal constrictions or "writhes."
9. What is the principle of the carrageenan-induced paw edema model?
   Answer: It measures the anti-inflammatory activity of drugs by inducing acute inflammation in the paw.
10. Which phase of inflammation is mediated by prostaglandins in the carrageenan model?
    Answer: The second phase.
11. What standard drug is used in carrageenan-induced inflammation?
    Answer: Indomethacin.
12. How is paw edema measured in inflammation screening?
    Answer: Using a plethysmometer.
13. What is the principle of the yeast-induced pyrexia model?
    Answer: It is based on cytokine-induced elevation of body temperature following yeast injection.
14. What is considered significant pyrexia in rats?
    Answer: A rise of 1°C or more in rectal temperature.
15. What drug is commonly used as a standard in antipyretic screening?
    Answer: Paracetamol.
16. What route is used to inject Brewer's yeast in antipyretic models?
    Answer: Subcutaneous route.

17. What cytokines are involved in yeast-induced fever?

    Answer: IL-1, IL-6, and TNF-alpha.

18. What effect do NSAIDs have on fever?

    Answer: They inhibit prostaglandin synthesis and reduce fever.

19. Which test differentiates centrally acting from peripherally acting analgesics?

    Answer: Tail-flick and writhing tests, respectively.

20. How is the anti-inflammatory effect calculated in the paw edema model?

    Answer: By measuring the percentage inhibition of paw volume compared to control.

21. What is the duration of the carrageenan-induced inflammation observation?

    Answer: Typically up to 4 hours.

22. What does a decrease in writhing indicate?

    Answer: Peripheral analgesic effect.

23. What is a biphasic inflammatory response?

    Answer: A response with two phases: early phase (histamine, serotonin) and late phase (prostaglandins).

24. Which model mimics supraspinal pain response?

    Answer: Hot plate test.

25. What is the method of inducing pyrexia in antipyretic models?

    Answer: Administration of Brewer's yeast.

26. What is the mechanism of action of paracetamol?

    Answer: Central inhibition of prostaglandin synthesis.

27. What parameter is used to determine fever reduction in rats?

    Answer: Rectal temperature.

28. What is used to calculate % inhibition in inflammation models?

    Answer: [(Control paw volume – Test paw volume) / Control paw volume] × 100.

29. Which model is suitable for studying the central effects of analgesics?

    Answer: Tail-flick and hot plate tests.

30. What type of pain is assessed in the writhing test?

    Answer: Peripheral nociceptive pain.

31. Why is the writhing test considered sensitive?

    Answer: It detects even weak peripheral analgesics.

32. Which standard drugs are used in hot plate and tail-flick tests?

    Answer: Morphine or tramadol.

33. What is latency in the context of analgesic models?
    Answer: The time taken to respond to a pain stimulus.
34. What is the stimulus used in the tail-flick method?
    Answer: Focused heat on the tail.
35. Which animal behavior indicates pain response in hot plate test?
    Answer: Paw licking or jumping.
36. What is the purpose of using control and treated groups in screening?
    Answer: To compare and evaluate drug effectiveness.
37. What is a suitable method for measuring anti-inflammatory activity in vivo?
    Answer: Carrageenan-induced paw edema test.
38. Which chemical is responsible for the second phase of inflammation?
    Answer: Prostaglandins.
39. What is plethysmography?
    Answer: A technique to measure the volume of a paw to assess inflammation.
40. What is considered a reliable parameter in the yeast-induced pyrexia model?
    Answer: Drop in rectal temperature after drug administration.
41. Which parameters are measured in hot plate tests?
    Answer: Reaction time to pain (latency).
42. What is the method of measuring inflammation in the paw edema model?
    Answer: Volume displacement using a plethysmometer.
43. What is the significance of using yeast in antipyretic models?
    Answer: It produces consistent fever via immune activation.
44. Which test is better for central analgesics: tail-flick or writhing?
    Answer: Tail-flick test.
45. What is used as a pain-inducing agent in writhing test?
    Answer: Acetic acid.
46. What are typical observation times in pyrexia models?
    Answer: 30-minute intervals for up to 3 hours.
47. What is the purpose of using standard drugs in screening models?
    Answer: To compare the test drug's effect against a known active agent.
48. Why are rodents used in pharmacological screening?
    Answer: They are small, cost-effective, and physiologically responsive.
49. What is the typical dose of acetic acid in writhing tests?
    Answer: 1% solution, 10 mL/kg intraperitoneally.

50. What is the principle behind central analgesic models?
    Answer: Measurement of the drug's ability to increase pain threshold in CNS pathways.

· Which test is used to assess central analgesic activity?

A. Tail flick test

B. Writhing test

C. Paw edema test

D. Pyrexia model

Answer: A

· What is the standard temperature for the hot plate test?

A. 45°C

B. 50°C

C. 55°C

D. 60°C

Answer: C

· Which of the following drugs is a standard for the tail flick test?

A. Paracetamol

B. Indomethacin

C. Morphine

D. Diclofenac

Answer: C

· What chemical is used in the writhing test to induce pain?

A. Carrageenan

B. Acetic acid

C. Ethanol

D. Yeast

Answer: B

· Which model is suitable for evaluating anti-inflammatory drugs?

A. Tail flick

B. Hot plate

C. Carrageenan-induced paw edema

D. Writhing test

Answer: C

· What standard drug is used in the paw edema model?

A. Morphine

B. Indomethacin

C. Paracetamol

D. Diazepam

Answer: B

· The yeast-induced pyrexia model is used to assess:

A. Analgesic activity

B. Anti-inflammatory activity

C. Antipyretic activity

D. Sedative effect

Answer: C

· Which parameter is recorded in the hot plate test?

A. Body temperature

B. Writhing count

C. Reaction time

D. Paw volume

Answer: C

· Which mediator is predominant in the second phase of inflammation?

A. Histamine

B. Serotonin

C. Prostaglandin

D. Bradykinin

Answer: C

· Which of the following is a peripherally acting analgesic?

A. Morphine

B. Ibuprofen

C. Diazepam

D. Tramadol

Answer: B

· What does an increase in tail-flick latency indicate?

A. Inflammation

B. Fever

C. Analgesia

D. Spasticity

Answer: C

· What induces inflammation in the paw edema model?

A. Ethanol

B. Carrageenan

C. Acetic acid

D. Histamine

Answer: B

· Which standard drug is used in yeast-induced pyrexia?

A. Morphine

B. Paracetamol

C. Diazepam

D. Aspirin

Answer: B

· What is measured in the writhing test?

A. Temperature

B. Latency

C. Paw swelling

D. Number of abdominal constrictions

Answer: D

· What is the route of yeast administration in pyrexia models?

A. Oral

B. Intramuscular

C. Subcutaneous

D. Intravenous

Answer: C

· Which test uses thermal stimulus to evaluate pain threshold?

A. Writhing

B. Tail flick

C. Pyrexia

D. Edema

Answer: B

· What is the early phase of carrageenan-induced inflammation mediated by?

A. Prostaglandins

B. IL-1

C. Histamine and serotonin

D. Bradykinin

Answer: C

· Which parameter is used in evaluating antipyretic activity?

A. Paw volume

B. Tail withdrawal time

C. Rectal temperature

D. Number of writhes

Answer: C

· What does a decrease in writhing suggest?

A. Antipyretic effect

B. Muscle relaxation

C. Analgesic effect

D. Diuresis

Answer: C

· What instrument is used to measure paw volume?

A. Plethysmometer

B. Thermometer

C. Sphygmomanometer

D. Oscilloscope

Answer: A

· Which model helps evaluate opioid analgesics?

A. Writhing

B. Hot plate

C. Carrageenan

D. Yeast-induced pyrexia

Answer: B

· What class of drugs is tested in the writhing test?

A. Antihistamines

B. NSAIDs

C. Antiemetics

D. Sedatives

Answer: B

· What is the typical duration of yeast-induced fever before drug administration?

A. 30 minutes

B. 1 hour

C. 18 hours

D. 3 hours

Answer: C

· Which model produces biphasic inflammation?

A. Tail flick

B. Pyrexia

C. Carrageenan

D. Writhing

Answer: C

· What is the role of prostaglandins in inflammation?
A. Anti-inflammatory
B. Vasodilation and pain
C. Antipyretic
D. Diuretic
Answer: B

· What type of pain is assessed in the hot plate test?
A. Deep pain
B. Chronic pain
C. Supraspinal pain
D. Neuropathic pain
Answer: C

· What drug is commonly used as a standard in the writhing test?
A. Ibuprofen
B. Aspirin
C. Diclofenac
D. All of these
Answer: D

· Which test is based on the reaction time to heat exposure?
A. Hot plate
B. Writhing
C. Carrageenan
D. Yeast pyrexia
Answer: A

· Which type of inflammation is caused by carrageenan?
A. Subacute
B. Acute
C. Chronic
D. Allergic
Answer: B

· Which phase of inflammation begins after 3 hours in the carrageenan model?
A. Vascular
B. Neural
C. Prostaglandin-mediated
D. Histamine-mediated
Answer: C

· What is the minimum temperature rise required to consider fever in rats?

A. 0.5°C

B. 1.0°C

C. 1.5°C

D. 2.0°C

Answer: B

· Which of the following is not an analgesic model?

A. Tail flick

B. Writhing

C. Carrageenan paw edema

D. Hot plate

Answer: C

· Which drug inhibits cyclooxygenase to reduce pain and inflammation?

A. Diazepam

B. Aspirin

C. Digoxin

D. Metformin

Answer: B

· The yeast-induced pyrexia model mimics which physiological condition?

A. Infection-induced fever

B. Autoimmunity

C. Allergies

D. Neuropathy

Answer: A

· What is the outcome measured in the tail flick test?

A. Reaction time

B. Paw edema

C. Fever

D. Writhes

Answer: A

· Which test is best for evaluating NSAIDs?

A. Hot plate

B. Tail flick

C. Writhing

D. Pyrexia

Answer: C

· How is the anti-inflammatory effect expressed in paw edema test?

A. Volume difference

B. Reaction time

C. Number of writhes

D. Percentage inhibition

Answer: D

· Which of the following is not involved in the first phase of inflammation?

A. Histamine

B. Serotonin

C. Bradykinin

D. Prostaglandin

Answer: D

· Which is the most direct indicator of central analgesic activity?

A. Reduction in edema

B. Rise in body temperature

C. Increased tail flick latency

D. Reduced food intake

Answer: C

· Which substance induces experimental fever in rats?

A. Lipopolysaccharide

B. Carrageenan

C. Brewer's yeast

D. Histamine

Answer: C

· Tail flick latency is expressed in:

A. Seconds

B. Milliliters

C. Degrees Celsius

D. Hours

Answer: A

· Which response indicates pain relief in writhing test?

A. Increased reaction time

B. Increased body weight

C. Decreased writhing count

D. Increased paw volume

Answer: C

· What type of drugs are best tested in the hot plate model?

A. NSAIDs

B. Corticosteroids

C. Opioids

D. Diuretics

Answer: C

· What is the typical dose of acetic acid used in writhing test?

A. 0.1 mL/kg

B. 1% w/v

C. 1 mL/kg

D. 10 mL/kg

Answer: D

· Which organ is involved in tail flick response?

A. Brain

B. Tail muscles

C. Spinal cord

D. Lungs

Answer: C

· What causes the second phase of carrageenan inflammation?

A. Histamine

B. Serotonin

C. Cytokines

D. Prostaglandins

Answer: D

· What kind of response is observed in hot plate test?

A. Vocalization

B. Jumping

C. Paw licking

D. All of the above

Answer: D

· What is the observation period in pyrexia test post-treatment?

A. 1 hour

B. 3 hours

C. 12 hours

D. 24 hours

Answer: B

· Which of the following is not used in analgesic testing?

A. Morphine

B. Tramadol

C. Paracetamol

D. Digoxin

Answer: D

· How is anti-inflammatory activity of test drug calculated?

A. Reaction time

B. Edema latency

C. % Inhibition of paw edema

D. % Drop in writhing

Answer: C

Fill in the Blanks

1. The tail-flick test is used to evaluate ___________ acting analgesics.
2. Morphine is a ___________ analgesic.
3. In the hot plate test, the typical temperature used is ___________.
4. The acetic acid-induced ___________ test is used for peripheral analgesia.
5. Prostaglandins are responsible for the ___________ phase of inflammation.
6. Carrageenan-induced paw edema is a model for ___________ activity.
7. The yeast-induced pyrexia model is used to screen ___________ drugs.
8. In the tail-flick test, heat is applied to the ___________ of the rat.
9. ___________ is a commonly used standard drug in the paw edema test.
10. The reaction time in the hot plate test is recorded in ___________.
11. Acetic acid induces pain by releasing ___________ mediators.
12. Writhing test involves the counting of ___________ in mice.
13. Inflammation in the carrageenan model is measured using a ___________.
14. The second phase of carrageenan inflammation starts after ___________ hours.
15. Paracetamol is the standard drug for ___________ activity.
16. The fever in the pyrexia model is induced by ___________ injection.
17. The site for temperature measurement in rats is the ___________ region.
18. Tail-flick and hot plate tests assess ___________ perception.
19. Carrageenan is injected in the ___________ region of the rat paw.
20. The ___________ test involves placing the mouse on a heated surface.
21. Paw volume is usually measured using a ___________.
22. In pyrexia model, fever is considered significant when body temperature rises by more than ___________ °C.
23. The early phase of inflammation is mediated by ___________ and serotonin.
24. In the writhing test, ___________ acid is injected intraperitoneally.
25. Tramadol produces analgesia through ___________ receptor activation.
26. NSAIDs act by inhibiting ___________ enzymes.

27. The test used to evaluate fever-reducing activity is called ___________ model.
28. The latency time in tail-flick test is measured in ___________.
29. ___________ is responsible for thermal pain sensation.
30. Acetic acid concentration commonly used in writhing test is ___________ percent.
31. Drugs like ibuprofen show their analgesic action at the ___________ level.
32. The yeast suspension is usually injected ___________ in antipyretic studies.
33. In the carrageenan model, inflammation is due to fluid ___________.
34. Indomethacin belongs to the class of ___________ drugs.
35. Thermal stimulus is a part of ___________ analgesic models.
36. The instrument used to monitor temperature in animals is a ___________ thermometer.
37. A decrease in paw volume after drug treatment indicates ___________ activity.
38. Morphine is ineffective in the ___________ test due to peripheral mechanism.
39. The number of animals showing writhes is used to calculate ___________.
40. Paw volume changes are expressed in ___________ (unit).
41. Tail flick latency increases with ___________ drug administration.
42. Inflammation is an immune response characterized by redness, heat, swelling, pain, and ___________.
43. Prostaglandin synthesis occurs via the ___________ pathway.
44. Central analgesic activity requires penetration of drugs into the ___________.
45. The drug used to induce inflammation in experimental animals is ___________.
46. Pyrexia occurs due to increased levels of endogenous ___________.
47. The percentage inhibition of inflammation is calculated by comparing with the ___________ group.
48. Antipyretics act on the hypothalamus to regulate ___________ set point.
49. The two phases of inflammation differ in terms of ___________ involvement.
50. The effectiveness of an analgesic is determined by the change in ___________ to pain stimuli.

Answer Key

1. centrally
2. centrally acting
3. 55°C
4. writhing
5. second
6. anti-inflammatory
7. antipyretic
8. tail
9. Indomethacin
10. seconds
11. inflammatory
12. abdominal constrictions
13. plethysmometer
14. three (3)
15. antipyretic
16. Brewer's yeast
17. rectal
18. pain
19. subplantar
20. hot plate
21. plethysmometer
22. 1
23. histamine
24. acetic
25. opioid
26. cyclooxygenase
27. yeast-induced pyrexia
28. seconds
29. nociceptors
30. one (1%)
31. peripheral
32. subcutaneously
33. exudation
34. NSAID

35. central
36. rectal
37. anti-inflammatory
38. writhing
39. analgesic index
40. milliliters
41. analgesic
42. loss of function
43. cyclooxygenase
44. central nervous system
45. carrageenan
46. pyrogens
47. control
48. temperature
49. mediator
50. response latency.

True/False Questions

1. The tail-flick test is used to evaluate peripheral analgesics.
2. Morphine is a centrally acting analgesic.
3. The hot plate test is suitable for evaluating opioid analgesics.
4. Acetic acid-induced writhing test measures anti-inflammatory activity.
5. Indomethacin is commonly used in the paw edema model as a standard anti-inflammatory drug.
6. Carrageenan is used to induce acute inflammation in rodents.
7. Prostaglandins mediate the first phase of carrageenan-induced inflammation.
8. The plethysmometer is used to measure writhes in the writhing test.
9. Paracetamol is used as a standard antipyretic in the yeast-induced pyrexia model.
10. The yeast-induced pyrexia model simulates bacterial infection-induced fever.
11. Hot plate test uses mechanical pressure to assess pain.
12. A decrease in tail-flick latency indicates analgesic activity.
13. NSAIDs act primarily through opioid receptor activation.
14. The acetic acid writhing test is sensitive to centrally acting analgesics.
15. The tail-flick and hot plate methods are used for evaluating central analgesics.
16. Rectal temperature is the preferred method for recording body temperature in pyrexia models.
17. The writhing response is triggered by acetic acid–induced release of prostaglandins.
18. A latency period in the hot plate test longer than baseline suggests analgesic effect.
19. Indomethacin has no role in reducing inflammation.
20. The second phase of carrageenan inflammation occurs within 30 minutes.
21. Inflammation can be both acute and chronic in nature.
22. The tail-flick model is useful for evaluating anti-inflammatory drugs.
23. Tramadol is considered a central analgesic.
24. Pain, redness, swelling, and fever are classic signs of inflammation.

25. The yeast-induced pyrexia model is not suitable for testing antipyretic drugs.
26. Acetic acid-induced writhing is considered a behavioral model of pain.
27. The reaction time in the hot plate test is recorded in minutes.
28. Aspirin can be evaluated in both analgesic and antipyretic models.
29. Central analgesics show poor results in peripheral pain models.
30. Acetic acid produces pain through neural mechanisms alone.
31. A reduction in rectal temperature indicates effective antipyretic activity.
32. Anti-inflammatory agents act by suppressing immune system responses.
33. Pyrexia is caused by endogenous pyrogens like IL-1 and TNF-alpha.
34. Morphine produces its effects by inhibiting prostaglandin synthesis.
35. The hot plate test is commonly used in evaluating skeletal muscle relaxants.
36. Acetic acid causes pain by increasing capillary permeability.
37. The writhing test is useful for detecting the analgesic activity of NSAIDs.
38. Tail-flick and hot plate methods cannot detect opioid activity.
39. Plethysmography is used for measuring body temperature.
40. A reduction in paw edema volume suggests anti-inflammatory action.
41. Antipyretics lower body temperature by resetting the hypothalamic set point.
42. Centrally acting drugs do not cross the blood-brain barrier.
43. Tail flick latency is recorded using a stopwatch.
44. Pyrexia models are used to test anxiolytic activity.
45. Writhing models involve oral administration of test agents.
46. A fever rise of 1°C is typically considered significant in rodent studies.
47. The latency in hot plate method must be shorter after drug administration to show efficacy.
48. NSAIDs like ibuprofen reduce both pain and inflammation.
49. The pain threshold is lowered in the presence of prostaglandins.
50. The tail-flick method evaluates nociceptive threshold by mechanical pressure.

Answers

1. False
2. True

3. True
4. False
5. True
6. True
7. False
8. False
9. True
10. True
11. False
12. False
13. False
14. False
15. True
16. True
17. True
18. True
19. False
20. False
21. True
22. False
23. True
24. True
25. False
26. True
27. False
28. True
29. True
30. False
31. True
32. True
33. True
34. False
35. False
36. False
37. True
38. False
39. False
40. True

41. True
42. False
43. True
44. False
45. True
46. True
47. False
48. True
49. True
50. False